D1472474

ALL OF
THE
ABOVE

For Russell, libraries are the heart of any community!!

ALL OF THE ABOVE

A NOVEL BY

Brian L. Cox

TWO WORLDS PRODUCTIONS
A MEDIA COMPANY
(CHICAGO)

Copyright © Brian L. Cox – 2018

ISBN-13: 9781546378785
ISBN-10: 1546378782

Printed in the United States of America

Set in Nova Scotia

Acknowledgements

It takes hard work, determination and support to complete a novel. Thanks to Paul McComas, Emil Ferris, Scott Blackwood, Mary Mrugalski, Christy Cox and Alex Luft, who read early drafts of this tale and helped me believe this is a story worth telling and that I am the writer who should tell it.
B+

Also by Brian L. Cox

Birthday Presence – 16 Stories With One Thing In Common
(www.birthdaypresence.org)

NU Rock Art - A coffee table book of photos
(www.nurockart.com)

Cover Photograph and Design – Brian L. Cox w/ Ted Glasoe
Photograph taken in Nova Scotia

Contact: www.brianlcox.com

For all the "strong" women in my life.
Christy, Connie, Bucket, Carol, Helen, Lynn, Mary, Nura, MB,
Molli and all the others. I have learned so much from you!

- 1 -

A few days after Kevin's funeral...I went for a long hike on the high bluffs overlooking the wide watery mouth of Halifax Harbour. An early June breeze had been blowing out of the south, and my armpits, forehead, and the back of my neck were slick with sweat. Pulling a bandana from my pocket, I mopped my brow, then made my way down through the woods, around Chandler's Cove and climbed the grass and stony slope in front of our house.

That's when I saw it...a dead bird under our living room window...a red-headed woodpecker. It was the third time that had happened in as many weeks. Gently cupping the bird, I was overwhelmed with sorrow. Nothing is as sad as a lifeless bird. Strikingly tri-colored...a brilliant red head and neck...oily black wings...a dark tail and back...a white underside that shimmered in the sunlight. It was so soft and delicate as to be weightless.

Melanerpes erythrocephalus...its Latin name. Red-headed woodpeckers usually aren't found as far north as Nova Scotia. It must have been blown wildly off course by a storm that swept in from the south the previous week. Just like the other dead birds, it saw the tree it was perched in reflected in the window, flew over to land in it, crashed into the window and had broken its neck. Its wings were spread open as if to embrace something.

People and events fly into our lives the same way.

Reckless...Stricken...Unforeseen...Head-on.

No one is immune.

A great and slashing change was gathering strength…poised to come crashing…smashing…tsunami like into my family's life. My parents and I were oblivious to the massive transformation that was about to be visited upon us. But who can know the future? Not Kevin. He was dead and I was the last person with him that endless night. Besides, I didn't have a future. All I had was a lethal mistake, a death and an awful secret. But life was about to get even more complicated! Two thousand miles away events were coalescing. A long distance phone call was coming that would alter the course of my family's life like, well, like a bird blown wildly off course.

I had pleaded hard with my father to cut down the bird-murdering trees, but he balked.

"I planted those trees when I built this house!" he had said.

In a desperate attempt to end the carnage I taped cutouts of owls on the inside of the window in the hope that they might scare off birds, stopping the slaughter. Birds are smart. It didn't work.

Still holding the woodpecker, I trudged into the backyard. My mother was sitting in the grass taking a break from hanging laundry…the empty sleeves of her blouses bellowing…like wind catchers against a cobalt blue sky.

She smiled as I approached. A floppy blue hat with a wide brim cast shade on her face.

"What you got there, Max?" she asked.

I showed her the dead bird and the corners of her mouth turned down.

"Another one?"

"I just found it."

She extended her hand.

"Help me up."

She grunted as I carefully held the bird in my left hand and used my right hand to hoist her to her feet. Specks of dirt fell from the knees of her jeans as she gazed down.

"What is it?"

"A red-headed woodpecker."

She shook her head.

"Mum, this is the third dead bird in less than a month! We've got to do something."

She planted her hands on her hips.

"Max, there's no way your father's going to cut those trees down. He planted them."

"They're killing birds!"

She pulled off her hat, fanned herself with it and motioned to the bird.

"What are you going to do with it?"

I had buried the others down by the cove.

"Put it with the others."

"I'll talk to your father," she said, then rubbed her belly.

"Your little sister's kicking up a storm," she moaned. "I feel lousy."

She was six months pregnant. She had been hospitalized as a precaution a few weeks earlier and was told to stay off her feet. I was surprised that she was hanging clothes if she felt sick.

"You shouldn't be out here. You should be inside lying down. The doctor said..."

She cut me off.

"I had to hang the laundry. Now if you don't mind I've got some weeding to do. Time in the garden will help me feel better."

She firmly believed in the healing and restorative power of gardening. It rose to the level of a religion for her. Digging in the soil…planting…watering…watching…weeding…cultivating…as something vital for the body and soul.

"Plugging in!" That's what she called it. It did replenish her, adding a pink tinge to her check. During summer there was always a vase of fresh cut flowers on the kitchen table and herbs and vegetables from the garden in everything she cooked. She tried to get me interested in gardening. It seemed like nothing more than another chore. Besides, my endless guilt had drained me of energy.

I was about to bury the dead bird when a shrill screeching stopped me in my tracks.

"Ziggy," my mother yelled, waving her hands in the air. "Get lost!"

Ziggy was a biggie…a large male Blue Jay who had been terrorizing us all spring. He had a nest across the cove and was being protective. Whenever anyone was in the yard, he would dive-bomb them, screeching, furiously flapping his wings.

My mother named him Ziggy after a David Bowie album. My dog, Homer was scared shitless of Ziggy. He bolted to the front of the house as Ziggy circled high above us, his white underside in sharp contrast to his blue feathers.

Birds are astonishing…their feathers a poem to nature…solid strong beaks…their community…ability to fly…glass-like eyes…hollow bones…winged and savage spirit. My first memory…birds. I was two or three…a large flock…probably gulls…in an indigo sky…I wanted to fly.

Ziggy…a *cyanocitta cristata bromia,* a passerine bird in the Corvidae family. Blue Jays are native to Nova Scotia, nesting here all year long. He dove at us again, passing a foot above my mother's head.

"Go!" she screamed, frantically waving her hat through the air.

Ziggy understood. He flew across the cove and took up a strategic position at the top of a majestic fir tree, his shrill call, scolding us like a teacher dressing down naughty grade school students. My mother had a heart the size of Canada and was always a good friend to birds, and all animals, a passion she made sure she passed onto me.

"He hates this hat," she said, studying the hat's wide brim. "He gets angry when I wear it."

The sun had created a series of shadows on her face. She looked really weary.

I shrugged.

"Then don't wear it."

She put the hat back on and pulled it down until the brim touched the top of her ears.

"It's my gardening hat! He's going to have to live with it."

Wiping her brow with the back of her gloved hand, she pointed to a head of lettuce.

"I'm making a salad to have with dinner."

"Need an help?"

She planted her hands on her hips.

"I'd love a glass of water."

"You got it."

I laid the bird in the grass and crossed the yard into the kitchen...turned on the tap, let it run until the water was cold... filled the glass and turned toward the screen door. I was just about to go outside when the phone rang.

Intuition whispered I should get it.

"Hello."

"Is this the Geoff Lipton household in Chandler's Cove, Nova Scotia?" a voice asked. "Geoff Lipton, middle initial B?"

She pronounced Nova Scotia "Nova Scot i-a" like people from away sometimes do. She was obviously calling long distance.

"That's my father."

"I'm calling from Colorado," she replied curtly. "Can I speak to him?"

5

From Colorado?

My father played violin with the Halifax Symphony Orchestra...I figured it might be a symphony related call.

"He's not here. He's at rehearsal."

"Who's this?"

"Max, his son. Who's this?"

Pause.

"Is your mother there?"

She sounded official.

"She's here. Who's calling?"

There was another long pause.

"My name is Sergeant Rene Norkett. I'm with the Colorado State Patrol. Put your mother on."

The police?

"I'll get her."

Hurrying to the backyard, I found my mother sitting cross-legged in the grass with strawberries in her apron, a gentle breeze playing with her hair.

"There's a call from the States. She said she's with the Colorado State Patrol."

Her face screwed up.

"What? The police?"

Peeling off her dirt-laden gloves, she dropped them in the grass and raised her hand.

"Help me up."

In the kitchen she grabbed the phone and leaned against the table.

"This is Karen Lipton. How can I help you?"

My mother's expression turned from tired to serious...offering terse two...three-word responses.

"Yes it is. They are..."

She raised her hand to her mouth and exclaimed "Oh my God!" in a traumatized tone I had never heard from her. She dropped into a chair, her face like porcelain.

"When? Yesterday? Oh my God. No. No!"

Lowering her head, she raised a trembling hand to her temple. "How…where?"

She wore a look of complete disbelief. Something was terribly wrong.

I slid onto a chair across from her.

"Are you sure it's them?" she asked as she rubbed her eyes. "Dear God. What about Molli?

"Yes, their daughter?"

There was another pause as she listened closely to the caller.

"Oh thank God," she muttered after a moment. "Where?"

Covering the phone with her hand, she motioned to a drawer on the other side of the kitchen.

"Get me a pen and piece of paper," she whispered urgently.

I grabbed them from the drawer and quickly handed them to her. She started scribbling furiously on the paper.

"Your name again? Your phone number again?"

She listened silently for a few more moments, her brow creased in concentration.

"My husband will call you. I'm calling him…at work… rehearsal…yes he will…today."

Her expression was drained as she hung up the phone.

"Mum, what is it?"

The shocked look in her eyes confirmed that the call carried very bad news.

"It's your uncle Harry and Aunt Beth, and their son, your cousin, Tim," she said, her green eyes wide. "Max, they've been killed. They're dead. Some kind of plane crash in Colorado."

"Plane crash?"

She shook her head in disbelief.

"Harry flew his Cessna into high voltage wires. Beth…their son Tim…they're gone."

- 2 -

Classical music was at the heart of my father's life, but my mother wasn't the least bit musical–unless you count whistling. I'd hear her in the garden…correcting homework… in the kitchen making tea…folding laundry…preparing a salad…anywhere…softly whistling. One time I was looking for her in the vastness of a Home Depot store and simply followed the sweet melody of her whistling.

Her face was ashen as she reached for the phone.

"I've got to call your father."

Uncle Harry was my father's older brother, his only sibling. A doctor, he lived with his family in Denver. They visited us when I was a kid, around nine or ten. Sitting there dazed, all I could remember was Uncle Harry telling me he'd take me up in his plane some day.

"Can I speak to Geoff Lipton?" my mother said into the phone.

They put her on hold, and she turned to me.

"Get me the red photo album in the living room."

Retrieving it, I rushed to the kitchen. My mother was still on hold as she dusted the album off with her hand and leafed through it.

"I'm still here," she said into the phone. "When he gets back, tell him his wife called and to call me right away, okay? It's important."

She hung up and turned back toward me.

"When he gets the message he'll probably think there's a problem with the baby and freak out."

She stopped leafing through the album and dropped it on the table.

"There they are," she said pointing down. "They visited eight years ago."

Kneeling beside her, I gazed at the photograph. It had been taken on a dreary overcast summer day near the high bluffs looming over Halifax Harbour where Kevin had been killed. My aunt and uncle were standing there smiling, the ocean a gray sheet behind them. My aunt's hand was resting on the shoulder of a little girl frowning beside them...Molli.

"This was before your cousin Tim was born," my mother said.

She pointed at the child in the picture.

"That's their daughter, Molli."

She turned toward me, her eyes wide.

"She was insistent everyone spell her name with an 'i' not a 'y.' She was adamant."

She paused as if thinking

"She's got to be fifteen."

"Was she in the plane?"

"Thank God, no. She was at home."

"What's going to happen to her? Is there any family out there?"

"No."

"What's going to happen to her?" I repeated.

"Her family's dead. She'll have to come here...there's no one else."

Molli was family, but we hardly knew her. We didn't have room for her in our lives, our house, and the baby was due in three months.

"I'm parched," she said.

I grabbed the glass of water off the counter, handed it to her and she took a long, slow gulp.

"I'm going upstairs to lie down," she said, placing the glass on the table.

"Are you okay?"

"Not today. I'm tired"

I carefully helped her up the stairs to my parents' room. Grunting loudly, she lay down on the bed covered with a colorful patch quilt she'd made.

"Wake me if your father calls."

"I will."

Slouched on the edge of the bed, I looked at her hair. She had become panicked that spring after she saw a few gray hairs. She gave herself a dye job but something went terribly and comically wrong. She was aiming for light brown but instead ended up with rusty red. My father called her a "punk rocker." I called her "Tomato."

"If the baby comes out with hair like that, I'm leaving," my father had joked.

She taught English literature at J.L. Isley High School, in Spryfield, on our side of the outskirts of Halifax. I was going into grade twelve in a few months. Chances were one in four that she would be my English teacher. Anyone who has ever had their mother as a teacher would understand my apprehension.

"I've got to rest," she said wearily.

I got up to leave but she placed her hand on mine and looked me in the eye, her soft gaze searching my core.

"You haven't been yourself lately. What's up?"

I glanced at the floor.

"Nothing."

"'Nothing?' Come on, Max."

She smiled lovingly.

"There's something on your mind. There has been for weeks. Tell me. I'm your mother."

God, how I wanted to confide in her! *I'm a thief and a killer!* Confessing was impossible. It would open a Pandora's Box of consequences that would destroy me and my family. The truth had died with Kevin.

"I'm fine," I muttered.

She didn't believe me. I didn't care. I'd take my secret to the grave rather than tell anyone.

- 3 -

The ocean current took three days to deliver Kevin Price's body to Chandler's Cove. In some kind of repulsive cosmic coincidence, death pretty much delivered him right to our door. Neighbors were paddling around the cove in their kayaks when they made the gruesome water soaked discovery. Kevin's dead eyes were wide in disbelief. He was floating a few feet from the rocky shore lining Chandler's Cove like a granite necklace. One of his Nike sneakers was given up to the ocean, just like his life. Do you know what a body looks like after three days in the ocean getting bashed into rocks like a piece of driftwood? Not a pretty sight. I didn't see his body. I had nightmares of it. Ghastly images of his grotesquely wrinkled corpse filled my sleep jarring me awake in the depths of the night, my sweat laden sheets clinging to my body like loose skin.

I longed to tell my parents what had really happened. I wanted nothing more than to unburden myself of the immense weights of guilt and fear. My parents could not save me from this. Even the best mothers and fathers will condemn a thief and killer living under their roof.

The coastguard had scoured the shoreline looking for Kevin. A red and white search helicopter flew low back and forth the day after he went missing, the whir of the rotor blades a solemn reminder of what was happening.

What a futile endeavor!

The Atlantic decides how long it keeps its watery arms wrapped around the dead. Sometimes, it gently releases them after a few

13

days or weeks. More often it holds them in its soggy embrace until the end of time. Every fisherman and sailor knows that as truth.

Kevin's sudden death cast a colorless pall over that entire summer. There were plenty of pleasant days but they seemed grim, without the healing warmth of the sun. No one knew the true story except for me, Kevin and God. Not that I believed I had a shot at redemption. I wasn't big on religion but if you killed someone you're going to jail then hell. Right? Could an afterlife be any worse than this?

On the deck, I gazed out over the rocky cove and beyond to the broad expanse of the ocean. The same breeze that was carrying spring away was delivering an uncertain summer. Blue jays, robins, finches, sparrows darted in and out of the evergreens swaying in the lofty June breeze. It was their season of dedication…hard work…mating…nesting. Their melodic songs filled the salty air. Seagulls rode the wind toward the ocean as clouds marched across a faint blue sky.

Violent. Spiritual. Beautiful. Alive. The ocean's surface is a living canvas. That day it was a breathtaking shade of laughing blue. Or more appropriately…mocking blue. Any attempt to capture that color on some paint sample would prove untrue. It changed every moment. Alluring. Deadly. Poetic. Ironic. Like a god…giving…taking life with equal blasé. Kevin could testify to that. People complain that the ocean doesn't care…or worse…it's vengeful. Untrue! Blustery blue it wore that afternoon. For that reason alone you couldn't help but fall in love with it. But many times I'd gazed into its mystical jade eyes. Deception is one of its greatest talents. I'd seen it change moods and its wardrobe so quickly, it took your breath away. Beyond magic. Enchanting. Personifying a watery melancholy, its pensive and ghostly sadness filling the salty air all the way to heaven.

Later, it could easily slip into something deeper, darker, its gentle translucent eyes suddenly turning black and evil. It could be your exquisite redeemer, and the same day, it could transform into a terrifying sea witch gleefully dragging your soul to the bottom.

Everything changed after Kevin's death. I can't really put my finger on what was different. But even the way I saw the ocean changed. It looked exactly as it had before he died. But now it was less perfect, as if a tiny particle of light had been removed from it. Considering all that happened that summer, maybe death was in it. Who am I kidding? Death was always there...a slender and hidden part of it, but this was the first time I was truly seeing it.

• • •

We gradually discover our "emotional selves" the way people discover new places: one decision...one experience...one mistake...one misstep...one death...at a time. Good...bad...happy...sad. Lost. Found. When you're seventeen, life is all about new...experiences. Your body and mind...discovering each other big time...everything is emotionally...physically...sexually...spiritually charged with a raw and abundant energy.

I planned on spending time with friends. Instead I was confined at home, waiting for my father to call. Back in the kitchen, I slid onto a chair and looked down at the photo album. What emotion was I feeling as my dead aunt, uncle, and Molli, looked up at me? Something I had never felt before.

Shock...morbid curiosity? Perhaps. I had never known anyone who had died in a plane crash. I stared into the photo and my eyes were drawn to Molli. She was frowning.

It hit me. *Molli's pain. She must be going through pure hell.*

Her family had been wiped out. A fifteen-year-old girl we hardly knew was moving into our home.

The phone rang. Thinking it was my father, I jumped to answer it. It was my best friend, Ricky Reid. People called him "Sticky

Ricky." He could get out of any "sticky situation." Everyone had a story or a nickname tethered to them like a flag…or an anchor. It was as if there was a wicked "nickname committee" somewhere dreaming up the most bluntly insulting, mean and mocking nicknames possible.

The nickname was usually tied to a ghastly tragedy, misfortune or even a birth defect. "Scarface Idiot" (real name Tony) earned his nickname after a forest fire in Herring Cove burned up 1,200 acres. Tony saw an opportunity to get rid of a small bungalow back in the woods. He doused the house with gas, lit it up and stood there admiring his crime assuming everyone would think it was a casualty of the forest fire. Somehow he caught fire and his face was scarred. The forest fire never came within a kilometer of the house. The authorities figured out he had burned it down for the insurance money. He lost the house, never got a dime and did time. When he got out of jail he moved down the road to a shack in Halibut Bay. People said he smelled of gasoline.

"Stubby" lived in East Pennant. His arm was ripped off. You could see people calling him "Lefty," something like that. The nickname committee wouldn't have that. Lefty wasn't mean enough. There were at least five contradicting stories as to when and how he had lost this arm. I preferred the story of a mackerel fishing accident. His arm got caught in a net going over the side of a fishing boat and got ripped off near the shoulder. He had to be airlifted to hospital and almost died. I later found out that drunk as a skunk, he crashed and rolled his truck near Purcell's Cove.

Speeding. Drunk. No seatbelt. The truth can be *so* disappointing.

The nickname committee dubbed me "Forklift." A few years earlier someone left a forklift running outside of school. I jumped in, accidently crashed it and was suspended for a week. "Deadeye" a mechanic at Wilson's gas station with a lazy right eye. Snake got his name due to his penis. Shitpants from, Terence Bay, had an unfortunate accident while drinking. Bloody Mary was wearing white pants during a party at Crystal Crescent Beach when her period unexpectedly started big time. I don't know how "Soupbone" got his nickname.

I wanted to scream at the nickname committee, to call them out for their cruelness. All it would elicit would be a smirk or blank emotion. Maybe such meanness and Gallows humor has something to do with living close to the ocean, a hard life, poverty, eking out a living.

Or maybe people everywhere are all of the above.

The guy with the most unfortunate "name" didn't have a nick-name. His real name was bad enough. "Yuron" Morash. Everyone called him "Urine." People did a double take when they heard his name "What did you say? 'Urine?'" He was probably named after his great uncle, Uncle Urine. It was pronounced "you're on." No one bothered to say it properly. He was a nice guy, and he'd spell it out for people. "Y-u-r-o-n. It's pronounced like 'You're on first base,'" he'd smile. He was an okay guy, kind of shy. He sure had a funny name.

My father had little time for these locals. He thought they had blown their chances in life by drinking, taking drugs or by just being plain lazy and stupid. Not me. I saw them as colorful, real people. Flawed and a bit tragic, but real in a way the world demands.

Ricky and I were classmates since grade one. His father was a lobsterman, as was his grandfather. Ricky's ride was a beat-to-shit, fire-engine-red Camaro that broke down every few days. When the car wasn't up on blocks with Ricky working on it, he'd pick me up and we'd go driving. I was determined to get my driver's license that summer, and he had been letting me practice with the Camaro.

"I'll come pick you up," he said.

"I can't go. I've got to wait for my father to call."

"Why?"

I didn't feel like getting into it.

"I can't talk about it right now, but it's important."

"What is it?"

"Family stuff. I'll tell you later."

Call waiting beeped and I glanced at the incoming number. My father.

"I gotta take this call. I'll hit you up later…Hello, Dad?"

"Max, your mother called and said it's important? Is she okay? Is there a problem?"

I could have told him what was going on. But there was no way I going to be the conveyer of such unbelievably tragic news. *Your brother's dead and so is his wife and their son…*

The thing is, I always wanted to please my father, to be his "golden boy." I was never able to meet his lofty expectations. If gold was the highest, I came in a distant bronze. I studied relentlessly and got a B+, he would ask why I didn't get an A? Did he love me? *Maybe.* Yes, I guess, as any decent parent loves their child. I always felt like I was a disappointment to him. It was probably one of those things where he believed his real genius son and I had been switched at birth. Everyone has a sixth sense, an ability to keenly and painfully understand when they have let down their parents. I would have given anything to not have been cursed with such a capacity. There was no more hellish scenario then having to tell my father that his only child was a thief…a killer.

"Mum's okay," I replied, trying to sound calm. "She's lying down. She said to get her when you called."

I put the phone down, climbed the stairs and rapped gently on my parents' bedroom door.

"Mum? Dad's on the phone."

Nothing. I knocked harder.

"Mum?"

I heard her stirring. She got up and pulled open the door.

"Is it your father?"

"Yeah."

She rubbed her eyes.

"Did you tell him?"

"No.

She pulled on her robe and we descended the stairs to the kitchen.

"Geoff?" she said. "Where are you? Come home. The baby's fine. I'm fine...I need you to come home...just get here...don't drive fast...bye."

She hung up and sat at the table. She looked even more exhausted than earlier.

"I didn't want him driving on that road after he got the bad news," she said wearily.

The Ketch Harbour Road is dangerous at the best of times and treacherous when it's slick with rain, snow or shrouded in fog. The orchestra was in Halifax, and could take my father a half hour or more to get home. When I was nine, we drove up on a horrible head-on collision on that road. An elderly couple from Quebec were hit head-on by a lobsterman driving a GMC Pickup truck. A sickening mess. Smashed lobster traps, glass, debris and shattered lives were all over the road. The couple were killed, the fisherman badly hurt. Driving slowly passed, we could see the dead woman clutching a coffee cup in her bony fingers.

My mother sank into her chair.

"Who knows what pills he's taking today," she moaned. "He'd be devastated if I told him what's happened."

My parents had been arguing over my father's misuse of his heavy-duty oxycodone pain medication for his bad back. She watched like a hawk when he took them. She'd checked the bottle to see how many he had taken. If she said something to him about it, he'd dismiss her with a wave of his hand insisting he needed them to get through the day.

After I... after Kevin died...I started stealing his pills. I'd wait until no one was home, and grab one or two. They were "painkillers" after all, and that's exactly what they did, take the sharp edge off my immense guilt. Painkillers and booze were a welcome addition to my diet.

Take the "t" out of "diet" and you get...

I had been doing my *one letter substitution game* a lot that summer. I'd hear a word and as if by reflex would substitute a letter, drop a letter, or add a letter and come up with a different word.

Dead...head...lead...fall...call...love...glove...hua...aua... flower...lower...sex...see...math...bath...kill...pill...rum...run... rain...pain...lift. Life is the same way. Substitute one letter for another and everything changes.

• • •

My father and Uncle Harry weren't close siblings. He would talk to Harry on the phone at Christmas and other times, but they rarely saw each other.

"What's Dad going to do? Does he, do we, have to go there, to Colorado?"

"Your father will have to go, but the doctor told me not to fly," she said rubbing her stomach. "So there's no way..."

"What about Molli? What's going to happen to her?"

She exhaled heavily and looked me in the eye...her face drained of color.

"Like I said, Max, she'll have to come here, for a while anyway. There's no one else in the world for her."

I could barely contemplate the possibility. Our house had three small bedrooms: my parents' room, my room, the baby's room.

"What kind of doctor is...was Uncle Harry?"

"Internal medicine."

She got up from the table and pulled the tie of her robe tight.

"I'm going back to bed until your father gets here."

"I was going to take Homer for a walk, but I can stick around if you want?"

She waved her hand through the air.

"I'm okay. You go."

I turned to leave but she grabbed my arm.

"Max, my God you're dripping with sweat. Are you okay?"

She pressed her wrist to my forehead.

"You're freezing!"

Even since Kevin...I had been cursed with cold sweats. I had absolutely no control over them. They weren't tied to physical exertion or the temperature. They came and went as they pleased, as if a vengeful demon was gleefully turning on an unholy tap with me standing under it.

"I'm fine."

-4-

Sex and death have walked hand-in-hand over the ages…as have the natural and spiritual worlds. It's no different in Chandler's Cove. It's no different anywhere.

Kevin's funeral was at Saint Peter's Church in Ketch Harbour. His coffin was so highly polished I could see my distorted reflection in it. Everyone from Sambro to Spryfield was there. Kevin wasn't "religious" and it's a safe bet that one of the only time he went to church was for his own funeral. But that's the way it is with people, right? The only time they set foot inside a church is when they are Christened as a newborn…or for their own funeral. What happens in the intervening years? They don't care? They're too busy? They don't believe? All of the above?

Kevin's mother wept so long and loudly…I sank…into the pew weighed down by her tears and my endless guilt. I gazed at the worn wooden floorboards for most of the service. At one point I glanced around and saw my friend's older sister…Hua. Her dark eyes met mine. She smiled faintly. That summer, we were having sex…lots of sex. No one knew. She had sworn me to secrecy. A couple of years older than me, she was a student at Dalhousie University in Halifax. The only time I wasn't thinking of what happened to Kevin, when I was with her.

The faint smell of incense from ten thousand services held in the church over the years hung in the air. It was a scalding June day…they threw open all the windows to allow in a refreshing ocean breeze. Half way through the service…a robin flew in…its rusty breast a blur of color...the soft sound of its fluttering wings causing a small commotion before it finally found a perch...high up in the rafters. It shit on some lady's head. Within a week the story of the bird made the rounds, embellished by everyone who told it. It went from a bird sitting on the woman's head...to shitting...to landing on Kevin's mother's head.

There are more superstitions than people in Nova Scotia. Superstition says that when a bird flies into a house, or in the case of Kevin's funeral, a church, it's an omen of some kind. Either someone is going to die, or have a lucky day, or who knows what? And if a bird shits on your head, you'll get money in the mail or lose money. One time I pulled a new pair of shoes from a box and casually placed them on the dining room table. My mother had a shit fit. She grabbed the shoes, put them on the floor and sternly admonished me to never do that again.

"It's very bad luck!"

I'm not big on folklore. But I'm a birder. I didn't care if a bird flew in through an open window as long as the bird didn't get hurt. Fishermen...lobstermen...are beyond superstitious. Maybe everyone living near the ocean is. Perhaps it's ignorance. Maybe it's true. It was true that summer. The previous July, I was with Ricky and his father getting ready to go day fishing on their lobster boat, *The Anna Gale*. We were on the wharf when I pulled a banana from my backpack. I started peeling it as the boat strained and creaked at the moorings. Ricky's dad's a gruff no-nonsense guy. He glanced at the banana then glared at me.

"You're not bringing that on my boat," he growled.

I was shocked.

"It's only a banana," I replied, holding it out for him to see.

That made it worse. He scowled and made his way to the wheelhouse as Ricky gently placed his hand on my shoulder.

23

"Lobstermen, fishermen are superstitious," he said with a shrug. "Never bring a freaking banana on a boat. It's bad luck."

"Bad luck?" I scoffed. "Why?"

He lowered his voice and cracked a smile.

"I don't want to get into it. They're weird like that. Certain things are no-nos, man."

He nodded toward the wheelhouse.

"I know it's strange," he continued, the sun reflecting in his aviators. "It's just the way he is, the way lobstermen are."

- 5 -

Homer is named after Homer Simpson, not Homer the Greek poet. He's a Golden Lab goofball. Purebred Labrador Retrievers have webbing between their toes. Labs are "duck dogs," bred for hunting and swimming. The webbing is in their DNA. Labs love the water, as if they're part seal.

We ambled down the dirt and gravel road leading out of Chandler's Cove and up into the woods. Within twenty minutes we reached the bluffs overlooking the broad and limitless expanse of the Atlantic. A few miles out a container ship the size of a skyscraper moved with determination and grace toward the mouth of Halifax Harbour. The sun was in the east as I shielded my eyes and gazed eastward across the ocean. A warm summer breeze tickled its tranquil surface as my mind swam with thoughts of foreign lands. I was seventeen, but the only time I had set foot outside of Nova Scotia was on a school trip to Ottawa the previous year. I wanted nothing more than to get away...to escape...sprout wings...take off...never look back.

I was only a stone's toss from where I last saw Kevin.

Sixty feet below me thick waves hurled themselves into the base of the bluffs. I was scared shitless of heights but stepped forward and looked down. A seven-foot thick wave thundered into the blackened rocks at the bluff's base. It exploded with a monstrous boom! Frothy surf raced into endless cavities the ocean had carved into the cliff base. A wondrous spray of fine salty mist blew up to where I was standing and gently touched my cheek. I can't think of a way to describe that sound except to say it was like the voice of

God. Maybe that's appropriate. It was the summer I came to know there is an awesome certainty and unwavering authority above anything else.

It was a sheer and deadly drop. Kev could testify to that. If the fall didn't kill you, you'd be smashed into the rocky cliff base by the ceaseless waves and drowned. Gazing down I realized that I wasn't afraid of falling…I was afraid of jumping…surrendering to the abyss like Kevin did.

It was mid-afternoon by the time I got back. My father had not yet arrived. Climbing the stony slope behind our house, I pulled open the door of the small "A-frame" my father and I had built three years earlier. He practiced violin there on occasion, but it was pretty much my domain. My refuge. I had even started hiding my liquor in there.

The A-frame was one room, fifteen feet long, ten feet wide and ten feet tall at the very top of the A. There's something wonderfully universal in the simple architecture of an A frame. It looks like a pair of hands clasped together in prayer. It had been hard work building it. My father made sure I paid close attention to every detail. I actually learned a lot about carpentry and the tools of the trade.

Built of pressure treated fir and cedar, it was cool in summer and warm in winter. My father believes in building for the long haul, so it was well constructed. Over and over he said that when it comes to building, you have to work to the same exacting standards of sturdiness and beauty required for a full-size house.

"Max, extra attention to detail only takes a little extra care, cost and materials, but it makes for a huge increase in longevity."

That was him through and through. The other thing he harped on was the foundation. If you knew him, you knew that a "solid foundation" wasn't a metaphor for anything less than how to live.

"Just like in life," he loved saying, "everything begins with a good foundation."

The familiar crunch of car tires on the gravel driveway pulled me out of my thoughts. I peered out the window. My father, a stern expression on his face, strode inside. Something told me to wait before following him in. I sat there wondering what he would do? How would he handle such tragic news? He was generally a serious man not given to sentimentality. A classically trained violinist, he could play any piece of music as long as it was written down. At the same time, he wouldn't sit in on Irish or contemporary music sessions. He had difficulty improvising in music and in life.

-6-

The afternoon sun warmed my shoulders as I crossed our backyard and went into the kitchen. Upstairs my parents were
talking, their voices muffled and serious. The stairs creaked and
moaned as I slowly climbed them. The bedroom door was ajar.
Instead of going in, I stopped…listened. My mother must have just
finished telling my father what had happened because he asked
what anyone in a situation like that would ask.

"Are they sure it's them?"

"Yes," my mother replied softly. "They said they're sure."

"This can't be happening," my father muttered. "In his Cessna?
Into high voltage wires? There's got to be a mistake. Harry was an
excellent pilot."

I looked around the doorframe into the room. My father, his
back to me, was slouched on the edge of the bed. My mother was
sitting next to him.

"Dad, are you okay?"

They both turned as I stepped into the room.

"I know what's happened," I said, looking into my father's
brown eyes. "I was here when the police called."

His face was pale, his shoulders slouched. I had never seen him
so seemingly vulnerable.

"There's got to be a mistake," he repeated.

"Maybe there is a mistake," my mother replied unconvincingly.
"Why don't you call the police?"

He was about to pick up the phone when my mother stopped
him.

"I didn't tell you," she gasped. "It's Molli. She wasn't with them. She wasn't on the plane. She's okay."

"What did you say?"

"She wasn't on the plane. She's alright."

She inhaled deeply.

"She's not hurt. She's at home."

"By herself?"

My mother claimed a seat beside my father and gently placed her hand on his.

"The neighbors are helping out, and there's a social worker with Molli."

"A social worker?" he asked in a tight faced grimace.

"Yes. They asked me if Molli had any family out there. I told them, 'no.'"

She paused then raised he hand to her mouth.

"Oh God, I didn't think to tell them about Abby. It never occurred to me."

"Good," my father replied wearily. "If she's still alive, she's probably in rehab."

Abby was Molli's aunt, her mother's younger sister. I had never met her. The only reason I knew of her was that I remembered my parents talking about her the previous summer. The proverbial "black sheep," she continuously got in trouble with the law, often turning to her sister and Uncle Harry for help, usually in the form of money.

My father raised a trembling hand to his temple as if thinking.

"Molli's a year or two younger than Max?"

"Fifteen," my mother replied.

He made the call. Confirmed it all. His brother Harry, Beth, their son, Tim…were dead.

Then he talked briefly to Molli.

"How is she?" my mother asked.

"Devastated."

He leaned forward and ran a hand over his lower back.

"My back's killing me."

Crossing the kitchen to the cupboard, he pulled out a prescription bottle and dumped out three pills. I glanced at my mother. She was watching him with narrowed eyes.

"Geoff, you took three this morning. I know you're upset but the doctor told you three a day..."

He cut her off.

"Please!" he replied, his voice rising. "You don't understand the pain I'm in."

He held up the bottle of pills.

"I need these, especially right now!"

My mother knew better than to push it. She crossed the room to the sink and poured him a glass of water.

"Be careful, okay?"

That long afternoon was the first time I really saw how death sets things in motion. Death, the final stop in life, is also a catalyst for so many things. Flights...funeral arrangements...lengthy phone calls...hurried packing. A feeling of deep loss and fog settled over our home that June afternoon, covering everything in a soggy gray shawl.

We were in the kitchen when my father asked me to get the mail. I pulled on my Montreal Canadiens cap and started toward the community mailboxes at the top of the road leading into the cove. I had almost reached them when I saw the mail carrier sitting in her boxy white delivery van. She was black and in her forties. Her head was slightly lowered...she was crying...weeping, her mournful sobs carried in the mist. She didn't see me. Why was she so upset? Maybe she had a secret and didn't feel like living? Maybe life demands tears. I didn't want to disturb her. I quietly went back to the house and returned for the mail later.

- 7 -

Later in life I came to understand that my father was best described as "aloof." He wasn't arrogant. He was aloof. He kept an emotional and often physical distance from everyone. People liked him, but he was not a "hugger." He often seemed to be thinking...his thoughts multi-layered and distant.

After dinner Homer and I went to the A-frame to finish the cleaning job I had started earlier in the day. I heard my father inside the house playing his violin. I don't know what piece of music he was playing, but it was heartrending and poignant, the notes giving voice to his immense grief. He always turned to his instrument when he was stressed or troubled. He had played it for hours when my mother was admitted to the hospital the previous month. After a while his playing stopped. I was sweeping the floor when he came in, pulled out one of the benches and sat down. It was dusk, the sky a striking shade of purple, orange and blue.

"Your mother and I were talking. The doctor says there's no way she can fly."

"I know."

He leaned back on the bench.

"I've booked a flight to Denver tomorrow."

"How long are you going to be there?"

He turned his palms skyward.

"It's open-ended right now, but your mother and I are figuring on two weeks."

His gaze fell to the floor.

"Dad, are you okay?"

"I've had much better days."

He paused and seemed to be thinking…his expression remote.

"No one ever plans for something like this. Someone you love is here and the next second…"

He snapped is fingers.

"They're gone."

It was quiet for a moment, then I asked him about Molli.

"What's going to happen to her?"

He patted the space on the bench next to him, motioned for me to sit, put his hand on my shoulder and looked me in the eye. It was an unusual show of emotional and physical closeness for him.

"She's going to have to come here to stay with us, for a little while anyway. We're all she's got."

He must have read my expression.

"I know that's a surprise. But she's fifteen, too young to stay by herself."

He paused then inhaled deeply.

"I just got off the phone with an attorney who's a patron of the symphony. He doesn't know exactly what the law in Colorado says, but he's pretty sure I'm now Molli's guardian. When I get there I'm going to see if Harry left a will, any instructions."

A faint smile formed on his lips.

"I'm Molli's Godfather."

"Really?"

"Yep. When Molli was born, Harry called me. He'd been celebrating, drinking. He told me he wanted me to be Molli's Godfather. He *insisted*. I was shocked. He was an atheist. When I pointed that out, he said, 'I am, but just in case I'm wrong, I think my daughter should have a Godfather.'"

He shook his head and grinned slightly.

"That's just *like* Harry, covering all the bases."

"What does that mean exactly, being her Godfather?"

"That's what I asked him," he shrugged. "He said it meant I'd look after Molli if anything ever happened to them. But he laughed and said he'd outlive me by twenty years. I agreed to be her Godfather, but I was sure as Hell that was the end of it. I never in a million years thought..."

He threw up his hands.

"But like I said, no one plans for something like this."

Still grinning slightly, he told me a story from his childhood.

"When I was ten, your uncle Harry was fifteen. He didn't want to have anything to do with me because of our age difference and the fact I was a pest. But on occasion he'd do the big brother thing, help me with homework, take me to a movie. I don't think he knew it, but I adored and admired him. He always had good grades, played sports and had a lot of friends."

I glanced out the window. The sun was slipping behind the evergreens. Night was quickly encroaching, the twilight giving accent to my father's heartache as tears welled in his eyes.

"There was this one time. I was thirteen. A twenty-dollar bill went missing from the top of my father's bureau. He was angry as hell. Honesty was a big thing to him. Huge. But he wasn't sure who had taken the money: me or Harry. He said it wasn't the money, but the principle of it. Harry was like, 'I didn't take it, Dad, and I was like, 'I didn't take it, either.' So your grandfather started giving us both a grilling threatening to ground us for a year. After a half hour of this, Harry finally copped to it and said, 'I took it and spent it.' My father grounded him, and he missed a dance and a few hockey games."

He looked me in the eye.

"That evening when I was in bed, Harry came in, pulled a twenty-dollar bill from his pocket, and handed it to me. 'You left this on your bedroom floor this morning.' He turned and walked out. I had taken the money. He knew it and took the blame for me."

"Did your father ever figure out the truth, that you took the money?"

"Nope. Harry never told him."

All I could do is shake my head in disbelief.

"He was my only sibling. I always knew I could count on him."

He paused, his lips pursed.

"Now I guess I want him to know, wherever he is, that he can count on me. His daughter will be looked after."

He squeezed my knee, stood and gazed down at me.

"I'm really counting on you."

"I know."

He went back inside and I stayed in the A-frame, lying on the bench thinking. A stranger was moving into our home. What was I feeling? Mixed emotions? I guess. For the second time that day, I was definitely feeling something new.

Do you know what's great for killing feelings? Any feelings? Alcohol. In the wake of Kevin's death, I had been drinking anything I could get my hands on. Gin, tequila, vodka, rum, coolers, wine, beer, whatever. It didn't matter as long as it got me quickly and totally hammered. It was an easy way to dull my guilty conscience and navigate the awkward life I was locked into. I had hidden a quart of gin under the floor of the A-frame. I quickly retrieved it. With Homer a few paces in front of me, we carefully navigated our way through the twilight to a group of large boulders out of sight of our house. Climbing up on the largest one, I sat crossed legged as Homer sniffed around then settled in a grassy spot. I chugged down three burning gulps from the bottle as I gazed out across the black ocean. Lights from Cole Harbor sparkled. The air temperature had plunged by fifteen degrees but the gin was warming my blood. Easing my conscience. The foghorn at Chebucto Head started blowing mournfully, its heavy two-tone blast familiar.

You had to get used to that foghorn, or it could keep you awake all night, like a dripping tap. Like your conscience. The mournful bellow of the foghorn never bothered me. It had always been part of my life. It was comforting, like a favorite piece of music or a wool blanket pulled from a closet and thrown across a bed on the first day of autumn.

I chugged down half the bottle of gin. With Homer at my side, I staggered down the hill falling twice. My head was spinning as I placed the bottle back under the floor of the A-frame and crawled inside. It was dark. My parents were in bed. Their lights off.

- 8 -

The next morning came early. Painfully.

A throbbing head...wished I was dead...my mouth like sandpaper. I had grown used to that. Killer hangovers were yet another new experience for me that summer. Dressed only in my underwear...i staggered into the bathroom...locked the door...hit the floor...turned on the shower at full blast to drown out the noise of my puking...dropped to my knees...leaned in over the bowl... threw-up...an explosion of vomit...tiny projectiles...half-digested food...booze and ooze...bile...from the very pit of me. Blindly reaching up...I pressed the handle...swirling water...caught my death...breath...dry heaving...beyond exhausting...my whole body contorted like a wet piece of clothing being rung out by hand...no control...a brutally painful spasm...rejecting everything in my stomach as if it were poison.

Who am I kidding? Alcohol is *"poison."* All day I'd be tired... sick. But you know what? Drinking *"poison"* was worth any hangover. Drinking took away the pain of life and numbed me.

Staggering to my feet I turned on the sink tap, guzzled down as much water as I could, took a long piss, examined my reflection in the mirror, wiped vomit from my chin with a facecloth, pulled back the shower curtain and got in. The water was cool and refreshing.

Back in my bedroom, sitting on the edge of my bed, I wearily pulled on my jeans, sneakers and a T-shirt as the familiar smell of freshly baked bread, toast and coffee wafting up to my room. I could hear my parents in the kitchen talking. Pulling myself together as best I could, I descended the stairs. Outside, light rain and heavy fog had chased away the perfect blue skies and warm breezes of the previous day.

"Morning," I offered weakly, padding into the kitchen where my parents were sitting at the table finishing breakfast.

My mother made bread from scratch in clay flowerpots. A half dozen were sitting on the counter cooling, their divine aroma rousing my hunger. The tops were overflowing with golden bread like oversized muffins. She made the best bread in the world. Everyone said that. She loved baking. Bread was the thing she loved baking the most. She'd make it twice a week and leave it on the counter to cool. Our house was always filled with the delicious aroma of freshly baked bread. She used to sell it at a church market and would sometimes give it to neighbors.

There are eight houses scattered on the stone and grassy slope that runs to the rocky water's edge in Chandler's Cove. Eight and a half if you include the A-frame. Our neighbors? Okay. We tend to keep to ourselves, but we see each other once in a while at the mailboxes or simply coming and going. Living beside the ocean takes a certain temperament. You love it or hate it. My par-ents loved it. My father had taught himself to tell the time... within seventeen minutes... by looking at the ocean level on the rocks...the seaweed, kelp and tide lines acting like primitive hands on a clock. It was my parent's idea of some kind of seaside Shangri-La. I would have jumped at the idea of moving to Halifax...turning my back on our shitty little cove.

"Max," my father said, pointing at his watch. "We have to leave in twenty minutes. Put my luggage in the trunk."

On the way to the airport I was sleeping off my hangover in the backseat.

"Max, your mother and I know that you want to help," my father said, jolting me out of a half-slumber, "that you want to make the transition easy for Molli."

"Molli? Transition?" I yawned. "Yeah, I do. I want to help."

My father's gaze was fixed on me in the rearview mirror.

"We want you to take the baby's room and for Molli to have your room."

"What?"

My mother turned to me.

"Your room is bigger, and we think Molli would be more comfortable in there."

"I've got everything exactly how I like it!" I protested. "Why can't she take the baby's room?"

"Max," my father replied sternly, his gaze now on the road. "The baby's room isn't finished, and we don't want to put Molli in there after all she's been through."

"Isn't finished" was putting it nicely. It was a wreck…the walls bare and unpainted…the floor rough unfinished…the room lit by a single dim light bulb hanging from the ceiling. My parents had been planning on finishing it before the baby was born but obviously still had much to do.

"Leave your bed in there," my father continued. "Move everything else out before Molli and I get back."

"What am I going to sleep in?"

"I'm going to buy you a new bed," my mother smiled.

"I love my bed!"

"Max," my father snapped. "This is the way your mother and I want it. Everyone's going to be inconvenienced. It's nothing compared to what Molli's been through."

- 9 -

What's in a word? Birds. Letters. Syllables. Meaning. Art. Wings…other things…Love. Hate. Death. God. Life.

All of the above?

We dropped my father at the airport then stopped at a discount furniture store in Halifax to buy me a new bed.

"I have a huge craving for McDonald's fries," my mother said as she turned out of the store parking lot. She loved those fries. She had been driving my father and me crazy with her cravings for months.

"Me too."

We stopped at a McDonald's in Spryfield. Big Macs, fries and cokes.

"Hi, Mrs. Lipton," the guy working the food window said as he handed us our food in a bag. It was Nathan McKenzie, a guy from school. He was a Herring Cover and a "grease monkey" who could take a car engine apart and put it back together the same day. Not surprising considering his father was a mechanic. Nathan would never go to university. That didn't bother him a bit.

"Hi, Nathan," my mother replied cheerfully.

He leaned out the window to see who was in the passenger seat.

"Hey Max, how ya doing?"

I waved.

"Good."

"Kevin's funeral was real sad?"

"Yes, it was," my mother replied.

I sank into my seat without replying.

"Birds flew into the church and landed on Kevin's parents?" Nathan asked. "Weird ehhh?"

"That is weird," my mother replied with a half-smile.

He leaned further out the window and handed us another bag

"Max, I put an extra burger in there for ya."

"Thanks," I mouthed.

Back on the road, the car filled with the smell of fast food. My mother turned to me, her eyes filled with empathy.

"I know how hard Kevin's death has been on you," she said quietly. "And I know you don't like talking about it because it's still very painful."

She paused, waiting for a reply, but I kept staring out the window.

"Max, it's not your fault. No one could have saved him."

"He was my friend. I should have…"

She took one hand off the steering wheel and placed it on top of mine.

"It's not your fault," she said softly.

Yeah, it was my fault.

We drove for a while, eating in silence, deep in our own thoughts.

"We've decided on a name for the baby," my mother said after a moment.

"What?"

"We considered Lori. Christy. Connie. Jerri. Jennifer. Theresa. And what the names mean. The name we settled on is…Grace."

I glanced at her.

"Grandma's name?"

"Exactly. It's a good name to have going through life."

"Why?"

"'Grace' is a divine influence working in humans."

"Dad signed off on this? Since when are you guys religious?"

She exhaled.

"More than anything, he was sold by the fact it was his mother's name."

That made sense. He put big value on family. He talked about family and family values...foundations...The funny thing is, he really didn't have any family besides us and Harry...and now... Molli.

"Grace' is a better name than, Maxamillian." I said sarcastically.

I hated my name. Who names their son, Maxamillian? My father does. Five hundred years ago a French emperor called his son "Maxamillian" and my father loved that. His first son, "Maxamillian. Thank God, everybody called me...Max.

"You grew into your name," my mother laughed. "Don't forget, I talked your father out of naming you Schnittke!"

I shook my head.

"Thank God for small miracles."

"So what do you think, Max?" she smiled. "You're going to have a little sister named 'Grace."

My immediate 17-year-old mind thought: *There's only one letter difference between Grace and Grave...*a tinge of guilt. I must be weird and morbid. Where do thoughts like that come from?

"Grave," I muttered, "yeah that's nice."

"'Grave?'" my mother blurted. "What do you mean, Grave? It's Grace. Not Grave!"

"That's what I meant to say, Grace!"

"Are you feeling okay?" my mother asked, her brow furrowed.

"I'm just tired and stressed like you and Dad."

"When we get home, you rest."

I turned toward the window as we raced past Long Lake, the faint afternoon light working in watercolors on its worried surface.

-10-

Over the next few days I started imagining Molli in bits... pieces...a jigsaw puzzle of memory and fiction...carefully put together...in the mind until...it becomes an outline. We were only two years apart...a lifetime at that age. She had lost her family and was coming to live with us. What was her state of mind? What would she be like? What did she look like? How would she fit in? We were the blank pages that she would write on and what a story she would tell.

The sun was breaking through the clouds, revealing patches of light blue sky as I ambled up the road leading from our home toward The Ketch Harbour Road. I had talked to Ricky and he said he'd pick me up. Like me, Ricky never travelled much, but unlike me, he had no desire to. He didn't even like going into Halifax. If I talked about travel he'd blow me off with a wave of his hand.

"I've got everything I need right here," he'd laugh. "What are you going to do in Europe? See some museum? Pay twelve bucks for a coffee? Go up the Eiffel Tower? See some old broken-down hundred-year-old building in Rome? If I want that, I'll go online or look at a book."

He was perfectly content living in Sambro. After high school he'd work fulltime on his father's trawler until his father retired, and then Ricky would take it over. Who knows which of us had the better life plan? In some ways I envied his simplistic approach.

I was close to the main road. I saw him driving toward me, blue smoke from the engine trailing behind his Camaro. He pulled up and stuck his head out the window. His normal dress...a ratty red T-shirt…jeans…ball cap with a Toronto Blue Jays logo on the front. He loved that team. Lived and died with them. He jumped out and punched me lightly in the shoulder.

"You drive, man. I'll ride shotgun."

One of his irritating colloquialisms, was the word "man" tagged onto the end of his sentences.

I climbed into the driver's seat and Ricky slid into the passenger's seat.

"Where do you want to go, man?"

I dropped the car into drive and turned to him.

"Crystal Crescent."

"Let's do it, man."

Crystal Crescent Beach was a ten-minute drive. It's on the Atlantic so the water is often freezing. My friends and I would hang out there or hike through the hills. I turned onto Ketch Harbour Road and tapped the accelerator. Ricky's Camaro was obviously much more powerful than my parents' Toyota, and I was quickly up to sixty clicks.

"What was the big deal yesterday?" he asked as I navigated a short uphill curve.

I told him what had happened and that Molli was coming to live with us.

"How old is she?"

"Fifteen."

"She's coming from the States?"

"Colorado."

He fixed his gaze on me.

"What's she like, man?"

I shrugged, my hands still on the wheel.

"I have no idea. The last time they visited was years ago. I barely remember her."

"Shit, that's heavy, man."

I pulled off the Ketch Harbour Road and onto the dirt-and-gravel tree lined road that led to the beach. I parked on a slight rise overlooking the ocean and turned off the car. A dozen other vehicles were sitting in the dirt parking lot. A handful of people were on the beach. Ricky punched up a rock radio station, pulled a joint from his pocket, lit it, took a long drag, then offered it to me.

I waved him off. He continued puffing on the joint, smoke swirling around his head.

I patted the stirring wheel.

"Your ride's great. What did you do?"

"I've been working on the fuel injection."

He offered me the joint again.

"Sure you don't want some? It's good."

"I'll take a pass."

He took a last hit on the joint and then flicked the butt out the window. We sauntered down to the beach and sat in the sand looking out over the cobalt ocean. The breeze had picked up. Waves crashed onto the shore and raced up the beach in a frothy sprint.

"They're looking for somebody to work the yard at the squadron," Ricky said. "Two to three days a week."

The previous few summers he had worked at the Royal Nova Scotia Yacht Squadron in Halifax as a kind of laborer. When school had let out that summer I had asked him to let me know if there were any job openings there.

I turned toward him.

"Two or three days a week?"

"Yeah, twenty hours a week, something like that."

"Doing what?"

"Same as me. It doesn't take any skill as long as you can push a broom, use a paintbrush and pump diesel for the boats. That's it.

Once in a while we'll have to launch a boat from the slip, but Drew and Richie do most of that, seeing it involves the tractor."

Drew was Ricky's boss. Ricky continually complained about him. The yacht squadron was one of the nicest in the province attracting lots of wealthy people with their expensive sailboats, yachts and cabin cruisers.

I nodded.

"Sounds great. What's the pay?"

"What pay?"

I swatted him on the arm.

"The pay for the job, you stoner!"

He laughed, turned his ball cap backwards, pushed his sunglasses up on his nose and leaned back, resting his elbows in the sand.

"You'd be getting two bucks an hour less than me, but that's only because I've been working there a couple of summers already."

The "squadron," as everyone called it, was about ten kilometers away, on the outskirts of Halifax, too far to ride my bike.

"How would I get there?"

He shrugged.

"I'd give you a ride."

Exactly what I was hoping to hear.

"That works."

"Good, I'll tell Drew you're interested."

"I've got to run it past my parents first," I said sheepishly.

Okay," he replied in a mocking tone, "check with your mommy and daddy and let me know by the end of the week."

-11-

Driving back, the afternoon sun tinted the windows as we discussed plans for a get-together with friends that night at "Champayne Dam." Up through the woods on the other side of Chandler's Cove, it was always a refuge for me. Literally and figuratively. But Kevin died not far from there so it was haunted with fresh memories and death.

It wasn't much a dam...or a metaphor...more like a roughly v-shaped cement wall...twenty feet long...a foot thick...six feet deep...built into the side of a rocky hill in the early 1940s by Canadian soldiers manning coastal defenses as a way to collect fresh water from a little stream for bathing and drinking. They named it "Champayne Dam." The water in the small reservoir behind the dam was filled with minerals from the rocks that gave the water the tint of pink Champayne. The soldiers imprinted "CHAMPAYNE DAM 1941" in the cement lip on top. Apparently soldiers are not the best "spellers." Our parties there were a highlight of my summers. We'd light a bonfire in the narrow, rocky inlet below the dam and spend the night talking, laughing and playing music on guitar.

"Who's going?" I asked.

"The usual."

We pulled off the Ketch Harbour Road, onto Chebucto Head Road and then turned down the short dirt road leading to my house. I jumped out and leaned in the window.

"Come by and get me."

He nodded.

"Eight o'clock."

He punched the gas and roared away as I sauntered down the hill toward home.

It was dinnertime. My mother was in the kitchen making pasta, steam rising spirit-like from a boiling pot on the stove.

"How's Ricky?" she asked, glancing up from her work.

I claimed a seat at the table.

"Good. They're looking for someone to help out at the yacht squadron. He asked if I was interested."

"And you said?"

"I said 'yes,' but that I'd have to check with you and Dad first, and since Dad's not here..."

Her eyebrows arched.

"What's the job exactly?"

I told her what Ricky had told me. She seemed to be thinking.

"I'm not sure, Max. With all that's happened and with Molli coming and the baby, we may need you around."

"Mum, it's only a few days a week," I pleaded. "You and Dad have been saying I should get a summer job. This is perfect for me."

"I know, but that was before..."

She turned her palms up.

"Everything's changed."

"I'm seventeen! I shouldn't have to ask you!"

She planted her hands on the counter and shot me a stern look.

"As long as you live under this roof, your father and I have a say in what you do, Max."

"Mum, please," I said, dialing down my tone. "I'll make sure I'm here if you need me. It's only a few days a week."

She exhaled heavily.

"I'll talk to your father when he gets back."

"That's too late! I've got to give Ricky an answer by the end of the week."

"I'll talk to him about it when he calls."

She looked me in the eye.

"I can't make any promises."

-12-

Ghosts are real...ask half the people in Nova Scotia. They'll swear they saw one or know somebody who saw one. Ask author, Helen Creighton. She wrote a book called *Bluenose Ghosts*. It's real stories of ghosts, devils, angels, foresight and phantom ships in Nova Scotia. But she left out one very important ghost. Kevin. His untimely death haunted me.

Ricky came by that evening at eight. The sun was sliding down the backside of the sky as I stepped onto our deck under a magnificent and bold sunset. Is Nova Scotia the only place with lilac sunsets like that? It was as if the amethyst so abundant below the province somehow magically joined the sky.

Homer sauntered in front of us as we followed the path around the cove and carefully navigated our way uphill, through the woods toward Champayne Dam. I had grabbed a bottle of red wine that I had hidden in the A-frame. Ricky and I were trudging along the path when a dozen seagulls flew low overhead squawking like crazy.

"Gulls," Ricky cursed. "They shit all over my car yesterday."

I grinned.

"That's good luck, or you're going to die."

He snorted.

"If the amount of shit is any indication, I must be in line to win the lottery or get hit by lightning!"

I pointed at the sky.

"Those are Ross gulls."

"You can tell by just looking at 'em?"

"Yeah, they're a small gull, white neck, thin black collar, white wedge-shaped tail and pink under parts. They have a short black bill and orange-reddish feet."

He shook his head.

"I don't get your fascination with birds, man. A bird's a bird. So what? What are you going to do, become one of those people who study birds? An entomologist?"

"You mean an ornithologist."

"Whatever."

"It's like you and cars. Except for me it's not cars, it's birds."

He seemed to be thinking.

"That don't make sense, man. You gotta have a ride."

"Imagine a world without birds."

He shook his head.

"I wouldn't miss em."

I shot him a look of disdain.

"Yeah, you would."

"No way, man. All they do is shit on my car and make a racket in the morning. Gulls are the worst. They eat a ton of fish and shit all over the wharf."

"They spread seeds and eat bugs, rodents and garbage. Gulls are like living vacuum cleaners."

He stopped walking and stared at me.

"See what I mean! People are going to think you're a geek. A bird geek. It's weird. It's like you care more about birds than you care about people, man."

Hmmm. Maybe.

"I know one group of birds you love," I said.

"What?"

"The Toronto Blue Jays!"

"Yeah," he chuckled. "You got me there, man."

By the time Ricky and I arrived at the dam, a few people were already there. They had started the fire, which bathed the inlet in a soft yellow glow. I was hoping Hua would come. When you're seventeen…parties like that are indelible…living in your memory…majestic light against darkness…in the deepest part of summer nights. You'll always be able to recall them because of the drama in your teenage life. You're finding your way on the path of life the same way you find your way…to the dam. Sometimes it's so black you have to "feel" your way along the path being careful not to fall or walk face-first into a tree branch. Other times….the path…well lit and easy to navigated. Nonetheless…just like life…there are always places to get snagged or tripped up. Then there was the, singing, laughing, talking, smoke from the burning driftwood adding incense to the whole night. The bottomless sky staring down at us…smiling. The moon and stars dancing.

We were about a short distance away when could see who was there. "Squidman," real name Frank, who got his nickname due to his lankiness. Trent, a.k.a. "Tuna" because he always had tuna sandwiches for lunch at school. Next to him were Antonio and his girlfriend, Janet. Jamie was tending the fire with the shaft of a broken hockey stick, and also beside the fire was Chen, Hua's younger brother. Hua wasn't there. Their family had moved to nearby Ketch Harbour from China when Hua and Chen were toddlers.

After a while the clouds cleared and the stars shined like pinpricks of light. I sat on the flat side of a boulder near the fire, opened my wine and took a swig as smoke wafted over me.

"Max, buddy," Ricky slurred. "When's your cousin get here from the states, man?"

Everyone looked at me, their eyes questioning.

"Your cousin's coming from the States?" Janet asked.

"Yep. I just found out yesterday."

I told them what had happened. Molli's family had been wiped out and she was coming to stay with us.

Tuna sat on a boulder and looked at me.

"A Cessna filled with gas into high voltage wires? Kaboom!"

He slowly shook his head.

"No way anyone's walking away from that."

I took a giant swig of wine, which dripped down my chin onto my shirt. A week earlier someone had snuck rum-spiked punch into a party. I lapped it up like a dog. Then I got sick as a dog in their bathroom. People were banging on the door.

"Max are you okay in there?"

I was far from okay, draped over the toilet puking blood and punch.

Janet came over and sat beside me, the fire lighting her face

"I'm really sorry. Are you okay? Are your parents okay?"

I hit the bottle again, then wiped my chin with the back of my hand.

"We weren't that close. We didn't see them much. They came to visit once."

I rubbed my forehead.

"I don't know."

There was the familiar sound of bottles clinking together on the path above us. Toby and Chris. They carefully descended the boulder strewn hill and I could see that Toby had a guitar case strapped over his shoulder.

"It's dark tonight," Chris said, claiming a seat on a boulder near the fire. "Impossible to see the path."

"Jan," Antonio said. "Tell them about Kevin's ghost."

"You guys didn't hear about this?" Janet replied.

"Hear about what?" I asked.

Janet leaned forward, elbows resting on her knees, her face pensive and lit by the flickering flames.

"Jade Walsh is driving back from Crystal Crescent last week and sees a figure along the road," Janet said, her voice low and serious. "It's foggy and she's probably stoned, right? But she slows down and looks, and she can't believe it because it's Kevin!"

The hair on my arms and the back of my neck prickled.

"Kevin Price?" someone asked.

"Do you know any other 'Kevin' who done a header off the bluffs this summer?" Antonio replied sarcastically.

Janet continued in a hushed tone.

"Jade said one of his sneakers missing, just like they found him. She said he looked right queer, eehhh. Weird, like he was lost or something. His face was all screwed up."

"Eels coming out of his eyes too, I bet," Trent chuckled.

"Shut up, Trent," someone said.

"Anyway," Janet continued. "Kevin's all dead and whatnot, and he looks right at Jade, and it's like he's trying to say something but can't."

"I've fallen and I can't get up," Trent blurted.

"Shut up Trent," Pete said. "I mean it!"

"Jade got the hell out of there," Janet continued, her eyes wide. "She drove home a hundred miles an hour and went screaming into the house. 'I just seen a ghost!' It took her father an hour to settle her down. He had to give her a pill."

Janet leaned back and shook her head.

"Right weird, ehhhh?"

"Bullshit," Kevin muttered. "Everyone knows that stoner girl's been crazy since her mother died."

The "ghost story" was likely bullshit. Still, it sent a chill through me. Kevin lived, in my conscience, anyway.

• • •

The next morning…a rainy and deeply gloomy day. I stumbled into the bathroom…turned on the shower…knelt in front of the toilet and emptied my guts. After my shower I went down to the kitchen. My mother was in her bathrobe at the table. A half dozen loaves of bread in clay flowerpots were cooling on the window-sill, filling the kitchen with the perfume of freshly baked bread. But thanks to my wicked hangover, even that normally welcoming aroma turned my stomach.

"I didn't hear you come in last night," she said, looking up.

"I tried to be quiet."

I poured a bowl of cereal and sat down across from her.

"What's that?" I asked, motioning with my spoon to what she was reading.

"I went online and pulled together some stuff on the history of Chandler's Cove," she replied. "It's for Molli."

"Why bother?" I asked. "She can Google it if she's interested."

"She's in mourning, and I want to help her get her mind off things. When you're travelling somewhere it's interesting to do research ahead of time. To get the lay of the land. Here, take a look."

She slid the printout across the table. It read like a boring history report. That made sense. She was a teacher.

"There's a geography of the land, but there's a greater geography of the soul, the spirit and the heart," she said softly. "That's what I'm worried about with Molli. The lay of the land is so much easier to see and navigate."

That was my mother through and through. She always thought of other people. She wasn't concerned we didn't have room for Molli. Or at least didn't let on she was concerned. If a neighbor was sick she'd make them soup. She volunteered to be a tutor for kids with bad grades and volunteered at the IWK Children's Hospital to hold newborns whose mothers were sick. She was compassionate and caring. There was always a hint of kindness in her green eyes.

"Your father called last night after you went out."

"What's happening?"

"He's very stressed."

She exhaled loudly.

"God, I wish I was there to help out."

"Did he see Molli?"

"He was with her."

"How's she doing?"

She shook her head.

"Not good."

I desperately wanted to ask if she had talked to him about me taking the job at the yacht squadron.

"Does he know when they're coming back?"

"He's just arrived. They're trying to find a will and make arrangements."

I placed my spoon on the table beside my bowl.

"Did you ask him about the job?"

"What job?"

"The job at the yacht squadron."

She sipped her coffee and looked at me over the rim.

"No," she replied, her eyes suddenly not so kind. "He was stressed to death. It wasn't a good time."

"I've got to give Ricky an answer!"

"I'll ask when he calls tonight, if I think he's not too stressed. Okay? That's the best I can do."

I got up. She took another sip of coffee and again examined me over the rim of the cup.

"It was late when you got home last night."

"I thought you were asleep, so I tried to be quiet. How did you know what time I got in?"

Her gaze was sharp.

"I'm your mother. That's how I know."

She paused.

"What did you guys do last night?"

"The usual. We sat around. Chris brought his guitar." I shrugged. "We hung out."

Her eyes narrowed.

"Was there any drinking?"

Her question caught me off guard.

"Drinking? No. No one was drinking."

"Are you sure?" she asked, her stare burning through me.

"We were hanging out," I answered as calmly as I could. "We weren't drinking."

"Interesting, because I ran into Norm Pinnet at the grocery store the other day, and he said he found a bunch of empty beer and liquor bottles near the dam last week. He said it looked like someone had a party."

Norm was our big-mouthed neighbor. A chef at some high-end restaurant in Halifax, he was continually sticking his nose into everyone's business. My father loathed Norm, referring to him as "the spy."

"I've seen empty beer bottles by the dam," I said. "Who knows how they got there? Probably Spryfielders."

"Could be," she said, picking up her coffee mug. "But I'm your mother, and you can't lie to me."

Once again she eyed me suspiciously.

"Your clothes have reeked of booze and…"

I jumped from the table.

"Someone spilled beer on me."

"Right," she scoffed.

"I'm going for a walk. I can get some cool pictures in this fog."

"Get back here, Maxamillian!"

She only called me, "Maxamillian," when she was mad…and she looked ticked off.

I ignored her.

"Get back here, Maxamillian! I mean it!"

-13-

I bolted up the stairs two at a time to my bedroom, grabbed my camera off my bureau, pulled on my boots, raincoat and cap. When I went back to the kitchen, my mother was on the phone, so I made a dash for the door.

Outside the fog was unusually thick, wet and cold. It was still better than being grilled by my mother on drinking. Visibility was less than thirty meters. I carefully navigated the muddy path at the end of the rocky cove. I heard a barking sound, and when I stopped to listen I heard it again. It was impossible to see very far to the fog, so I cautiously made my way over the seaweed covered rocks to the water's edge, then crouched and listened. Out on the water a dozen feet in front of me something was on the surface. At first I couldn't make out what it was, but then I realized a seal was looking at me. Its head peeked above the water. It seemed as surprised to see me as I was to see it. Seals swam into the cove on occasion, but usually stayed further from shore or lazily sun themselves on a tiny island near the mouth of the cove.

Two worlds meet at the ocean's edge...the ocean...earth... world of man...world of nature...conscious...subconscious... lust...love...a unique balance...energy there. I had begun to believe there was another world there as well...an unseen spiritual world...a liminal space...

The seal, bobbing at the surface, continued to watch me with wide black eyes. I slowly removed the lens cover from my camera and snapped its picture.

People are drawn to seals because of their cuteness, large oval eyes, long whiskers and half-smiles. They're the dogs of the ocean. But fishermen hate seals. Seals eat a ton of fish. If that seal were to surface near a fishermen's boat in Sambro, the fisherman would blow its head off. There's no room for sentimentally in a fisherman's life. It's hard, dangerous work.

The seal looked at me quizzically for a few more moments, then silently dipped below the still surface. It was a thrilling and wondrous moment. As it slipped away, disappointment welled up inside me. I wanted to keep that moment alive, to jump in and swim with the seal, to see the murky and mysterious depths of the ocean as the seal saw it, to glide effortlessly under the water free of the cares of the broken world above the surface.

I stayed there for a few more minutes hoping the seal would reappear. It didn't. I pulled up my collar and continued walking up past Champayne Dam, and through the woods until I was on the high bluffs. It was like a dream. Everything was silently shrouded in the dense fog. The only noise was the thunderous impact of waves pounding relentlessly into the cliff's base and the occasional muffled blast from the foghorn at Chebucto Head.

There's something mystical about walking through the fog. It alters the scenery and imagination with echoes of whimsy like the first snowfall of winter. Everything you thought you knew so well is suddenly unfamiliar. *That stand of birch trees? Those boulders? How did they get there?* Sometimes the fog isn't cloaking anything. Instead it's making things easier to see. At the same time I was keenly aware of my oneness with God or an absolute of some kind. My father would have scoffed if he had heard me talking about God. He was an atheist. He had absolutely no doubts about the nonexistence of God. "There is no God. Religion is a disease. Opium of the people. Period." I wasn't sure. When I looked out over the ocean, at a spectacular sunset, a lone maple leaf or into a baby's eyes, there seemed to be something magnificent at work there, an intention, a guiding hand or a grand design.

It was impossible to see the ocean through the fog. As I gazed eastward it seemed like it would be possible to keep walking over the edge of the cliff, that the fog would hold me up. Illusions are false…dangerous. Sitting on a moss-covered boulder, my thoughts tumbled like Kevin had tumbled over the edge a few weeks earlier. He could be a jerk but I missed him. My mind couldn't accept the brutal fact that he was gone. My phone would ring. For an instant I'd think he was calling. I'd catch myself thinking I should call him. I heard his voice in crowds. Kevin's parents knew we liked the same bands and had asked if I'd like to have some of his CDs. I said yes, but in reality I couldn't face them.

It started raining, so I pulled up my hood and made my way back home. The previous night Ricky and I had agreed that I'd do some city driving because traffic would be light. By the time I returned home, the rain had stopped and patches of blue sky were visible. I rounded the corner of the house and saw something dark in the wet grass by the windows next to the fir trees. A robin, its neck broken. I gently poked it with my foot. Nothing except deep remorse. Even in death it was strikingly beautiful. It's eyes wide…wings open. I buried it with the others down by the shore, called Rick, and checked on my mother, wrapped in a blanket watching TV. She was in a better mood than earlier and thank God didn't ask me about drinking.

"Hey Mom, how you feeling?"

"Not great."

She was pale. Exhausted. Her pregnancy had been a huge surprise to everyone. My parents had been trying to have a second child for years and had tried everything to ensure success. The doctors finally told my mother she couldn't have any more children. She was beyond devastated. Three years earlier she had fallen into a deep depression that required she be hospitalized for more than a month. When she found out she was pregnant, she was astonished, as was my father. I'd never seen them so unbelievably happy. I wasn't as enthusiastic. I hadn't expressed my doubts but I wasn't sold on the idea.

Who has another kid at their age? Isn't that kind of selfish and potentially dangerous?

I sat by her feet.

"I'll stay if you're not feeling well."

"That's okay. You go."

I turned to leave but she called me back.

"There is one thing you can do for me."

"Sure."

"I have a serious craving for caramel swirl ice cream. Can you pick some up?"

"Absolutely."

I heard a car horn and figured it was Ricky.

"I'll be gone a few hours. Call me if anything happens."

She waved me off.

"Don't be a worrywart."

I started to leave but stopped and turned back toward her.

"There was another dead bird under the living room window. A robin."

She frowned.

"We've got to do something. That's the fifth one this summer."

She nodded.

"I know."

Outside, Ricky was sitting in the passenger seat…smoke belching from the tailpipe. I climbed in and flicked on the windshield wipers, which fell into rhythm with a Metallica song blaring on the radio. He loved that band. Not me. I was more of a U2 fan. In high school you *are* your music. You represent the band you love.

You buy their records, wear their T-Shirts and brag to your friends about them.

"Can I turn this off?" I said, facing him.

"What? Turn it off? It's *Sandman!*"

"I know, but it's hard to concentrate and drive with this on and I'm hung over..."

He reached over and turned it off.

"You okay now, pussy?"

"Thanks."

He lit a cigarette, exhaled a large plume of smoke, and then motioned to the outside.

"I want to see how you drive in this pea soup."

By the time we reached the Ketch Harbour Road the car was filled with cigarette smoke.

I coughed and waved my hand through the air.

"It's harder to see in here than in the fog."

He smirked.

"Crack a window, dumbass."

I did and was immediately pelted in the face with cold rain. Ricky shook his head and chuckled.

"Not the front windows. The back windows, dumbass!"

I opened the back windows a few inches, which helped clear the smoke.

"Watch your speed here," Ricky said as we approached a long downhill curve.

The road is narrow, flanked by trees on both sides and curvy and hilly with a few straight stretches. Like I said, there had been plenty of accidents on it over the years, usually involving drunk fishermen or teenagers like Ricky and me. But surprisingly, Ricky was always careful. He paid attention to the speed limit and continually admonished me if I was driving too fast or recklessly. His concerns had more to do with protecting his car than anything else.

"Quite a night last night, man," he said. "Bit hung over today though."

"Me too."

He glanced at me.

"That was some bullshit story about Kevin's ghost, huh?"

I shook my head.

"She's nuts."

"Yep but it was weird eh?"

"I don't believe in ghosts."

Yet another lie! Lies give birth to more lies…until your whole miserable life…is a lie! Of course I believed in ghosts. Kevin had been haunting me all summer.

"I should have stayed with you guys that night," Ricky said sheepishly. "I would have helped get him back and…"

"What were you going to do, go take a leak for him? He was drunk and stumbled off and fell. There wasn't anything anyone could have done. It was his time to go I guess. We all have…"

Ricky threw up his hands in surrender.

"Relax, man. It's no one's fault."

I turned toward him…truth welling up inside me like vomit. I desperately wanted to tell him what happened. Impossible.

"I could have…If only I had insisted he stay near the fire, everything would be…"

"Max, buddy, don't go beating yourself up. He made his own choices."

We stopped at Sobey's to pick up ice cream for my mother and bananas for Ricky.

"Three pounds for a loonie!" Ricky grinned. "And you know me. I'm ape over bananas!"

That was true. He loved bananas.
I glanced over at him.
"Better not bring one on your old man's boat."
He grinned as he slapped my arm.
"You're thinking like a lobsterman!"

-14-

Arrogance is not a good thing. Arrogant people say "arrogance" is another word for "confidence." They're not the same. Arrogance is haughtiness. Self-importance. Egotism. Pride. If arrogance were given a name it would be...John King.

Ricky dropped me off, and when I went inside I found my mother in the kitchen on the phone with my father. I threw the ice cream in the freezer and then sat at the table and listened as my father gave her an update on the situation in Colorado. I grabbed a pen and scribbled: "Ask dad about me taking the job at the squadron!!!"

She looked down at it and nodded.

"Max just walked in," she said, handing me the phone. "Your father wants to talk to you about the job."

"Hi, Dad. How's it going?"

"Busy. Sad. Crazy."

He sounded tired.

"How's your mother?"

I glanced across the table at her.

"She's fine. She was worn out this morning, but she's okay now."

My mother nodded and smiled faintly.

"Your mother told me about the job at the yacht squadron," he said, then paused. "Max, I'm sorry, but with everything that's going on, your mother pregnant and everything with Molli, I'm going to need you around home this summer. There's no way..."

"It's only 20 hours a week," I blurted. "I'll be around to help and..."

He cut me off.

"Max, please! I don't want to get into an argument over this, especially right now. The bottom line is there's too much going on around home. I need you there. Understand?"

"I *understand* I want this job!" I replied angrily. "I *understand* I need the money. I *understand* that this is wrong!"

I threw the phone down on the table and stormed outside, slamming the screen door behind me. Livid! I paced around the yard for a few minutes then called to Homer so we could walk to the dam and cool off. There were two things I really wanted very badly that summer: to get my driver's license and to take the job at the yacht squadron.

The rain slowed to a drizzle, but it was still gray and overcast as I trod on the soaked path beside the cove and up through the woods. I had almost reached the dam, when I saw a middle-aged man in a red raincoat and ball cap on the path coming toward me. John King. He and his wife were from Toronto, Vancouver or from some place from away like that. They were universally despised. They built their "dream house" on top of one of the nicest look-offs in the area. It was only a ten-minute stroll from our place. Their "dream house?" A tragic combination of money, arrogance and colossal bad taste. It drew hateful snickers from everyone. It resembled a castle. Anyone with even a mild imagination could see it…turrets and all. The Kings were out-of-town arrogant snobs who didn't give a care about us "locals." A security camera stood guard by a big gate they had built on the road. A sign warned that it was private property and to "stay off!"

Homer, his tail wagging, started toward him like he did to all people. When we were a few feet apart, King stopped and pointed up the path.

"That's private property."

I pointed at the ground.

"This isn't private property."

He pointed up the path again.

"I said that is."

"You're John King, right?"

He nodded smugly.

"Yes. I'm John King."

"I've been hoping to run into you."

His expression was a grotesque mixture of condescension and entitlement.

"You have?"

"Yes, I have," I replied, staring right at him. "You can't come down here from Toronto and act like you own the place. It's wrong. People used to walk out here until you put your gate up. They weren't bothering anyone. We were here long before you built your ugly ass disgusting castle."

"Where do you live?" he snapped.

"What's it matter where I live?"

He turned to leave but then stopped.

"You and your mutt stay off my property!"

"Go back to Toronto!"

"I'm not from Toronto!"

"Where you from?"

He scoffed.

"That's none of your business."

"Go back to wherever you're from! We don't need your type around here."

"Stay off my property!" he repeated angrily.

"It's not your property!" I scoffed. "You don't own it. You're renting it. Fifty years from now, or hopefully sooner, you'll be gone. Dead. You'll be under ground! No one owns anything!"

I really believed that! The ocean…air…planet…belong to everyone…now and forever. I didn't have to look far to see the horrendous crimes that were being committed against nature. There was illegal ocean and stream dumping in Nova Scotia. Immense deforestation. Erosion. Problems with old mines and quarries. It was all caused by greed. People had a bottomless appetite for destruction of the land…air…sea. The planet. Massive overfishing around Nova Scotia over the decades had led to a point where the ocean was almost literally fished dry. Strict catch quotas were in place.

I recycled whatever I could. Plastic. Glass. Paper. Everything. It's willfully blind not to see we all have a vital stake in the future of the planet we share. There's an old expression: "Don't shit in your kitchen." That's what was happening in Nova Scotia and around the planet with climate change and massive amounts of carbon being pumped into in the atmosphere. It's destructive and wrong, but maybe that's just how the world works. Still, nature doesn't reveal all its prevailing truths at once. It has a vengeful streak and will strike back…hard.

King and people like him didn't care. They put money and status above everything. They'd take the "nicest view" from everyone without a care.

He muttered something spiteful and inaudible then stomped away up the path. It felt good to tell him off, like a balm for my simmering anger.

With Homer in the lead we cut through the woods on a narrow path so we wouldn't have to set foot on his property. It started raining again, the drops tapping out a soft jazz beat on the leafs. We cleared the woods and continued walking south. It was liberating to be out of the house but my thoughts were still there. I didn't know Molli, but I was already starting to resent her. If she hadn't been coming there wouldn't be a problem with me taking the job. I wouldn't have been tossed from my bedroom. I'm not heartless. I felt for her...for what had happened...her huge loss. My emotions were mixed. Volatile sympathy. Caring begrudgement.

-15-

Imagine a room…a bedroom…is in grief. All you have to do to get rid of the grief is to paint the room…end the gloom. Imagine Kevin were still alive…you can turn back time…unring a bell…avoid hell…pray that what you did to your friend isn't true…it wasn't you…imagine…

The next few days dragged by as my mother and I got my bedroom ready for Molli and did a quick patch-and-paint job on my new room. Drained of color and energy, she talked to my father at least once a day. He updated her on what was happening in Colorado, and she updated me, or sometimes I got on the phone with him. When I spoke to him the evening after the funeral, he was totally exhausted.

"How's your mother?"

"She tired, but she's fine," I replied, trying to reassure him that things were okay on our end.

"It's difficult being away when she's pregnant. It's comforting for me knowing you're there."

I gazed out the window.

"I'm helping as much as possible."

"Max, I'm real sorry about the job at the yacht squadron. I know you're upset. The timing couldn't be worse."

I didn't want to get into it.

"How was the funeral?"

He paused, as if fighting back tears.

"Heart breaking."

"How's Molli?"

"In shock."

My mother was hovering anxiously nearby so I handed her the phone. She talked to my father for ten minutes before hanging up.

"I forgot to ask him when they're coming back."

She peered at me over the rim of her reading glasses.

"On Friday."

In three days.

Molli didn't want to come to live with us. She wanted to stay in Colorado. No big surprise there. If the circumstances had been reversed, if my family had been wiped out, I certainly wouldn't want to be pulled away from my home and friends and taken to live with relatives I didn't know in Colorado. There had been a big ugly scene... deep tears...Molli...my father...a social worker...yelling...the police. She didn't have a choice. She had to come live with us. She was just fifteen and my father was her legal guardian.

My mother had lined up a grief counselor for Molli and had checked out books from the library dealing with grief and loss.

"Dad sounds exhausted."

She sat at the table and rubbed her eyes.

"Don't I know it. We all are."

"He's worried about you."

"Don't I know it," she repeated.

I sat down.

"How can I help?"

"All that's left to do is finishing Molli's room."

She reached over and patted my hand.

"I'm giving you the afternoon off."

"Really? Chen, asked me if I wanted to go sailing. But if you're not feeling good I can stick around. "

She smiled.

"I'm fine. You go!"

. . .

Anytime a family moves from China to rural Nova Scotia they're going to be the "proverbial fish out of water." It doesn't matter how smart they are or how hard they try to fit in…they're vulnerable and exposed. That was Chen's family. They moved to Ketch Harbour from China when Chen was a baby and Hua was three. Chen was my age, 17, and just like Ricky, I had known him for as long as I could remember. Chen's father owned a 26-foot sailboat, which he kept moored near their house.

*Breadth Of Heart…*was painted on the stern.

Chen was a superb sailor. I loved being on the water and wished I had my own aluminum boat and motor for puttering around the cove. A boat like the one I was going to buy with the money Kevin and me split.

Sailing with Chen was the only way I had of getting out on the ocean. It's liberating being in a sailboat on the grand expanse of the ocean powered only by wind-filled sails. It was also a good way to get away from home for a while.

I jumped on my bike and started toward his house, the sun warming my back. When I hit the main road I switched gears and pedaled harder. I liked physically testing myself on that road… pressing my limits…peddling hard…fast…sweating…the feel of my leg muscles burning. I'd time myself.

I was hoping Chen's sister, Hua, would be there. She was nineteen, and like I said, she had seduced me. I had been stealing lusty glances at her for a year but hadn't been sure how to act. She sensed that. She'd come to parties at Champayne Dam or I'd see her at her parent's house. She caught me checking her out one time when I was waiting for Chen.

"A penny for your thoughts?" she had smiled.

I fumbled some sort of flimsy reply and she chuckled.

"Not very fast on your feet, are you?"

Her eyes, dark and mysterious, always revealed a hint of sexuality.

That spring, Hua had picked me up when I was hitchhiking home from Isley. I always missed the bus and it was the third time that she had done that in a few weeks. After we had been driving and talking for a few minutes, she pulled a joint from her jeans jacket pocket and held it up.

"Do you wanna smoke this with me?"

"Sure." I didn't like smoking dope, but since *she* was asking...

We turned onto a narrow dirt road outside of Bear Cove, drove for a few hundred feet, and parked in a clearing of high grass under a stand of birch trees.

"I'm exhausted," she said lighting the joint.

"Hard day of classes?"

She inhaled deeply.

"My worst day of the week," she moaned. "I've been running around all day."

She passed me the joint. I took a long, slow drag and handed it back to her.

"Chen said you're planning on medical school?" I asked, exhaling a plume of smoke

"That's what my father wants."

"What do you want?"

She laughed and kicked off her sandals.

"I want you to rub my feet."

I smiled widely.

"Okay."

She sat sideways in her seat...leaned against the driver's door...
her bare feet in my lap...her mischievous smile.

"I like you," she whispered. "I don't know why, but I like you."

Desire flared in her gaze...she sat up...wrapped her long
slim arms around my neck...her breath...hot and delicious as
she drove her tongue into my mouth, tore at her clothes and
climbed on top of me.

That's how it started. I lost my virginity to her. She was fun,
horny, curious and patient. We wore out the springs in her red
Honda that summer, throwing ourselves into a thoughtless
and abundant passion. It was like something from out of time,
that probably saved me from myself. I lived for it. If "sex is the
opium of the people" I was addicted to Hua. It wasn't a dangerous addiction...more like...a lusty, sweaty in the moment
freedom...that didn't have a downside...until later...that was
to come...but for a few precious month the only times I wasn't
moping around plagued with guilt and fear were the times I was
having sex with Hua.

-16-

I changed gears along a straight section of road as a string of cars whizzed past...the sun propelling...untelling me...a fresh afternoon breeze...invigorating against my knees...leaning into the wind...changed gears...peddling hard...attacked a hill...flew into ketch harbour road...coasted to a stop...breathlessly looked at my watch...9:17...no where near my best time...7:43.

Sweat stung my eyes as I wiped my forehead with a bandana and looked around to see if Hua's car was there? Nope. I laid my bike in the grass and knocked on Chen's door. His father answered it and invited me in.

"Chen's getting ready," he smiled.

He motioned to a cushy sofa in the living room.

"Please sit."

Their tiny house was different from any I had ever been in. They had a television and "regular" furniture but also colorful hangings depicting Chinese scenes...jade dragons...figurines... pagodas...waterfalls...scenic landscapes. It was like getting immersed in another culture, and I imagined visiting China someday. Their home always had funky aromas from Chinese dishes Chen's parents were cooking. This time was no different. I'm not sure what they were making, but the whole house smelled very fishy. I think Chen was slightly embarrassed by his parents, the decor of their house and the unusual smells from the cooking. I was really the only person he had invited in, and it took him years to do that.

"Bro!" Chen said, emerging from a hallway, his ball cap on backwards.

He was dressed in his usual summer garb, denim cutoff shorts, a t-shirt and sneakers.

"Let's go."

He said something to his father in Chinese, and his father nodded.

"Where's Hua today?"

"At the library," Chen replied, without looking at me.

She had taken a summer job at the Dalhousie University library...a drag...I didn't get to see...fuck...her as much as I wanted. She had sworn me to secrecy. It was as serious as I had ever seen her. She said her father would fly into a rage if he knew she was dating...let alone having sex. He wanted her to devote all her time and energy to her academics so she could get into medical school.

The sailboat....a 26-foot...Albin Nova sloop with a small cabin and a fiberglass hull painted blue. Just stepping onto the boat was like stepping into another world. Sailing is the closest thing there is to...flying.

"There's not much wind in the cove, so I'm going to motor out and then put the sails up," Chen said.

I rarely got out on the ocean unless it was with friends. But I always felt its inviting call and presence. My family didn't own a boat because my father had an irrational fear of boats. He got queasy if he got in a boat, or a ship, no matter the size. Our neighbors had an aluminum boat with a twelve horsepower outboard motor for puttering around Chandler's Cove, but it was too small to take out on the open ocean. They'd let me use the boat on occasion, but my father always refused to get in.

"You go ahead," he would say, his face screwed up in anxiety. "Just don't leave the cove."

The boat was fun for about 30 minutes but quickly got boring because the cove was small. I wanted to be out on the ocean where the horizon was endless!

Chen had taught me about sailing. I always jumped at the chance to go out on the water with him. Chen's real name was, Whack Lee. Imagine the cruel and endless teasing he took in rural Nova Scotia with a name like that.

He made friends easily and most of the kids and parents liked him. But the meaner…older boys…broke his toys…they all had a shot at his name…starting in grade school…whack lee…became… whack off…quack lee…whack me…always pronounced with a condescending Chinese accent. Complaining was useless because all that did was elicit spiteful snickers from small hearted people… who despised the Chinese…their massive factory fishing ships in the atlantic…five time the size of the titanic…lurking off the coast taking all the fish. We all called him Chen, his middle name. Being a first generation Chinese immigrant with parents that spoke broken English was hard as hell for Chen and Hua, but they never let it get to them. Talk about fish out of water.

-17-

Chen and I ambled down the grassy slope behind his house, climbed onboard the sailboat and untied it from its moorings. Sailing is total freedom. If you set a course…you can leave your problems onshore. But if you don't know what you're doing…you can easily get into trouble. The ocean can be merciless.

Once we motored out of the harbour, Chen scampered over the deck to the mast and unfurled the mainsail. There was wind, but the ocean was calm except for swells that gently rocked the boat. After a few minutes the wind filled the sails. The boat seemed to sense it and creaked in response as we moved gracefully ahead.

"Where we headed?" I asked as Chen took the tiller.

"Gull Rock."

Gull Rock was a tiny island offshore that seagulls and seals sunbathed on. It would take hours to sail there and back. But the weather was nice, the sun was warm, and a steady wind was gently propelling us forward.

"The wind's at our back. That means our point of sail is running," Chen grinned. "This is great. We're going to run straight out there."

Sailing allowed me to escape my fathomless feelings of guilt and fear. Looking back on that summer, I can see that being out on the ocean in Chen's sailboat saved me from myself, free of the burdens on shore. The ocean was old and new at every moment. Everywhere at once. It spoke of life…death…mystery…grandeur. I imagined the tall wooden sailing ships of two hundred years earlier, their sails bellowing as they entered Halifax Harbour.

Slipping on my sunglasses, I leaned back taking in the magnificent and broad expanse of the ocean...the salty air...sparkling sun...the sound of the boat cutting through the water...wind playing in our sails and rigging. There's something undeniable mystical about being in a sailboat, the wind moving the boat the same as it has for thousands of years.

Thirty feet off to the right, a plastic milk container was bobbing on the surface.

"Chen, I want to get that milk container."

"Why?"

"So I can recycle it."

Whenever I saw anything plastic on the shore or in the water, I grabbed it, took it home and dropped it in our recycling container. Plastic can last ten thousand years and picking it up here and there was my small way of trying to make a difference.

We sailed over to it, and using the boathook I was able to snag it and pull it onboard. Grinning, I held it up like a trophy.

"One less plastic thing in the ocean is a tiny victory! If everyone did this the oceans would be pristine."

Chen nodded in agreement and we continued toward Gull Rock.

We weren't saying much as I gazed down into the ocean's jade eyes. Sun danced on the surface as if God had dropped an immense glowing orb of white light that shattered into thousands of tiny pieces flickering on the lips of the waves.

Chen pointed forward.

"Check out the set of the sails."

He smiled widely.

"We're wing-on-wing, buddy. The mainsail is on port and the jib is on starboard. I love this set of the sails. We've got to be careful though. We don't want to do an accidental jibe. That could really mess us up."

I could see where the "wing-on-wing" term must have come from because the sails, now perpendicular to each other, resembled angels white wings.

"When's your cousin get here?"

"Tomorrow."

He adjusted his ball cap.

"Wow! How long's she going to be here?"

I shrugged.

"Who knows? A few weeks. A few months. Forever? We're the only family she has."

"Jeez, suddenly you have an instant sister."

I shot him a harsh look.

"She's not my sister!"

I wasn't ready for Molli's arrival. No one was.

"You take the tiller," Chen said. "I'm going below to grab a couple of Cokes."

"What should I do?"

"Like I showed you before."

He pointed forward.

"Keep her steady and straight ahead. Pick a spot on the horizon. Point the bow of the boat at it."

I grabbed the tiller and he scrambled into the cabin. I was a little unsure at first and the boat seemed to sense that. We had been sailing pretty much in a straight line before, but now the boat jerked slightly from side to side, responding every time I moved the tiller even a little.

Chen emerged from the cabin with the cokes and cracked them open.

"You're doing great."

Steering a sailboat with a tiller is a counterintuitive. Kind of like a watch going backwards. It's not like driving, because when you when you want to go left you push the tiller to the right and vice-versa. After a few minutes I got into the quiet rhythm of it. It was very Zen. The tiller was an extension of my body. When we reached Gull Rock, Chen took over.

"We're going into the wind now, so we're tacking," he said as we zigzagged back toward land.

What's up tonight?" I asked as we approached the mouth to Ketch Harbour

"I'm playing Dad in chess."

A big deal. Chen continually talked about playing his father, who was one step below a grand master or something like that. I don't think Chen had ever beaten him.

"Good luck."

He shot me a dismissive look.

"Chess isn't a game of luck like say, Monopoly. Chess is a game of skill. It's a little like sailing. Every time you trim a sail, adjust the tiller even a little or pull in a rope, there's a reaction. It's the same with chess. Every time you move a piece, it changes the whole complexity of the board."

"Okay. I won't say 'good luck.' How about 'kick ass?'"

He laughed.

"He's beaten me two hundred and thirty-four times straight, and we fought to a draw a year ago. It was a miracle! I played him to a draw! When he was a teenager he played in the Chess Olympics representing China."

Chen's father was quiet and nice but I think he had a ruthless streak. Why wouldn't he let Chen win once in a while? If he was such a great player, he had an obligation to help less talented players, especially his only son. Chen wouldn't want that because it would represent, in his mind at least, pity. He was proud.

"I always want to play someone better than me, so I can improve," Chen said. "I beat everybody I know. Nobody will play me anymore, except at tournaments. But if I move up a level in a tournament they kill me. I'm getting my pawns killed like crazy, throwing them against walls."

He made a comic face like someone getting killed.

"The best players are always ten moves ahead," he continued. "If you're only five moves ahead, they'll slaughter you. It's about setting up defenses and strategies and counteracting things done to you. It's about skill, not luck."

I didn't play chess, at least not well. But I respected Chen's passion for the game. He loved it as much as sailing.

It was a fantastic afternoon on the ocean. By the time we got back to Chen's house I felt as if a burden had been lifted from my shoulders. It was close to dinnertime and Chen invited me to stay. I had looked for Hua's red Honda as we crested the slope in front of Chen's house but didn't see it.

"Thanks, but I've got to go home," I replied. "Mum's getting things ready for Molli. She probably needs my help."

"Call me after she gets here," Chen waved. "Let me know what's up."

"I will. Good luck in chess tonight!"

"No need for luck," he scoffed.

I took my time pedaling home, and when I got there I found my mother upstairs in Molli's room, lying on the new bed. The whole house smelled of fresh paint.

She motioned around the room.

"How's it look?"

It didn't look anything like my old bedroom. The walls were a refreshing light blue, the trim a fresh white, like a blue sky with a few clouds. *Maybe a fresh coat of paint does make life a little less glum.* My posters had been replaced with framed seascape photographs my mother had taken.

"Looks nice."

She sat up on the edge of the bed.

"Your father called."

"How's it going?"

"Not great."

"He must be beat."

"He is. I'm worried about him."

"When do they get in?"

She sighed.

"Tomorrow night."

-18-

Eyes have a language all their own...expressing joy...pain... hurt...when words fail us. They reveal the state of the spirit. I remember people's eyes. The color. The shape. Eyebrows. It's as if my eyes are drawn magnetically to their eyes. Birds do that.

On the day Molli arrived my mother made pizza from scratch. She had stressed all day over what to make and finally settled on pizza.

"Everyone loves pizza, right?" she had said as she rolled dough in the kitchen.

I spent the day reading in the A-frame and then went for a long walk along the bluffs. It was overcast most of the day, but just as I got home a rainstorm blew in. It was so fierce that it rattled our windows, making it a grim and stormy night in every sense.

It was midnight by the time my father and Molli got home. My mother and I were watching TV, waiting, when we heard the taxi pull up. The front door opened, and my father's voice echoed in the front hall. My mother and I exchanged glances and then got up and went to greet them.

There Molli was...rain dripping off the hood of her raincoat... like an endless stream of tears. My mother rushed to my father and hugged him.

"Geoff, thank God you're back."

"Molli," my father said calmly, "this is your Aunt Karen and your cousin Max."

She pushed back her hood...a pained...tired expression... evoking misfortune...great loss...smoky blue eyes...a color that mutely told the story of the ocean on certain days…red and badly swollen from days of crying…a deeply wounded gaze beyond mere words. She appeared younger than fifteen…more like a tall twelve-year-old. Never had I seen…such a miserable human being. A loose tangle of brown curls…tumbled over her face….down her back. She tried to smile…but it collapsed.

"Hi," she said weakly.

My mother embraced her.

"Come in."

Molli didn't see me…in a daze…a soul dark and grief filled…a void of some kind…inaccessible.

"Hi, Molli," I said, awkwardly holding out my hand for her to shake. I don't know why I did that. It was pure reaction more than anything.

She looked at my hand and then at me. She seemed confused.

"Hi," she replied, softly taking my hand.

"Come in and get warmed up," my mother said, ushering us toward the kitchen.

My father grabbed my shoulder and held me back.

"Get our suitcases out of the taxi."

I ran outside in the rain and pulled the suitcases from the truck. After lugging Molli's suitcases and a snowboard to her room, I went back downstairs to the kitchen. Without her jacket she looked a little older. Her frayed Nike sneakers looked as exhausted as she did. Her sagging light brown sweater matched the color of her hair. Slightly heavy and lanky, her arms and legs were too long for her body, like she had yet to grow into them. Her pale skin made her thick eyebrows stand out like rocks in the snow. I recognized her eyebrows from somewhere. I realized they were exactly like my father's. A single hoop earring dangled from her right ear.

My father got up, pulled a glass from the cupboard above the sink, filled it with water and then popped something into his mouth, probably a painkiller. My mother was watching him but didn't say anything.

I glanced at Molli. I had never been in such an uncomfortable situation in my life. It was as if the air in the room had suddenly been charged with raw energy. I didn't know what to say. What not to say. How to act. How not to act. Where to put my hands. Where to look. My mother finally broke the silence and offered Molli pizza.

"I made it this afternoon," she smiled.

Molli sat motionless without responding.

"Molli," my mother repeated. "I've got pizza?"

"I'm not hungry."

"She hasn't eaten," my father said.

"You poor girl," my mother said. "You've got to have something. What about some nice hot soup?"

"No thanks."

My mother placed her hand on top of Molli's.

"You must be famished. There's got to be something I can get you?"

Molli pulled her hand away, her expression suddenly hard.

"You can get me my family back," she snapped. "You can take me back to my home! That would be nice!"

There was an appalling silence.

"You're probably nice people," she continued coldly. "And uncle Geoff helped a lot."

She paused and seemed to be collecting herself.

"But I want you to know something," she said, her voice more deliberate. "I can't stay here. This isn't my home. I was forced to come here. I don't belong here..."

My father cut her off.

"She's exhausted. What you really need, Molli, is a good night's sleep."

Molli slumped in her chair...a totally devastated human...right there...across the table from me. I could not reconcile myself to the fact she had actually arrived. I was mentally prepared for her arrival but obviously not emotionally ready. Everything had a dull dreamlike quality. I'm not sure what I had expected. All I could see was her raw grief...like a freshly scarred knee. No spark...a painful nothingness...as if her spirit had been in the plane and died with the rest of her family.

Her bedroom was next to mine. Later I could hear my mother's hushed voice in Molli's bedroom. I don't know what my mother was saying but it was a one-way conversation. Molli didn't utter a single word. After my mother went to bed I laid there wondering if I'd hear her weeping. I didn't. It was completely quiet...the only sounds...gusting wind...rain.

Take the "r" out of rain and replace it with a "p" and you get...

-19-

It took three endless days for Molli to leave her bedroom. My mother went in faithfully bringing Molli meals and books on grief while gently coaxing her to come downstairs.

"She'll come down when she's ready," my father said.

It was as if there was a ghost...in the house. We quietly went about our lives, careful not to disturb her. Sometimes I'd hear my mother's hushed voice coming from Molli's bedroom and what sounded like a single word reply from Molli. Other times it was as if they were sitting in there for hours without uttering a word.

On the third morning, I was sitting in the kitchen checking email on my laptop. It was a beautiful and warm sunny day. My parents had agreed that someone would always be in the house for Molli. Since my father was at work and my mother was out, I was the only person around. I heard a noise and turned. Molli was standing in the doorway, wearing the same clothes she had on when she arrived.

"Molli," I blurted. "How are you feeling?"

I pointed to a chair.

"Sit down. Do you want breakfast, apple juice? Mum and Dad are out. I can make you some..."

I was practically stammering.

"Juice?" she replied weakly.

I jumped up.

"I'll get it."

She sat at the table.

"Thanks."

My hand was shaking as I poured the juice, handed it to her and sat down. She slowly sipped it. Saying I was uncomfortable would not even come close to describing how I felt. I was at a total loss as to what to do or say.

"Your father's at work?" she asked.

"Rehearsal, yep."

"And your Mum?"

"The grocery store."

She nodded and took another sip of juice.

"Is your room comfortable?" I managed to ask. "How are you feeling?"

She looked me in the eye.

"Like anyone who's lost their whole family, I guess."

My gaze fell to the table.

"Your mother's pregnant?" she asked after a moment. "When's the baby's due?"

"In a few months."

"Where's the baby's room?"

"It's ahhh...it's..."

She exhaled heavily.

"You're in the baby's room and I'm in your room, right?"

I didn't know what to say. I could have lied but she would have known it.

"They're trying to decide who goes where. We're..."

"I'm in your room," she repeated flatly.

"You need it more than I do." I'm not sure why I said that. It just came out.

"I *need* my own bedroom back in Denver," she moaned.

I didn't know what to say so I changed the subject.

"We have cereal, toast, bananas. I can make bacon..."

She turned toward the window then back toward me, her eyes heavy.

"I can't believe it's sunny, that it's not raining."

"Really?"

"Remember when I was here like ten years ago?"

I leaned back in my chair.

"Kind of."

"It rained the whole time."

"The weather can suck sometimes, but..."

She cut me off.

"It rains in Denver too."

I motioned to what looked like three small stars tattooed on the back of her right hand.

"Is that a tattoo?"

She gently stroked them.

"I forgot I had this. I got them two days before we left Denver as a way to pay homage to my family."

"Nice."

She shook her head.

"Your father got mad as hell when he saw it. I told him I had a right to remember my family anyway I wanted."

I imagined my father seeing the tattoos and going bonkers. Earlier that summer, after Ricky was showing off a new tattoo during a barbeque at our house, my father admonished me to never get one, "like that idiot friend of yours."

"You must be hungry? What about some cereal?"

"Okay. A little."

She was all arms and legs with a thick neck. Her skin was white as milk. I went to the cupboard and pulled out a box of Cheerios.

"Do you like these?"

"Yep."

I forced a smile.

"Mum calls them 'holes.'"

It was as if she didn't hear me. I grabbed a bowl and a carton of milk and put them on the table. She poured herself cereal and was eating quietly when I heard a car in the driveway. After a minute my mother came in carrying groceries.

"Molli!" she exclaimed. "You're up!"

She dropped the groceries on the counter then rushed over and hugged Molli.

"How are you? Are you hungry?"

"Fine, thanks. I had a bowl of cereal."

My mother started pulling things out of the grocery bag for Molli to see.

"I bought you soy milk, like you asked."

"Thank you, Aunt Karen."

"It's a beautiful day," my mother said. "Max, maybe Molli would like to go for a hike?"

My mother knew what anyone who enjoys hiking knows. There are times when a long walk or hike gives you a new perspective and changes for the better how you see the world.

I glanced at Molli.

"You up for that?"

She exhaled heavily.

"No. I..."

"It's a gorgeous day," my mother repeated. "You should get some fresh air, stretch your legs a little."

"Okay," Molli replied softly. "Let me put on my sneakers."

• • •

We had just stepped outside when I heard a dull thud. Molli and I both turned in time to see a bird falling to the ground beneath the living room window ten feet away. *Shit!* I strode over and looked down at the bird. A sparrow. Like the others before, its neck was broken. After a few moments it stopped twitching. It was dead.

Molli was standing a few feet behind me.

"Why did it do that?"

"They see the reflection of the trees in the window, fly over to land in them and break their necks."

I exhaled heavily.

"This is the sixth one this summer!"

She moved in a little closer and gazed down at the bird.

"That sucks."

"I'll bury it when we get back. Come on. Let's go."

It was low tide, and the familiar aroma of the ocean hung in the air as we made our way around the rocky cove, through the woods and up to the rocky bluffs. The sun and a warm breeze out of the south had chased away any trace of a chill. Despite it being a spectacular day, Molli was withdrawn and quiet, her thoughts obviously miles away.

"I've been coming out here forever," I said, trying to break the silence. "We have a picture of you and your parents out here from your visit ten years ago."

"It was out here?"

"Yeah, not far from here."

She stopped walking and brushed her hair back, exposing her tired smoky blue eyes.

"Every summer Dad said we were going to come and visit but it never happened."

"My father said the same thing about visiting you guys in Colorado."

Shielding her eyes with her hand, she looked out over the whitecaps dancing over the ocean.

"You can see forever from here."

I smiled.

"That's why I love it. It's endless."

We walked a little further until we reached "the crack." Anyone who ever hiked those windswept bluffs had looked in awe and horror into "the crack." Another way to describe it…a menacing crevice…a bottomless fissure…a shear deadly drop down a demon throat tumbling past eighty feet of black rock face into the gnashing teeth of the Atlantic. Waves thundered in there with an unambigu-ous…KABOOM…announcing something great and magnificent. But it might also be the last thing you heard. If you fell in…you were dead. Killed by the fall…smashed into the rocks like a doll. A tourist fell in once, getting her picture taken. She didn't have a chance. She shattered her leg and arm in the fall and drowned in minutes…her screams thankfully muffled by the roar of the waves. Her friend…a true friend to the end. He jumped in, in a heroic attempt to save her. He died with her. A rescue boat got there two hours later.

Kevin died in, the crack. A twelve foot wide jagged and danger-ous fracture…a violent crack…in the rock bluffs…straight down to the black boiling ocean…carved by glaciers…time. The crack wasn't a metaphor for anything…except death…if you wanted it… surrender to the void…to the crack…I never got that close to, the crack, except the night Kevin died. If you looked down into the very gut of it…you faced yourself…what you were made of…your fear of heights…of death…or a marvel of time and the natural world.

With Molli trailing behind me, I nervously skirted the crack, climbing twenty feet higher on a rocky path above it. That was the closet I would get. But it summoned you to the edge. Every fifteen seconds a five-ton wave threw itself into, the crack, with wild abandon…an explosion…then a fine ocean mist rode the air to your cheek.

Instead of following me, Molli walked to the edge of, the crack. The wind was brisk and gleefully grabbed her curly brown hair, whipping it around like crazy.

"Careful," I yelled. "It's windy out here."

Ignoring me she leaned forward to get an even closer look into, the crack.

"Molli," I yelled. "You're too close to the edge."

She just looked at me, her eyes wide. A strong gust could have carried her into, the crack.

"Come on, let's keep going!"

She looked down again, then back at me as waves continued their thunderous assault into, the crack. Her steely stare said it all.

If she wanted to jump I wasn't close enough to pull her back.

"Come on!" I yelled, waving her toward me. "It's windy, dangerous."

She looked perplexed, as if she didn't understand English. I was shaking, but I mustered up my courage, strode over, grabbed her arm and pulled her back.

"Let's head home."

It was a terrifying moment. Not just because of what might have happened, but also because of the awful insight it gave me into Molli's fractured soul, her devastated state of mind.

Walking through the woods she knelt to pick from a patch of purple wild flowers by the path.

"Do you ever think of doing it?" she asked softly without looking at me.

"Doing what?" I asked. But I knew what she meant.

She was gripping the flower stems tightly.

"Jumping...ending it all."

"No. I never thought of that."

That was a lie! Ever since Kevin died...

A wicked smile formed on her lips, her eyes suddenly as mean and dark as a thunderstorm.

"Of course you don't. I bet you're a 'happy person,'" she continued, spitting out the words "happy person" like poison. "Your kind never thinks about killing themselves."

"I'm not happy!" I blurted. "I mean, what's wrong with being happy?" *If only she knew how truly miserable I was!*

Still, I couldn't imagine the depth of pain she was in. Her grief was almost palatable.

"Listen to me," I pleaded. "You can't do it."

"Why?" she demanded angrily. "Why can't I do it?"

"Why? Because...because I won't let you. Because people love you!"

"Who?"

"My mother and father...me."

A deeply wounded expression formed on her face.

"I don't care. They'd get over it. You'd get over it."

She stood and looked me squarely in the eye.

"I don't belong with your family. I'm an imposition. Get real! Your mother's having a baby in a few months. You don't have room for me."

She leaned against a moss-covered rock and stared up at me, broken sunlight on her face.

"I'd do it except..."

Her gaze fell to the ground.

Except what?

Maybe it was the stress of everything, but instead of comforting Molli, as I should have, I lost my temper.

"Do you know what families do when there's a problem? Families work through it. They find a way. They make it work. They lean on each other. Is it always easy? No. But together they find a way, and that's what we're going to do. Find a way."

She shook her head dismissively.

"It must be a curse," she hissed, "to be *so* optimistic."

"Good! Not only am I a happy person, I'm also optimistic!"

Back at home, Molli gave my mother the wild flowers she had picked then went upstairs to lie down. I heard her door close then urgently whispered to my mother about what had happened with Molli at the edge of, the crack. The color drained from her face.

"I've got to get her into grief counseling right away."

She called the counselor and made an appointment for the following day. Then she sat and rubbed her temples.

"I can't imagine what a hellish state of mind she's in."

That night, I dreamed I was out on the cliffs with Molli. Just the two of us, exactly as it had been earlier that day. Molli was next to the crack, the wind blowing her hair around like crazy. I could tell she was going to jump, but when I tried to grab her arm, she pulled away.

"I'm not going to jump," she laughed. "I'm going to fly!"

She stepped off the edge, and to my utter dismay she started flying as if she were floating in the air. She laughed and coaxed me to join her.

"Come on," she grinned wickedly. "I'm flying. You can too. Come on, you can do it! You're an optimist!"

I nervously peered over the edge as mighty waves crashed into the crack.

"Stop it, Kevin. Come back here."

"I'm not Kevin," she laughed hysterically. "Come on. It's easy. Just spread your wings. Come on! Don't be afraid."

-20-

The next morning Ricky picked me up. I slid into the driver's seat, and we chugged down the road to Crystal Crescent Beach.

"Molli's gotta be going through hell," he said, shaking his head. "Does she talk about it?"

I glanced at him.

"Not really. And if anyone asks her how's she's doing, they get a one-word reply. 'Okay.' 'Alright.'"

She was the queen of one-word answers.

"It's got to be tough, man," Ricky replied softly, "real tough."

The dirt-and-gravel road leading into the beach was filled with deep potholes, and navigating them was a challenge, especially with Ricky constantly admonishing me to be careful.

"This road is like the surface of the moon," he muttered. "It's murder on my suspension!"

"I'm trying to be careful," I replied, keeping my eyes on the road.

We finally pulled into the dirt lot and parked in a spot over-looking the beach.

A gorgeous summer day…flawless blue sky…a delightful warm breeze chasing away any hint of the cool weather and fog that had dropped in on us just a few days earlier.

Ricky punched up a rock station and lit a joint. We were sitting there idly, windows down, listening to the radio and not saying much when I noticed a guy sitting in a fold-up beach chair smoking a cigar. Even from fifty feet away you could see his arrogance like an aura around him. He was wearing wrap-around sunglasses, but I immediately recognized him. It was John King. I tapped Ricky on the arm and pointed.

"Look, there's your buddy, John 'asshole' King!"

A sinister look crossed Ricky's face.

"Tis his highness himself. Go back to Toronto, shithead!"

"He's not from Toronto."

"Yeah? Where's he from Calgary? Vancouver?"

I shook my head.

"Who cares!"

King got up, dropped his cigar in the sand and strolled down the beach. He had only been gone a few minutes when a big old crow landed next to where he had been sitting. It hopped onto the chair and started rooting through a light jacket King had left there. It carefully plucked something from one of his pockets and flew off. A few minutes later it returned and took his watch!

"Look at that!" I said laughing. "That crow's picking his pockets!"

Ricky slapped his knee and started howling.

"That's one clever bird!"

"Crows are one of the world's most intelligent animals. They have an encephalization quotient approaching that of some apes."

He glanced over at me, his face a blank.

"A what?"

"An encephalization quotient. It's a measure of relative brain size between actual brain mass and predicted brain mass for an animal of a given size."

His face was screwed up like a question mark. Obviously he was expecting a more detailed explanation.

"It's used to help estimate the intelligence or cognition of the animal."

He motioned out the window.

"If you're saying that's a smart bird, I got to agree with that."

"They're from the Corvidae family of birds, which are bitching smart!"

"Oh yeah" he yawned.

"Ricky, they're an incredible bird!"

"Okay, if you say so, man."

"Yeah, I do say so," I replied somewhat indignantly. "Crow use tools and tool construction."

He smirked.

"Can they pass woodshop?"

"Maybe," I grinned. "In medieval times crows were thought to live an abnormally long life, and it was thought they could predict the future, predict rain and reveal ambushes."

He leaned back in his seat and pushed his sunglasses up on his nose.

"I've got to get myself one of those."

"What you need is a 'forest owlet.'"

"Huh?"

"A forest owlet. It's a very endangered species of owl."

"An endangered owl?"

"Yeah. The 'Heteroglaux blewitti.'"

I cracked a smile.

"That's its Latin name."

"You know its Latin name?"

I shrugged.

"They thought it was extinct until one was spotted in Maharashtra."

"Where's that?"

"Central India."

He slowly shook his head.

"You're telling me you want to travel to India to help save some stupid owl from extinction?"

"Yes, and it's not stupid. There's only like a few hundred left because lumber companies are destroying deciduous forest in central India, the only place they're still found."

"You're kidding right? You don't speak Indian."

I suppressed a chuckle.

"Have you told your parents about this?" he asked.

"No. Not yet."

"Why this owl, man? Jeez, isn't there something closer to home you can save?"

I glanced over at him.

"Maybe, but this is the one I want to help. It's a little owl and looks unassuming, but man-oh-man, you sure wouldn't want to get between it and a meal. It's got these huge talons and can snatch up animals twice its size."

Ricky grinned widely.

"Yeah? Sounds impressive."

I nodded.

"It's beyond awesome. I can't wait to see one in the wild."

-21-

Sex with Hua was a potion…a lotion…replacing the throbbing pain of life with intense pleasure. One afternoon she showed up at our house on her bike. My father was at practice and my mother and Molli were in town. It didn't take long for Hua and me to tear each other's clothes off and get down to business in my bedroom.

Her pallid skin was warm and silky. I gently rolled her onto her back…kissed her on the mouth…ran my hands over her nipples…which became erect. She was aggressive…which I really liked. She answered my kiss with a passionate one of her own…plunging her tongue into my mouth. After a few minutes she pulled back and smiled.

"Do you like oral sex?"

Before I could answer she started sloppily kissing her way down my naked torso. Every nerve in my body pulsed with sexual desire. Nothing in this world or the next would stop our singular moment of sexual bliss.

When we were done we lay in a loose embrace…sweating lightly in the warm afterglow of our lovemaking. No one knew me as well as Hua did. Not my parents or friends. Only she saw the full palette…the colors…dark…light…which completed me. The unending lust I worked so hard to hide from everyone, I gladfully revealed to her. I felt I could tell her…almost anything. She would be my trusted confidante if I only let her in. I propped myself up on one elbow and gazed over her long…slim…nude…body. She was on her side facing me…eyes closed as if she had fallen into a light slumber. She mumbled something inaudible.

Hua I desperately need to tell you something. There's a terrible secret I can't share with anyone else. It's eating me like cancer. I killed Kevin. I murdered him. I pushed him to his death. I killed him. Please help me! I can't go another day like this…

She opened her eyes and smiled.

"I drifted off."

"You were talking in your sleep."

She stretched like a cat.

"What did I say?"

"I couldn't make it out."

Sitting on the edge of the bed, she slipped her panties on and turned to me, her expression more serious.

"How's Molli?"

I flopped back on my pillow.

"Who knows?"

She pulled on her denim skirt, buttoned her blouse, then stepped into her sandals.

"I brought her something," she said. "Come on, I'll show you."

It was midday; the sun at its apex as we walked over to her trail bike leaned against the side of the house.

"I'm giving this to Molli."

"Your bike?"

"Yeah, she needs something to get around on."

"But it's your bike."

She shrugged.

"I've got another bike. I don't need two."

"Really? For Molli?"

She nodded.

We were standing there looking at the bike and talking when my mother and Molli got back.

"Molli," I said as they got out of the car and approached us. "Hua's giving you this bike."

Molli looked beyond shocked.

"I can't take your bike."

"Too late," Hua replied, "and besides, like I was telling Max, I have another bike."

"Hua, that's really sweet of you," my mother said.

"Try it out," Hua said to Molli.

Once on the bike, Molli pedaled unsteadily for a few seconds but then found her balance. She continued carefully up the driveway, then coasted back and stopped in front of us. I think she was actually smiling, albeit slightly.

"I don't know what to say," Molli said shyly.

I glanced over at Hua, who was standing next to my mother, both of them smiling. Hua constantly thought of others. She also had a fiercely protective side, especially when it came to her parents or Chen.

Looking at her standing in the driveway, giving away her bike, I was struck by her act of thoughtfulness. Basically there are two kinds of people: those who continually think of themselves and their own needs and desires, and those who think of others first. What makes us one or the other? Who knows? Maybe it has something to do with upbringing or perhaps people are born either selfish or generous. There's a big risk to putting others first. But if you can do it, there's also a huge reward. Hua's generosity and wisdom were as much a part of her as her dark eyes and toothy smile.

"Max, would you take the groceries in?" my mother asked.

Grabbing the bags from the car, I put them in the kitchen, poured myself a glass of apple juice and quickly drank it. When I went back outside my mother was weeding in her garden, the sun on her back. Hua and Molli were chatting.

"Molli and I are going to walk to Chebucto Head," Hua said.

"I'll grab my hat and come with you."

"Girls only on this trip," Hua replied.

"What? Why don't I just..."

"We'll be fine, Max," Molli added reassuringly.

Considering what had happened when Molli and I were hiking on the cliffs a few weeks earlier, her suicidal thoughts, I was leery. But she seemed to be doing better, and I sensed it wasn't a good idea to argue. They wanted to be by themselves.

"Okay."

They walked up the driveway, the gravel crunching under their feet, and I went to talk to my mother. She had pulled a bunch of weeds from her garden that were in a pile.

"How's it going with Molli and the counselor?"

She stopped weeding, and still on her knees, looked up at me.

"Hard to tell. She's the queen of one-word answers. She's not saying much."

"Is the counseling helping?"

She nodded.

"It can't hurt."

"How are you?"

"Groggy."

"Need anything?"

"No, I'm fine."

I spent the next hour and a half in the A-frame leafing through travel magazines. I heard my father pull up and get out of his car. He stuck his head in the door of the A-frame, and Homer, his tail wagging, got up to greet him.

"I've finally nailed the second movement!" my father exclaimed.

His upbeat mood was in sharp contrast to the previous week, when he seemed dour, distracted and moody. The symphony was opening its season in a little more than a month with a performance of, Alfred Schnittke. Rehearsals had been disastrous. My father had been struggling with a critical violin segment even though he practiced it every night following rehearsal. Schnittke was a little-known Russian composer, and my father adored him. Schnittke, the Mozart of the twentieth century. He beamed when he talked about Schnittke's Concerto Gross for Two Violins, call-ing it one of the best classical pieces written in the last hundred years. He'd gush about Schnittke when my friends were around, which was beyond embarrassing. He had wanted to name me "Schnittke," but my mother talked him out of it.

"Check this out!"

He pulled his violin from its case, and grinning widely, started playing, slowly drawing his bow across the strings. His eyes were closed as if he were in a blissful dream. To an untrained ear like mine it sounded exactly the same as it had for weeks. But he was a perfectionist in all he did. He stopped playing and smiled.

I applauded.

"That's great."

He bowed.

"I adjusted my bow and that made all the difference."

"It sure did."

He carefully put the violin back in its case and closed the lid.

"I'm going inside to play it for your mother."

His face was radiant, like a kid with a new toy.

I heard him in the house playing it when Hua and Molli got back.

"Your father's getting better," Molli quipped.

"Go in and tell him that. He'll be beyond happy to hear it."

She turned to Hua and hugged her.

"Thanks," Molli said. "I really appreciate everything, not just the bike. *Everything*, okay?"

"Now you can ride down to see us," Hua replied.

"I will," Molli smiled before going inside.

Hua dropped onto the bench beside me.

"How was the walk?"

She grinned.

"Nice."

"What did you do?"

"Walked and talked."

"What did you talk about?"

"How she's doing. What she's thinking, stuff like that."

She paused.

"I told her about the accident...Kevin...what happened."

Accident. If only!

"Why?"

She exhaled heavily.

"He was your friend. It's a big deal. She should know about it."

She was right, I guess.

"How is she?"

She leaned over and kissed me.

"Hmmm. A little better."

-22-

Grief is not a spirit…nor is it memory.

Grief is a journey of heartache…anguish…woe…a depth of pain known only to those who have been forced to survive it…a deep crack…you have to claw your way out of. That was Molli's existence. I had been thrown into a different kind of hole. The chief emotions I was cursed with regarding Kevin were fear and guilt. They refused to let me grieve for my friend. They got down in the hole with me, always reminding me of what I had done. They were wicked and vengeful.

On Friday I went with my mother and Molli into Halifax to hang out while they were meeting with the grief counselor. I bought a Coke and then walked a few blocks up Spring Garden Road and strolled through, the Public Gardens. I loved it there. It was a leafy refuge from the real world. A city block sized Victorian garden with ponds, swans, ducks, ornate gardens, gnarly old trees providing shade, statues, fountains, pathways, a gazebo, a canteen and cool lawns you could lay on. It was mid-afternoon, and the warm July sun bathed everything in a delightful golden hue under a pale blue sky. I was sitting on a bench in the shade of an old maple tree when I heard someone call my name. It was Russ Devlin…a guy from Bear Cove…in his late twenties…with a reputation as a lowlife career criminal…and worse. Let me put it this way, if the Public Gardens were a kind of "Eden" then Russ was the snake.

That summer, he was my eye-opening introduction to genuine evil in the world. Not that I had been willfully naïve before that. But he was about to run off with my youthful innocence, like someone stealing my sneakers. You can't go back to who you were after that. I wondered how someone could turn out like Russ? Maybe life is like a chessboard. You're either born on a dark square or a light square. If you're born on a dark square you're going to do bad things. If you're born on a light square you're going to live a good life. Who am I kidding? Life isn't a chessboard. It's a battlefield. Besides, if life was like a chessboard, we'd all be born on gray squares.

The nickname committee had dubbed Russ, Mister D. Apparently he thought that his "Mister D" moniker was associated with the devil. In truth the real devil probably wouldn't want to be associated with Russ because Russ was a lowlife idiot. He had "Mister D" tattooed on his right forearm in two-inch Gothic lettering. If you didn't call him "Mister D" he'd get pissed off. He stabbed some guy from Spryfield in the foot because the guy wouldn't call him Mister D. After high school he said he was going to college to study "Medieval history." He was real disappointed when it was explained to him that it was not spelled "Midevil" and had nothing to do with anything "evil." He would have been comically criminal if it were not for a palatable aura of malevolence around him. It was always present in his hooded eyes and deranged grin. His mother had had some sort of nightmare before he was born, which was supposed to be a premonition that he would always be trouble.

Mister D was a nice kid, until grade ten. Then he changed for the worse. He became mean, started drinking and taking drugs. By seventeen, he had fallen down a well of trouble and never got out. When I was ten, he was the prime suspect in the rape and murder of a seventeen-year-old girl from Purcell's Cove…Diana Fitzgerald. He had dumped her body in the ocean, cleansing her of anything that would implicate him. Her mother had a stroke and died a year later. Her father started drinking and died a few years after that. I was beyond scared shitless of Mister D. But even reprobate criminals like that have some redeeming characteristics. He had a reputation as a great mechanic who could fix anything. I never saw him without a toothpick in his mouth, which he worked side to side with his tongue. His ratty horseshoe mustache added to his menace. That June day he was wearing a tattered blue T-Shirt that had "Smoke Meth. Worship Satan." printed in big white lettering on the front.

Who in Hell wears a T-Shirt like that?

"Hey there, dickwad," he said.

I looked up at him.

"Hi, Russ," I muttered.

He glared at me…bloodshot eyes bulging from their sockets.

"I meant, 'hi, Mister D,'" I stammered.

"What are you doing here, dickwad?"

"Waiting on my mother and cousin," I replied nervously. "What are you doing here?"

"I met my girlfriend for lunch. She loves it here."

He sat on the bench, pulled a pack of tobacco and rolling papers from his pocket, rolled a thin smoke, wet it with the tip of his tongue and lit it. He was slurring, his eyes bloodshot. He reeked of booze. I figured he was drunk.

"Your cousin?" he asked. "From the states, right?"

"Right."

"I heard about that," he said exhaling a large plume of smoke. "Her parents got killed?"

"And her little brother."

There were scabs on his arms and he kept scratching his face.

"You'd never get me in an airplane."

I figured someone must have told him. It seemed like everyone knew. He took another drag off the cigarette, then examined me with narrowed eyes.

"You were friends with dickwad Kevin Price, right?"

"Yeah."

He seemed to be thinking.

"That was screwed up."

"It was."

"You were there when he went over the edge?"

"I was with him that night. It was real foggy. He went to take a leak and never came back."

He shook his head.

"Imagine that. You go for a piss and fall off. You'd think he'd know better."

The conversation was making me uneasy...beads of sweat forming on my forehead. He leaned toward me and grinned fiendishly.

"I've been looking for you."

"For me? Why?"

"Because I know you done it."

I had no idea what he was talking about.

"Did what?"

The corners of his mouth turned down.

"You helped dickwad Kevin rob the station, and then you pushed him off the bluffs."

He stared at me, waiting for a reply, a malicious smile forming on his unshaven face. My blood turned to frost. *How could he know?*

"That's crazy," I muttered. "I don't know what you're talking about!"

"Bullshit you don't."

"I swear I don't," I replied, my voice breaking.

"You can't bullshit a bullshitter, kid," he sneered. "Come on. Where's your half of the money?"

"This is crazy!"

I jumped to my feet to leave, but he grabbed my arm and yanked me back onto the bench.

"Listen to me, kid! I was in the station the day after you guys pulled your little robbery. I asked Kevin about it. He was nervous as hell. He admitted it and told me you helped him."

My heart was pounding...unable to speak.

"That, that's…"

"Listen to me kid."

He looked around to make sure no one was watching, then slapped me.

"I'm not asking you, kid, I'm telling you, you done it! You helped him rob the station and then you pushed him off the bluffs because he was going to squeal."

"That's crazy!"

"It was you, kid!"

His eyes dark…wild…animalistic…terrifying.

"Where's the money, you little prick? That's all I want. Give me the money or I'll burn your house down."

He stared at me, or *through* me was more like it.

"It wasn't like that," I blurted. "It was supposed to be easy."

He smiled widely and snorted.

"How did you throw that big shithead off the bluffs?"

"It was an accident!" I half cried. "I didn't mean to hurt him. He hit me, he, he…I'll get you the money. Don't tell anyone."

"Tell anyone?"

He threw up his hands.

"Why would I do that? I'm not a cop. All I want is the money."

"I'll give you the money. Just please don't…"

"Shut up, dickwad," he sneered. "Your little secret is safe with me."

He leaned in, his voice barely above a whisper.

"But I want that money."

He took a drag off his cigarette and seemed to be thinking

"What's today, Thursday?"

"Friday."

"Friday? I want that money on Monday afternoon. Bring it all to the parking lot at Crystal Crescent Beach at two o'clock."

He glared at me.

"Do you understand? Crystal Crescent Beach parking lot, two o'clock Monday!"

I was so scared I could hardly talk.

"I understand," I muttered. "I'll be there with the money."

"Don't mess with me or I'll burn your damned house down," he growled. "Understand?"

"Okay, Russ," I muttered. "I understand."

"What did you call me?" he demanded angrily.

"I mean okay, Mister D. Sorry, Mister D. I'll give you the money."

"Good."

He seemed to be thinking.

"You know something, kid?"

"What?" I replied weakly.

"You should never play poker. Kevin didn't tell me shit, but I figured he had something to do with it. I wasn't sure it was you two until just now. I bluffed your ass off."

An evil smirk crossed his face.

"Nothing is sweeter than plundered treasure."

He stood...dropped his cigarette...ground it out with his foot...slipped on a pair of sunglasses...started walking....stopped and turned back toward me.

"You're in my world now dickwad," he grinned wickedly, "and it's a dangerous place."

● ● ●

I slouched on the bench in stunned silence...my mood swinging violently between shock and revulsion. If there was *one* person in the whole world I didn't want to know the truth about how Kevin died, it was Mister D. I didn't have any option other than to give him the money. I believed it when he said he'd burn our house down. Little did I know that his reign of terror in my life was just beginning. I'd hand him the money and hopefully he'd just go away and wouldn't tell the police. What else could he do, kill me? And you know what? That might actually be a release from everything!

By the time I met up with Molli and my mother outside the counselor's office I was nauseated. Molli was drained, her eyes red and swollen from crying. My mother didn't look any better. It was as if she had taken some of the heavy burden of Molli's grief onto her own slender shoulders.

"I need to pick up a prescription and run a few errands," my mother said. "Do you guys want to come with me or meet back at the car in half an hour?"

I didn't feel like tagging along with my mother. I felt like jumping off a bridge.

"Want to get some 'Bud the Spud' fries?" I weakly asked Molli.

"I'm not hungry."

"Neither am I," I exhaled, "but you don't have to be hungry to eat 'Bud the Spud' fries. They're delicious. It's a chip wagon."

I pointed down the street.

"A few blocks that way."

My mother pressed a five-dollar bill into my palm.

"Good idea. I'll see you at the car in thirty minutes."

She hurried down the sidewalk, and Molli and I headed in the opposite direction toward Spring Garden Road, the sun on our backs.

"How's it going with the counselor?"

She pulled her sunglasses out of the pocket of her blue jean jacket and slipped them on.

"It sucks."

"Is it helping?"

"It sucks," she repeated, still staring straight ahead. "Everything sucks."

Well that's true!

"Yeah, but if you keep going it'll help you put the pieces back together. Everyone says talking about it is a good way to…"

"Right," she replied flatly.

"I'm just saying that talking, seeing the counselor…facing your emotions…your great loss…"

She stopped walking and glared at me.

"Can we please not talk about it?"

"Of course," I shrugged. "Whatever you want. But I'm just saying it's important to put the pieces of your life back together. Talking about it will help you do that. You need to…"

"Please Max, I mean it. Please stop."

"Okay, but I want you to know that talking about it will help. Everyone knows that. Just expressing your…"

She cut me off and motioned to the ornate front door of a shop we had stopped in front of.

"I want to look in this place."

It was "Kirks" a high end store that sold jewelry, ceramics, crystal, china and other expensive gift items. Halifax's wealthy families registered there for weddings.

"You want to go in here?"

"Yeah," she replied as she brushed past me. "I want to go in here."

Inside she browsed the aisles…stopping once in a while to pick up a fancy ceramic tray…vase…or to simply gaze at the glittering merchandise. I wasn't sure what she found so interesting and was hanging back a little, deep in my own thoughts not saying much. Stopping in front of a shelf of beautiful crystal vases…she seemed to be studying them…then using both hands…she carefully picked up the largest most ornate one…raised it above her head…stared at me hatefully… and intentionally dropped it…a tremendous boom…smashing into a thousand pieces that rocketed across the floor.

I was stunned!

"Go ahead, Max!" she said, her voice mean and mocking, her eyes swelling with pain. "Go ahead! Put the pieces back together. Talk them back together!"

I was speechless, my mouth hanging open. She stormed past me out the door just as one of the people working there rushed up, obviously alerted by the boom of the vase shattering.

"That's a four hundred and fifty-dollar vase!" he exclaimed. "You're going to have to pay for that, young man."

I was completely flustered.

"It's called 'breakage,'" I finally blurted. "Every store has it. It was an accident. It was too close to the edge. You really have to be more careful!"

I bolted for the door with him yelling behind me. I couldn't find Molli anywhere and was relieved as hell when I finally got back to the car and saw her sitting on the curb as if nothing had happened. Clearly the solemnity of her grief was beyond understanding.

"Geez, you sure know how to make a point," I said, claiming a seat on the curb beside her. "I guess I really don't understand what you're going through, no one does, but..."

"Can we please just not talk about it?' she said softly, her eyes imploring. "Sorry if I got you in trouble, but I just can't talk about my feelings anymore. And besides, it's like I don't have any feelings. I can't feel anything. Can we please just not talk about it? I'm begging you."

"Okay, no problem."

We sat in silence until my mother got there. I didn't tell her what Molli had done because it would have upset her. Besides, I could barely believe it myself.

-23-

The next two days dragged past as if they had an anchor chained to them. On Monday afternoon I got the money from the A-frame and counted it. $1,768. I stuffed the wad of bills into my backpack, jumped on my bike and started down the Ketch Harbor Road toward Crystal Crescent Beach. I wanted nothing more than to escape the very real consequences of my deadly actions. Maybe paying off Mister D would be the start of that. Or maybe I was lying to myself...abdicating responsibility...letting an indifferent world chart my course.

Once I reached the dirt road leading into the beach parking lot, I slowed down, trying to avoid potholes. An SUV sped past me, sending up a cloud of dust that forced me to stop and rub my eyes with the sleeve of my T-shirt. When I got to the parking lot I got off my bike, looked around and realized I had no idea what kind of car Mister D would be driving. I was standing there when I heard a car horn blare. It was Mister D. He got out of his car and waved me over. I rode to his car and he motioned to the passenger's side door.

"Get in, dickwad."

The car interior was a mess...adding to my stress...the floor littered with fast food wrappers...seats cracked and worn... upholstery torn...foul stench...like something had died in there.

"You got the money?"

He looked like shit. His bulging eyes were bloodshot and he was unshaved.

"Yes."

I reached into my backpack...pulled out an inch-thick wad of cash...handed it to him.

He carefully counted it, then turned to me.

"This is a hundred bucks short!"

"I counted it. It's all there."

"Are you calling me a liar?"

"No. I counted it. It's all there. I swear it is."

He scowled at me.

"I counted it twice, and I'm telling you it's a hundred bucks short, dickwad."

My reply got lodged in my throat. The money was all there. He was blackmailing me for more. He grabbed my wrist and squeezed it.

"I want that hundred bucks by Wednesday, get me? Otherwise I'm telling the cops what you done. Understand dickwad?"

There's no use arguing with the devil. He's a liar, but that doesn't mean he doesn't get his way once in a while.

"Okay," I muttered. "I'll get it."

-24-

The following day was glum…like a dreary February day… dropped into the heart of summer. The stress of everything was weighing on everyone. That afternoon I was in the kitchen when I overheard my parents on the deck arguing.

"Geoff we have to make plans. School starts in a month and the baby's coming a month after that."

"Who can plan for something like this?" my father replied, his voice rising.

"What's happening in Denver?"

"I'll know more tomorrow. There's only so much I can do from here. The lawyers are working on it and…"

My mother interrupted him.

"We need answers."

"I'm trying to get answers," my father replied, his voice filled with exasperation. "Please, just a little more time."

It was quiet for a few moments, and then my mother asked my father about his painkillers.

"Geoff, the pill bottle is almost empty. Those should have lasted you a month. I'm very worried about you."

"There's no problem!" he snapped. "I'm careful. My back's been acting up, so I need more pills. Let it go! I can't handle this right now."

There was another short silence, which was broken by my mother.

"Have you seen Molli's fingernails?" she asked softly.

"No. Why?"

"My God, Geoff, they're chewed down to the flesh. Her finger-tips are raw. It's the stress of everything."

• • •

Molli stayed in her room sulking for most of the day. Despite my mother's pleas she refused to eat with us. As for me, I couldn't wait to get plastered...wasted...blind drunk...smashed...during a party at Champayne Dam that night.

After dinner my father called me into his tiny wood paneled study, where he was tying a fishing fly. He loved tying flies. It took him hours. He worked with the focus and steely dedication of a surgeon. Maybe for him at least there was a connection between that and playing music. It definitely seemed to soothe him. He always looked totally relaxed after he was done.

"How's it going with Molli?" he asked, as he looked through a magnifying glass at the fly he was working on.

My mind conjured up an image of the vase Molli had dropped. *No use in telling him about that.*

"Okay, I guess."

"Just okay?"

"Yeah, I don't know what you expect. She's not easy to talk to, to get along with...if I ask her anything, I get a one-word answer."

He looked up at me.

"We all get one-word answers from her. You have to understand what she's going through."

"I know. It's hard for her."

He put down the needle he was using to tie the fly and glared at me.

"'Hard?'" he replied angrily. "You're damned right it's hard! Imagine if the situation were reversed. If your mother and I were killed and you were shipped off to live with an uncle in Colorado you barely knew."

"That wouldn't happen. I'd live with Aunt Carol."

"I know! I'm just trying to get you to see where she's coming from. What she's been through. We're all she's got, her only family."

Molli emerged from her room just before seven...eyes swollen and bloodshot from crying. I was able to convince her to go to the party. When I told my father where we were headed he turned from his fishing fly...concern on his face.

"Make sure you're back here no later than ten. When you're a teenager nothing good happens after ten o'clock."

We stepped out of the house into a tender summer evening... dusk encroaching...long dark fingers of night slowly feeling their way in from the east...summer taking hold...all of nature proclaiming it.

"Wait here for a second," I whispered to Molli.

I grabbed my bottle of Gin from the A-frame and slipped it into my backpack.

Homer knew his way to the dam and led us along the path, stopping every once in a while to sniff or to piss on a bush or tree.

"Sorry about breaking the vase the other day," Molli said ruefully. "You must think I'm the 'gong show.'"

"That vase cost four hundred and fifty bucks!"

She looked shocked.

"I don't know what got into me. It's..."

"You were right about one thing. No one can understand what you're going through."

She stopped walking and turned to me, a sad half-smile on her face.

"Thanks, Max."

We walked a little further in silence, careful not to trip over any of the boulders or thick tree roots crisscrossing the path.

"What's up with your father and those painkillers?" she asked as we walked through a stand of birch trees. She stopped and looked at me, her brow creased in worry.

I hoisted my backpack up on my shoulder.

"Mum's worried about it. She's tried to talk to him. He says he needs them for his back."

"He may have a problem," she said thoughtfully. "My Dad was hooked on painkillers a few years ago and finally had to get into treatment."

"He says there's no problem. He'd never go into treatment. That means admitting he had a problem, something he couldn't control."

We walked a little further then Molli asked me about Kevin.

"Hua told me about what happened," she said as we climbed a slight incline in the narrow path. "Did it happen at the dam?"

"No, on the cliffs not far from there."

"You guys were friends?"

"Yeah. He was a... I really don't like talking about it."

Another big lie! All I wanted to do was to talk about it to someone. Anyone! To unburden myself. That was impossible. I would take it to my grave.

"Okay," Molli replied softly. "I can relate to that."

We walked in silence, the only sounds gravel crunching under our feet, our heavy breathing from the hike, birds singing and insects buzzing as they got ready to settle down for the night.

As we approached the unmarked trailhead leading up to the dam, Molli pulled a small spool of red ribbon from her backpack.

"What's that for?

"To mark the trail."

She shrugged.

"I want to be able to come out here by myself without getting lost."

Smart move. I knew those woods. But if you didn't…easy to get lost…paths unmarked… trees…narrow…boulders…rocky overgrown…broken tree branches jutting out like daggers.

Molli carefully cut off a piece of ribbon a few inches long and tied it around a tree branch. She did the same thing every thirty feet or so or when the path took a turn.

Wouldn't it be nice if we could do that in life? Mark the trail with ribbons for turns of danger, heartbreak, mistakes, and love. Mark the path with ribbons and never get lost…

For years afterwards…whenever I'd see one of the ribbons faded pink by time…i'd think of Molli.

When we got to the dam it was almost dark, the early night sky a magical shade of indigo blue. A half dozen people, Ricky, Chen, Antonio, Janet and Tuna, were already there and had started a bonfire lighting the entire inlet. Sitting on a rock near the fire, I pulled out my bottle of Gin and took a big swig.

Molli seemed surprised I was drinking.

"It's my medicine," I joked.

"What is it?"

"Gin and orange juice."

Ricky held up a can of beer and offered it to Molli.

"No," I blurted. "She's too young."

"Don't get your knickers in a knot, Max," Ricky snapped. "I was just asking."

"Fine," I replied, "and I've answered. She's too young, okay?"

Ricky and Antonio starting talking about a guy from Halifax who owed Antonio money for work he had done on the guy's truck.

"He's a major asshole," Antonio said in disgust. "I've been chasing that prick around for the money for weeks."

"You know who's a 'major asshole?'" Molli asked to no one in particular.

I glanced over at her. She was gazing into the fire, her face stern and tired.

"My dad's a major asshole," she said flatly. "He'd smoke dope and fly his Cesena. He loved it!"

● ● ●

The story of a fresh death is like a story of new birth. Both mean something transcendent and important. You get one of each. Bookends of time and life.

Molli gazed at us, her blue eyes wide, her expression distant.

"He flew it with my mother and little brother right into high voltage electricity cables carrying power into half of Denver."

An uneasy silence settled over our gathering. Everyone knew what had happened to Molli's family. I wanted to say something comforting, but suddenly language seemed to elude me.

"It was a Saturday afternoon," Molli continued softly. "I was working at Anthropologie and the power went out. Twenty square blocks of downtown Denver just blinked out. We didn't know what it was. My boss, Lisa, said a transformer probably blew somewhere. It was already four thirty, so they let me go early."

Everyone was watching her and listening.

"My mother, father and little brother, Tim, had flown up to Aspen for the day and they weren't back yet. A note from my mother was on the counter. 'There's spaghetti in the fridge. We'll be back by 8.' I was like, 'Great!' I was kickin' it. You know…not a care in the world. There was electricity in our part of the city, so I was all stretched out of the sofa watching TV. I was *so* glad I had the whole house to myself. Mum, dad and my little brother were nowhere in sight. I was making plans to go snowboarding the next day. They weren't home by nine, but I didn't think anything of it. I figured they probably stopped in Pagosa Springs because there was a store there my mother loved. I was channel surfing and stopped on the news. They said the power outage was caused by a small plane hitting electrical wires somewhere. I didn't put it together at all. It never occurred to me that it was them. Small planes hit the wires sometimes. It happens."

She paused again…the only sound…crackling of wood in the fire…a breeze in the trees above us…waves gently lapping against the rocky shoreline.

"By 10 o'clock it was dark and I was starting to wonder where they were because my father didn't like flying at night," Molli continued. "I checked my phone. Nothing. I started thinking I heard my dad's car, but it was someone else on the road. By 11 o'clock I was like, 'Where are they?'"

She paused and rubbed her eyes.

"Just before midnight the doorbell rang. I muted the TV and answered it, thinking it was the pizza I ordered. I pulled open the door and two cops, a man and woman, were standing there. 'How old are you?' one of them asked."

"'Fifteen.'"

"'Do you have any older brothers or sisters, anyone else living here?'"

"'No. Why? What's going on?'"

"'Do you know your neighbors?'"

"'Yes, why?' The cops exchanged glances."

"'Does your father fly a Cessna?'"

"'Yes.'"

"'Is his name Harry Lipton? Is your mother's name Beth? Do you have a younger sibling, Tim?'"

"'Yes…why, what's going on?' I was starting to have a chilling realization that something was terribly wrong. They asked if they could come in. We sat in the living room, and that's when they told me…There had been an accident involving my father's Cesena. Everyone was dead. Gone."

She looked over at me, her smoky blue eyes large.

"When you get news like that, it's weird," she said with a painful half smile. "It doesn't register at first. 'What did you say? My family is dead?' It's unreal, like a bad dream. They wanted to know if I had any relatives close by. No. Was there anyone they could call? No. One of them, I can't remember which one, went to get my neighbor. I was sure they were mistaken. I told them that. My parents and brother were going to walk through the door at any minute. That wasn't my father's plane. No way. There must have been some kind of a mistake, a misidentification of some kind."

"That's horrible," someone muttered. "Sad."

It was as if Molli didn't hear them. She gazed into the fire and slowly shook her head.

"They call those small planes 'doctor killers' because doctors with their big egos think they can do anything," she said spitefully. "They're all like, I completed medical school so I can fly this. This is nothing. That was my father. He thought he was smarter than everyone else. But somehow his plane hit electrical wires, exploded in a fireball and crashed to the ground in flames. They didn't have time to scream."

"Oh Molli," Janet said softly.

"That night, lying in bed, I kept asking myself one question," Molli said in a voice just above a whisper. "Why didn't I know when it happened? Why when they were killed at that moment, why didn't I feel something? A chill...breeze...whisper. Anything. My family was killed in an instant and I was making out with a guy while on my break."

Janet got up and sat beside Molli, but Molli barely acknowledged her. It was almost like she was in a trance.

"The three coffins were closed," Molli continued softly. "I didn't have a chance to say goodbye...so long. They were gone forever, puff, into thin air. Now my family lives in the sky."

"Oh Molli, that's so sad," Janet said, her voice cracking.

"It's okay," Molli replied. "I'm an orphan. I was brought here against my will. My choices were come here or run away. And who knows? I may still do exactly that."

Once again I desperately wanted to say something comforting, but drew a blank.

"Our house, the house I grew up in, is for sale," Molli continued. "I was only here in Nova Scotia once. I was six or something, and it was summer. The whole time we were here it rained, and the only time it wasn't raining there was this weird thick fog that settled over everything."

She looked around and then continued.

"I'm sorry to offend anyone," she said apologetically. "You grew up here and probably love it. But for me that trip was horrible and beyond depressing. I hated every moment of it and never wanted to come back."

"That's true," Ricky offered. "The weather does suck sometimes."

Someone elbowed him in the ribs and he gasped.

"They waited until after the funeral to tell me I was coming here," Molli said, the orange light from the bonfire dancing across her face. "They cornered me in our living room, my uncle Geoff, our neighbors, a social worker and a cop. I told them, 'You're crazy! I'm not leaving this house!' They were all like, 'Molli, you don't understand. It's just for a little while, while we get everything straightened out.' But I told them, 'This is my home. I'm not going!' They said some stupid law said I was too young to live there by myself. I remember screaming, 'What law?' and crying for three days. I didn't sleep for five days. Then I slept for five days."

She stopped and looked at us, or *through* us was more like it.

"That's how life is, right?" she asked no one in particular. "Good and bad right down the middle."

"Right," someone muttered.

"I think they medicated me," Molli said. "Suddenly I was on a plane to…here. All I had was two suitcases, the clothes I was wearing and my snowboard."

A heavy silence.

"I don't remember the flight," Molli continued. "I slept, I think. It took forever to get to Max's house from the airport. It was pitch black and raining so hard I thought the sky was going to explode. I wanted to die. That would have been easier. And you know what? It was like I was halfway between life and death in some sort of twilight zone. It was the darkest night ever. There would never be another sunrise. When we got there, to their house, all I remember was the appalling rain and their horrible awful yellow porch light."

She looked around again, the trance seemingly broken.

"I'm sorry," she said softly. "I don't want to depress everyone, but what happened and why I'm here is like the big elephant in the room. Now you know all the details."

Tears streaked Janet's cheeks as she leaned over and hugged Molli.

Molli's story was definitely a downer. How could it be anything else?

Her face was blank. Not a tear. No real emotion. It was as if she were reciting something, telling a story about someone else and that she was emotionally detached from it.

After a while the party gradually picked up again and Ricky gently nudged me.

"Hey Max," he smirked softly, "better get a new porch light, man."

-25-

I polished off half my bottle of gin...again and found myself gazing into the fire as if it held some great secret. Fire hypnotizes...provides warmth...two of its better qualities. It can also burn your house down. As I stared into the flames all they gave up was smoke and sparks, which climbed into the dark night sky.

Tuna was hammered. He half-climbed, half-crawled up the rocky path to puke in the bushes. Janet almost fell in the fire twice, laughing hysterically after each close call.

"So what do you guys do here besides sit around a fire?" Molli asked no one in particular. "Is there any snowboarding or skiing?"

"Snowboarding?" Janet chuckled. "Hardly. But Ricky can always pull you waterskiing behind his dad's trawler."

"There's a little snowboarding in Annapolis Valley, Wentworth or whatever," someone said. "There's no mountains in Nova Scotia like Colorado, though."

"The valley's a two-hour drive, and you'd be down the hill in about three minutes," someone else pointed out.

"I don't get the attraction of snowboarding or skiing," Ricky said. "I'd freeze to death and probably get killed by an avalanche."

The corners of Molli's mouth turned up. I think it was the first time I'd actually seen her smile, albeit an echo of a smile.

"You'll never understand snowboarding until you've tried it," she said. "After you learn the basics, you want to go faster and make tighter turns. Then you start jumping rails and thinking about dropping into a half-pipe. Then there's riding amazing powder on the mountains in Colorado. It's magic."

She shifted her weight and sat up straight.

"There's nothing better," she continued, her voice now more deliberate. "I love the speed, being outdoors, the feel of the board under my feet. It's like it's alive. You want to throw up giant rooster tails in powder and grab big air off jumps. When you're on the hill or drop into a half pipe, it's a total escape from reality. Nothing else matters. I'm alive when I'm snowboarding. Then you've got your snowboarding friends. They love it as much as you do. You show off your tricks and compete against each other. You meet other snowboarders. It's a community of people as hooked on it as you are."

Her faced glowed and her eyes grew wide, as if the thought of snowboarding had lit a fire within her.

I had never snowboarded and never wanted to. The big winter sport around here was hockey, and I only played that with friends on a nearby lake.

"What about skateboarding?" Molli asked. "Does anyone do that?"

"I don't know anyone who skateboards," I replied.

"So let me see," Molli said, her voice filled with sarcasm. "There's no snowboarding, skiing or skateboarding. So what exactly do you do around here for fun? I mean, besides drinking and puking?"

There was a pregnant pause.

"We fish!" Ricky said after a moment.

"Are you serious?" Molli groaned. "Fishing?"

"What about sailing?" Chen asked. "You ever sailed on the ocean?"

"No," Molli replied.

"Then that's what we'll do!" Chen grinned. "We'll sail my boat to McNab's tomorrow."

"McNab's?" Molli asked.

"McNab's Island," I replied. "It's in the mouth of the harbour. It's cool. There's an old fort, stuff like that."

"Yeah?" Molli said. "That sounds like fun."

"What about the Titanic graves?" someone asked. "Has she seen those yet?"

They were referring to a cemetery in Halifax where some of the people who died when the Titanic sank were buried. It was a must-see for tourists.

"I've seen enough graves lately," Molli replied softly.

There was another awkward silence that was thankfully broken by a noise on the path above us. Two dark figures, one with a guitar, carefully made their way over the boulders down to where we were sitting.

It was James and his girlfriend, Kim, friends from school. They settled in, and after a while James started playing his guitar. He was a talented musician with a deep repertoire of songs. He started playing The Beatles song "Hey Jude," as light from the bonfire flickered in the shiny finish of his guitar.

Molli gently nudged me.

"When I was twelve I loved The Beatles," she said quietly. "I had a bad case of Beatlemania."

"They're okay."

"'Okay?'" she shot back. "They were more than that, and it didn't matter one bit to me that they had broken up more than twenty years before I was born. It didn't matter that John Lennon and George Harrison were already dead."

"I'm more of a U2 fan."

"My middle name is 'Jude' after the song 'Hey Jude.' It was my Mum's favorite song."

"Your middle name is 'Jude?' Cool."

I drained my bottle of Gin and started in on Ricky's beers. Molli and Janet were chatting. I was among friends on a beautiful summer night, wallowing in guilt and fear, getting progressively drunker. At some point I crossed the dreadfully thin line where drunken euphoria gives way to a spinning world and nausea.

"Max, are you okay?" Molli asked.

"What?" I slurred.

"Are you okay?"

"I'm not feeling very good."

"Maybe we should head home?"

"Good idea."

I tried to get up but fell and banged my knee.

Molli grabbed my arm.

"Let me help you."

"Don't forget," Chen said. "We're going sailing tomorrow."

"Right," I replied. "Sailing tomorrow. Right."

We struggled up over the boulders to the path above the dam and staggering toward home. Suddenly I started violently cursing Kevin. I don't know why, besides the fact I was as loaded as I had ever been and Kevin never far from my thoughts. Who know? Maybe Molli said something to trigger my drunken rant.

"Kevin, you jerk! Jerk. Jerk. Jerk!"

I tripped over something and fell into the bushes.

"You dumb ass drunken shit. Kevin, you jerk…"

"Max," Molli pleaded. "Take my hand. Get up."

I grabbed her hand and she hoisted me to my feet.

"Kevin, you…"

Crying…weeping…puking…I let loose a ten-minute torrent of drunken curses while Molli carefully guided me along the path as Homer sauntered a few feet in front of us. We passed through a stand of fir trees…I dropped to my knees to puke. I wanted to curl up in a ball and die. I was leaning against a tree trying to catch my breath when Molli placed her hand on my shoulder.

"Are you okay?"

"No!"

"Let it out."

I gagged as vomit flowed from my mouth and nose.

"Thanks."

What was normally a pleasant twenty-minute walk home through the woods and along the cove took us at least twice that because I kept falling and stopping to empty my guts.

"Just kill me and get this over with," I said at one point, looking up at Molli.

"Come on," she replied, tugging my arm. "We're almost there."

The truth is I was as drunk with misery as I was from Gin.

By the time we got home it was after midnight, and my parents were asleep. Thank God, or I would have been busted big time. Molli quietly poured me fully dressed into bed and I plummeted into…a deep and dreamless slumber.

-26-

The next morning...pain...a murderous hangover...pounding head...wished I was dead...pain...severe cotton mouth...pain... throbbing knee...scratches...pain...bruises...from my drunken falls... pain!

I peeled off my clothes...limped to the bathroom...puked...took a long piss...guzzled greedily from the tap...stumbled back to bed. I had just closed my eyes when there was a soft knock on my door.

"I'm sleeping!"

"It's me," Molli replied. "Can I come in?"

"Not now."

She moved closer to the door.

"I need to talk to you."

God now what!

"Okay. Come in."

"How you feeling?"

"Terrible."

She put a glass of water and bottle of Anacin on my bedside table.

"That'll help."

"Thanks."

Gulping down two of the pills, I flopped back on my pillow.

"Your parents are gone to town for a Lamaze class."

"Good."

"Chen called to remind us about the trip to McNab's Island today," she continued cheerfully. "He's got the boat all ready."

Considering how sick I felt, nothing sounded like less fun.

"Today?" I muttered. "Not today. I'm tired and..."

"Come on, last night you promised," Molli said, tugging my arm. "Get up."

"Molli, I'm sorry but there's no way..."

She planted her hands on her hips and glared at me.

"I've sat around here for weeks with nothing to do," she said angrily. "We agreed we'd go sailing, and I'm going with or without you."

She started toward the door but then turned back toward me.

"You shouldn't have drank so much last night."

I didn't want to get into it.

"Okay!" I blurted, angrily throwing off the top sheet. "I'll go. Let me get ready."

"I'll be in the A-frame."

Stumbling back to the bathroom, I threw up again...showered. Returning to my bedroom, I pulled on a pair of shorts, sweatshirt and my sneakers then limped down to the kitchen and poured three glasses of water. Sun flooding into the room, forced me to squint. Outside, I crossed the yard and went into the A-frame where Molli was sitting on one of the fold-out benches sipping a glass of apple juice.

"I made something for your hangover."

"What?"

She pointed to a glass of brown liquid on the bench.

"What is it?"

"Chocolate milk, a few other things. Drink it up. You'll feel a lot better."

"What are the other things?"

She smiled shyly.

"A raw egg, your father's Bailey's Irish Cream and a few things I found in the cupboard."

I sat and took a sip. It had an odd taste but was cool and refreshing.

"How did you learn to make something like this?"

She grinned.

"I'm into homeopathic remedies. I used to make the same thing for my Dad when he was hung over."

I took another sip.

"You talked to Chen this morning?"

"He called. He's expecting us. Some other people are coming."

I was sipping the drink, not saying much, trying to pull myself together when Molli asked me about the previous night when I had been drunkenly ranting about Kevin.

"You were real angry at him."

"I was drunk."

"You kept cursing him! You were angry as hell."

"I was *drunk* as hell."

She was studying me, her unwavering gaze searching my core.

"What really happened, Max?"

"What?"

"What really happened that night Kevin fell?"

"He went to take a piss and fell. That's it!"

Maybe she sensed how weak and tired I was.

"There's more to it than that. What happened? Did he jump?"

"Jump?" I scoffed. "No! He was crazy but he'd never jump! He fell over the edge...into the crack."

"What was all that stuff last night when you were calling him a jerk? I thought he was your friend?"

"He was my friend," I blurted. "Just leave it alone."

I wanted nothing more than for her to shut up and stop pestering me. I got up to leave, but she grabbed my shoulder.

"Leave what alone?" she demanded.

"Just leave it alone, okay? Stop asking me about it."

"Not until you tell me the truth," she said accusingly. "Not the bullshit story you told everyone."

"It's not bullshit," I protested. "It's...kind of true."

She leaned back.

"Kind of true? So what's the true story? Come on out with it!"

I was extremely hung over...in pain...vulnerable. Who knows maybe she had worn me down. If anyone tells you that heavy secrets are easy to carry...tell them they're a liar.

"We fought," I blurted. "I didn't mean for it to happen. He went over the edge. The crack...I couldn't..."

"You were fighting?"

"Yes. He was going to...we had stolen money. I begged him not to..."

I was hyperventilating.

"My God, Max, slow down. Just tell me what happened."

"The drinking part was true," I continued, the truth welling up in me like vomit.

• • •

The truth? The truth is flimsy justifications are at the epicenter of all crimes...misdeeds.

Kevin was dead because I wanted a stupid boat and motor.

In the weeks before anyone knew Molli was coming to live with us, I helped Kevin rob the gas station in Halibut Bay where he worked. Robbing the station was wrong and I was hesitant. I had never done anything like that before, committed a robbery. My conscience flared at the thought of it but...my doubts were quickly and soundly extinguished.

For the previous two weeks my entire focus had been confined to buying an aluminum boat and outboard motor a guy in Sambro was selling for fifteen hundred bucks. I wanted the boat *so* badly. It was as if it had a voice calling to me. It would be perfect for puttering around Chandler's Cove, providing a welcome distraction from the seemingly boring summer laid out before me. I could even take the boat out on the ocean on calm days.

When you live next to the ocean, getting a boat like that is equal to a city kid getting a car. But I didn't have nearly enough money to buy the boat, and there was no way my parents were going to give it to me.

"A guy's paying cash for a rebuilt motor job," Kevin had smiled slyly as we sat in McDonald's munching burgers. "It's more than three grand. We never have that much cash at the station. Dave won't be there. I'll be there all by myself."

Dave was his boss, a hothead jerk, another thing that helped me further justify my soon-to-be-criminal actions.

I wasn't sure Kevin could pull it off without getting us caught. Everyone joked that grade six was the happiest three years of Kevin's life. He wasn't "the sharpest tool in the shed," not a criminal mastermind by any means. But at least he had a plan for the robbery. An inside job. What could go wrong? Still, I had serious reservations.

"What if we get caught?" I had asked.

Kevin scoffed and bits of food from his mouth landed on the table.

"There's no way we'll get caught, buddy. I'll be the only one working that night. The security cameras don't work half the time, and I can make sure they're not working on Friday."

"Yeah, but…"

He cut me off.

"Max, buddy, we got robbed for real last year, so this won't seem weird, ehhh."

All I'd have to do was go into the station on the agreed evening and take the cash. Kevin would give me time to get away, then he'd call the cops and make up a fake description of the robber. We'd split the money later. On the agreed night...my heart pounded...as I walked into the station...Kevin handed me a wad of cash...i shoved it into my backpack...jumped on my bike...raced three miles home. The following day we split $3,423.14.

I'd wait a week before buying the boat because I was paying in cash and didn't want to raise any suspicions. I'd tell my parents that the guy sold it to me on an installment plan...i'm paying him a hundred bucks a month.

Two days after we did the "robbery," Kevin and I got together with a few friends for a party. A dozen of us trudged around Chandler's Cove, up through the woods and out onto the high bluffs overlooking the Atlantic. It was supposed to be a fun evening under the stars celebrating the end of the school year. Instead the unforeseen events of that terrible night ended forever the youthful and naive folly of my adolescence.

Laughing under a blissful amethyst sunset, we were ecstatic... birds released from a cage. Our collective state of mind...buoyant like seagulls bobbing on the ocean's placid surface. I would come to despise that place, but in the fading twilight of that warm spring evening the panoramic view still held wonder.

My friends were joking around, starting a bonfire as I climbed up on a car-sized boulder and gazed out over the ocean. Its darkening surface stretched to the distant shores of England and Europe and into my imagination.

"Hey, Max," a voice cried out behind me. "Get your ass over here. We got the fire going."

I jumped off the boulder and joined my friends. Night was falling, the stars and moon dancing. Someone lit a joint, its orange tip glowing in the encroaching darkness.

"Here you go, Max, buddy," Kevin said as he handed me the joint. "Have a toke"

I shook my head.

"I'll take a pass."

I didn't like pot. I didn't have a moral imperative against it. Smoking it made me anxious.

Kevin smirked.

"Pussy!"

He held up a bottle of spiced rum. He was the only one of my friends who really drank, and that night he drank like someone who was trying to drown his feelings in alcohol. I was about to find out why.

This is more your speed, right?" he asked. "Go ahead take a swig. Fill your boots."

I waved him off.

"No thanks. I'm fine."

"You're not fine!"

He thrust the bottle toward me.

"It's Captain Crazy! Don't be a pussy. Come on, have a drink."

I could have continued saying no, but Kevin was hard to say "no" to. I'd done this uncomfortable dance with him before. We all had. He'd offer you a joint or a bottle…if you refused…which I usually did…he'd pester and tease you until you relented. He was eighteen, a year older than me, and a lot bigger than the rest of us. He was a mean drunk…and he drank a lot. He was intimidating when he wanted to be. He worked at the gas station during the school year but worked his father's lobster boat in the summer. He had developed massive arms and shoulders from all the heavy lifting.

I grabbed the bottle, took a swig and winced sharply as the rum burned going down.

"Thanks," I coughed, passing him the bottle.

"Go ahead," he said, his expression now fiendish in the glow of the bonfire. "Take another one."

"No! I'm fine."

"You're not fine," he scoffed. "You're a pussy."

He held out the bottle in front of him, the rum sloshing around inside it.

"Hey everyone," he slurred. "Max here won't take another drink. I say that makes him a pussy, right?"

The situation was getting a little tense.

Ricky got up and grabbed the bottle.

"You're a pussy, Max, buddy," he laughed.

He hit the bottle and then passed it back to Kevin, who grunted, took a long guzzle and then placed the bottle at his feet. He was getting progressively more drunk. Slouched on a log, he started leaning slightly to his right like a ship listing to starboard.

Al Duggan had brought a beat-up guitar and started strumming it as night dropped in on us. We were talking about our summer plans when Kevin staggered to his feet.

"Screw the gas station," he slurred. "I'm working on the *Crystal Dream* this summer."

The *Crystal Dream* was his father's lobster boat.

"I'll make more than the teachers at Isley do!" he said, referring to our high school, J.L. Isley.

He flashed a drunken smile.

"I'll make more money than any of your parents make."

We all murmured in agreement. A lobsterman could easily make a grand a day. It was hard and dangerous work, but it sure paid well, especially when lobster prices were up.

After a few hours the ocean brought in a chill, and people started to leave. Within twenty minutes only Kevin, Ricky and I were left.

"I'm headed out," Ricky said, stretching. "I got to work on my car in the morning."

"I'll go with you."

I stood to leave, but Kevin grabbed my arm.

"Max, buddy, can you hang on for a little while?"

He held up the bottle of rum.

"Just until I finish this?"

He grinned.

"I'm way too loaded to make it back over that path in the dark by myself. I'll break my neck."

Ricky and I exchanged worried glances.

"Come on," I said. "Pour it out or bring it with you."

"No, no, I can't pour it out," he slurred. "I just need a little time to get my shit together. Just fifteen minutes."

He smiled sheepishly.

"Sorry for busting your balls earlier. You don't have to drink if you don't want to. I'm a jerk. Stick around for a little while and give me a hand, okay?"

"I got to go," Ricky said with a wave. "Make sure he gets back in one piece."

He trudged off into the darkness, and I claimed a seat on the log beside Kevin. He was gazing into the fire, his face sad and lonely. He turned and offered me the bottle.

"Sure you don't want some?"

I was going to refuse, but I figured the quicker we got to the bottom of the bottle the sooner we could leave. I took a swig, then wiped my mouth with the back of my hand. A short distance away waves thundered into, the crack.

"Shit," I muttered, "that's like jet fuel."

I was definitely getting drunk, the alcohol chasing away any trace of a chill in the air.

Kevin turned to me, his eyes dark, his expression serious in the flickering light of the fire.

"I got bad news, buddy," he said slowly.

He looked me in the eye.

"They know."

My heart leapt.

"Know what?"

I really didn't have to ask. I knew.

"That we, that I, did the robbery."

My heart stopped.

"How could they know!?"

He slowly shook his head as his gaze fell to the ground.

"They were grilling me, right? Asking me a bunch of questions. I told them the robber was a white guy, but I forgot. Then I changed it to a black guy and then to an Asian guy."

An awful sinking feeling welled up from the soles of my feet as I gripped my forehead. Kevin had a perspiration problem and I imagined sweat pouring off him as the cops grilled him.

"This can't be happening," I muttered.

"They tricked me!" he said. "Cops should not be allowed to trick you!"

God no!

"They asked me what kind of vehicle he was driving, and I said a "Volkswagen Ford.""

"A 'Volkswagen Ford?' I blurted. "There's no such thing!"

He shot me a sideways glance.

"I know. When I was making up the story I was trying to decide what kind of car I was going to say the guy was driving. I was going to say a Volkswagen or a Ford. But when they asked me I kind of combined them because I was nervous."

No! No! No!

"That's not all, buddy."

"There's more?"

"Yep. The cops found a wad of cash in my car yesterday."

He looked at me and threw up his hands.

"I forgot it in the glove box! They asked me where I got it, and I drew a blank, ehhh. I said I got it working but couldn't tell them where. Finally they're like, 'This is half of what was taken. Where's the other half? Who did you split it with?'"

Once again his drunken gaze fell to the ground.

"They were right in my face!"

"What did you tell them?"

He shook his head.

"Nothing yet. But they know they got me."

"They can't prove anything. Just..."

He cut me off.

"Sorry, buddy, but I gotta tell them we did it together."

"No way! That's crazy. Don't tell them anything. It was your idea. I just helped you."

He exhaled heavily.

"I know, but the only way I'm going to get a avoid big trouble is if I tell them who was with me. I gotta go in tomorrow."

My blood was starting to boil.

"That's crazy! You're just scared. It'll blow over. Don't say anything."

He seemed to be thinking.

"You still have your half?"

"Yeah."

"Let's give it back. That's all they want anyway. I'll be fired, but I hate that job and I'm working on my Dad's lobster boat this summer so..."

"What about me? Have you told anyone I helped you?"

"Not yet," he frowned. "But I gotta tomorrow."

He staggered to his feet.

"Sorry, Max. I messed up. I can't take this fall alone."

Fear and anger swept through my veins. Being found out would be humiliating and I'd go to jail or get grounded all summer.

"My father will kill me!" I yelled. "My parents will be so disappointed."

Kevin looked at me through narrowed bloodshot eyes.

"We all let people down."

He shrugged.

"Sorry, buddy. I know this sucks."

He got up to leave as I jumped to my feet and grabbed his arm.

"Wait!" I said in a pleading voice. "Come on. Let's talk about this. There's got to be another way."

He pulled away.

"Don't be grabbing me."

"Kev, come on. Let's think about this."

He stepped back and stared at me, the glow from the fire lighting his face.

"There's no other way, Max. And besides, I've made up my mind."

He turned to leave but I grabbed him again.

"Wait!"

He pushed me, and I stumbled backwards.

"Screw-off!" he snarled. "Don't make things worse than they already are."

I lunged forward and pushed him.

"You can't tell anyone!"

He smashed me on the right side of the face. I flew backward and fell dazed to the ground.

"What are you doing?" he growled as he towered over me.

I jumped up...took a wild swing...not a thing...he wasn't fazed...
not even dazed...grabbed me...to the ground...outweighed me by forty
pounds...got to my feet...another swing...not a thing...he smashed me
in the face...i was losing this race...the back of his hand...slumped to
the ground...mouth full of blood...rage...i turned the page...picked
up a rock...harder than a sock...smashed him in the head...he collapsed dazed like a big bear...as if looking for a set of car keys there...
blood dripping down my chin...i was about to commit a mortal sin.

"What's wrong with you?" I yelled.

He looked up, his gaze distant. Then he held out his hand.

"Help me up."

Blood filled my mouth.

"What are you doing?"

I grabbed his hand and tried to hoist him to his feet.

"Are you crazy?"

Instead of getting up, he pulled me onto the ground and tried
to get on top of me. But once again I was able to slide out from
under him and jump to my feet.

"You're out of your mind!" I yelled.

I strode over and kicked him in hard in ribs.

"Jerk!"

He rolled onto his side. He was so drunk he couldn't stand. We
were only a few feet from, the crack. Sixty feet below...I was about
to see how things sometimes go.

He looked up at me and let loose a wicked laugh.

"I'm going to beat your ass!"

As he tried to get to his feet, I kicked him hard in the side. He
teetered on the edge. Our eyes met. I didn't reach out to help. He
fell into the crack...onto the rocks...stopping all clocks...black
waves slamming into the base of the bluffs...the end of fisticuffs...
gone...he'd never see another dawn...right...he had not simply dis-
solved into the night.

How long did I stand there dazed...crazed, angry, bleeding? The only sound louder than the waves hurling themselves into the crack...the pounding of my heart...a mere silhouette of shock and unwavering reality trembling in complete disbelief.

My God, what did I just do? Now what?

Kevin was dead. If the fall didn't kill him he'd be unmercifully pounded into the rocks by the ceaseless waves and drowned in minutes.

I staggered home...stripped off my clothes...my humanity... and lay in bed in a panic all night... staring at the ceiling wondering what to do. An immense guilt and remorse welled up within me. I had killed my friend! Drunk, and in a blind rage, I had killed him! How I wished I had followed Kevin to my death. I urgently prayed I would die before daybreak. *God please take me now!* I quick death would allow me to escape the harsh realities that awaited me in the morning.

Somewhere in that restless and endless night my immeasurable guilt blossomed into something darker and more hideous than simple guilt. *Fear!* When everyone found out I had killed Kevin, I'd go to jail. There'd be no bail. My life would be over. Everyone would revile me...a pariah. There would be huge legal bills and Kevin's parents would sue my parents. We were all witness to the wheels of justice destroying a family after a similar incident the previous year. A drunk woman from Bear Cove crashed her car and killed her friend. The dead girl's family sued the drunk woman's family for everything they had. When everyone found out I had killed Kevin there would be a lawsuit and my parents would lose their house. The reality of everything was so suffocating I felt as if I was trying to breathe underwater.

At some point in my blackest hour a simple thought emerged from the very depths of my soul. *I had to come up with a story that everyone would believe.* It came to me as if whispered by a malevolent spirit. By the time I fell into a fitful slumber it was daybreak.

There is an intersection in the mind…a crossroads…the truth ends…when you kill a friend…lies begin…you start drinking gin… your soul retches.

I had only been asleep for two minutes when there was a rap on my door. Exhausted I staggered to my feet and pulled it open. My father was standing there holding the phone, his hand cupped over the receiver.

"Kevin Price's father's on the phone," he said in monotone. "Kevin didn't come home last night and they're calling everyone trying to find out where he is."

I tried to act surprised.

"He's not home?"

"No. Did you see him last night?"

"Yeah, he was with us, a bunch of us. Everyone left and he ditched me. He didn't get home?"

"I guess not."

He eyed me up and down.

"Max, you look like crap."

Later that day we found Kevin's rusting Toyota parked in a wide spot fifty meters up the road from our house, in the place he usually parked for parties near the bluffs. The windows were down, the floor littered with fast food wrappers.

In the midst of my staggering guilt and fear I carefully fabricated my lie. I told it to everyone, always pausing thoughtfully at the right moments. I told my parents, Kevin's parents, the police and coast guard. Eventually I told everyone I knew or anyone who would listen. Maybe I thought that by telling the same lie over and over it would somehow become real. Details are important when you tell a big lie. It also helps if you mix lies with the truth.

…a bunch of us were celebrating. Kevin had a forty-ouncer of Captain Morgan rum. It was Kevin's favorite. He called it "Captain Crazy." We

built a bonfire in a sheltered area 50 feet from the bluffs. We were hang-
ing out talking about girls and our summer plans. Kevin was hitting the
bottle really hard. Huge swigs. The rest of us were taking it easy. We don't
drink. Everyone started bitching that they were cold and left. Finally only
Ricky, Kevin and I were left. Then Ricky took off because he had to work
on his car in the morning. I stayed to help Kevin over the path, because
you know, he was really loaded. I was trying to get Kevin to stop drinking
and to leave. Finally, drunk as a skunk, he said he was going to take a
piss. He staggered toward the bluffs and I asked him where he was going.

"I told you, to take a piss."

"Over the edge of the cliff? Are you crazy? Go in the trees."

He laughed.

"Pussy!"

He staggered through the fog toward the edge. He was only 50 feet
away, but the fog was thick and the night enveloped him. When he didn't
come back after five minutes I figured he was messing with me.

"Kevin, where are you?" I yelled into the darkness. "Get back here, you
piece of shit."

Silence. Another ten minutes passed, and I called to him again.

"Kev, I know you can hear me. Get back here."

I picked up his bottle of rum and waved it through the air.

"Kevin, I'm pouring your rum out if you don't get back here right now."

Nothing except for the mournful sound of the foghorn at Chebucto
Head.

I put the bottle down, stood and strained to see through the darkness.
Moving carefully toward the cliff's edge, I call out Kevin's name, thinking
he was going to jump out of the darkness and scare me. He didn't. I was
worried about him. Despite the darkness and fog I could make out the jag-
ged edge of the crack and hear the familiar roar of waves slamming into it
sixty feet below. I looked around. I was like, where is he? I figured he was
messing with me, that he had snuck away in the night. I pissed on the fire
and left. It was real dark and I fell on the path and cut my lip. By lunch

they had started searching the area below the cliffs for him figuring he had fallen off the cliff while drunk.

• • •

I could not believe that Molli had pried the awful truth out of me. Her face was thoughtful, and suddenly she looked older than fifteen.

"It was like slow motion," I muttered. "A horror movie."

"Awful," Molli replied softly.

"It was a nightmare," I choked. "I didn't mean to kill him!"

I was trembling. The dam holding back my endless guilt was crumbling and I didn't care!

"I ran home in a panic," I half-cried. "I didn't sleep. My guilt was too deep. I lay in bed staring at the ceiling going over it in my mind. Everyone knew what a nut Kevin could be, the crazy things he'd do. He would walk on his hands right on the edge and laugh."

My gaze fell on Molli, as I desperately tried to gauge her reaction. She was staring at me, her smoky blue eyes unwavering.

"That's horrible."

I buried my face in my hands. *Could this morning get any worse?*

"I killed my friend," I muttered.

Molli moved to my side and gently placed her hand on my knee.

"You have to tell your parents, his parents, what happened, or you'll always have this like an anchor around your neck."

I looked up at her in astonishment.

"Are you crazy? I can't face them. I'll go to jail. My life will be over. My parents will lose their house!"

I stared at her unflinchingly, suddenly and painfully aware that she had pried a deep and destructive secret from me.

"Promise me you won't tell anyone!" I blurted angrily. "I mean it! Promise me!"

She seemed to be thinking.

"I promise *I* won't tell anyone," she said after a moment. "*You* have to tell them."

"I can't!"

She exhaled loudly.

"Max, your life will be over if you don't unburden yourself. It's only been what, a little more than a month since he died? And you're already drinking yourself to death out of guilt."

"Good, I hope I die. I deserve to die! I'd rather die an alcoholic than tell anyone what really happened."

"Kevin's mother deserves to know the truth."

Who did she think she was? She was fifteen, for God's sake, and she thought she had an answer for everything!

Blood pounded up through my neck.

"The 'truth?' That I killed her son!?"

"You didn't kill him. He was really drunk."

She looked me in the eye.

"It was an accident."

"Accident or not, he's dead and I killed him! Don't you see? I killed him!"

We sat in a brutal silence for what seemed like an eternity.

"That's not all," I muttered. "Mister D knows what happened and he's blackmailing me."

Molli's eyes widened.

"Mister D?"

I told her all about Mister D and how he was shaking me down for money. Once again all she could do was shake her head in complete disbelief.

"Is there anything else?"

"Isn't that enough?"

She stood and looked down at me, her expression judgmental.

"Tell your parents and Kevin's parents what happened Max," she said emphatically. "Tell them!"

That was the start of her relentless and covert campaign...confess to the world what really happened. Every few days she'd write "Tell Them!" on a post-it and stick it to the fridge...my bedroom door...the kitchen table. Or she'd write "Tell Them!" on a magazine and leave it out for everyone to see. She even used a stick to write it in the sand at Crystal Crescent Beach.

-27-

We all have "dams" holding things back. Secrets. Loves. Desires. Sorrows. Words we too afraid or too ashamed to speak. Confessing to Molli relieved my conscience a little. But despite her pleas and "Tell Them" campaign, there was no way I was going to *tell* anyone else about what really happened. I was too ashamed. Too scared. Molli was right. My endless guilt was making me drink and take the painkillers. I didn't care. It was a small price to pay for what I had done.

With the sun and a scattering of clouds high above us, we rode our bikes to Chen's house. It was the slowest bike ride I'd ever taken to Ketch Harbour, made worse by the fact I was extremely hungover and Molli and I didn't exchange a single word the whole time. When we got there Chen was waiting for us in the sailboat. Ricky, Phillip and Janet were also there.

"Take these," Chen said, passing lifejackets to Molli and me.

We all settled into the boat, and then Chen untied it from the pier, carefully stepped onboard and grabbed the tiller. The wind was steady but not too strong, and the harbour was calm, conditions that Chen assured us were ideal for our sail to McNab's Island.

"The wind's at our stern so we're going to run right outta the harbour and then broad reach to McNab's," he smiled.

"Just get us there and back safely, captain," Ricky joked. "Don't hit any icebergs."

Molli sat beside me...a red bandana around her neck...cargo shorts...hiking boots...black socks...a light blue windbreaker. The breeze was tossing her hair around and she seemed somewhat contented. I was glad to see that, especially after the ugly scene with the vase and my tearful confession to her about Kevin that morning.

Within ten minutes we had cleared the mouth of the harbour and were out on the broad expanse of the ocean. Another world.

Wind filled the triangular sails as the boat slipped giddily over small whitecaps sending up a fine salty spray. The ocean air and sun…refreshing as a good nights sleep. I was starting to feel a little better, my hangover and guilt gradually lifting.

"Good party last night," Ricky said. "How you feeling today?"

He laughed and pretended to puke over the side.

"Idiot," Molli muttered.

"I'm getting a new tattoo," Ricky said. He rolled up his right sleeve. "A big Celtic Cross on my bicep. It's going to be awesome!"

Molli pushed the hair from her face.

"Why a cross?" she asked. "Are you religious, a Christian?"

"Hell no," Ricky scoffed. "I just like the way it looks."

"That figures," Molli muttered under her breath.

"I'd get a Star of David," Phil said, pointing to his chest. "Right here over my heart."

He was Jewish, so that made sense.

"I've already got a tattoo," Janet smiled. She pulled down the back of her T-shirt, revealing a tattoo of a tropical fish on her shoulder.

"It's an angel fish," she cooed. "I love it."

"I'd get Popeye," Chen chuckled. "You know, the sailor man."

He flexed his bicep.

"Right here."

"What would you get, Max?" Ricky asked. They all looked at me waiting for a reply.

"I don't know," I said. "Maybe a tattoo of a guitar."

154

"A guitar?" Ricky scoffed. "You don't play guitar."

I shrugged.

"I didn't know there could be a wrong answer."

Molli held up her hand for everyone to see.

"I've got these stars."

She smiled faintly.

"A friend told me I should get tears to remember my family, not stars."

She paused as if thinking, then looked at everyone, her eyes wide.

"The way I see it is there are enough tears in the world already, right?"

We all murmured in agreement.

"But if I was to get more tattoos," she continued with a slight smile, "I'd get the snow-topped Rocky Mountains. I'd get a full-on snowboarder. I'd get a killer whale and her pup."

The ocean swelled below us...the sailboat answered gently to accommodate it...the wind playing a symphony in the rigging.

"That's right poetic, ehhhh," Ricky said wryly. "A killer whale and a puppy."

He howled loudly.

"What's wrong with this picture?"

He held up his arms like two giant jaws, his fingers as teeth, and slowly closed them together.

"The puppy gets it," he laughed.

"Shut up, Ricky," Janet blurted. "She said 'pup' not puppy, you idiot. A pup is a baby killer whale that could eat you."

"Whatever."

Molli gently elbowed me in the side.

"I know he's your friend," she whispered, "but is he intentionally dense? Does he think that's funny?"

I looked over at Ricky and nodded.

"Yeah, probably."

Then...everyone was quiet...wrapped in their own thoughts... silently taking in the bold magnificence of the cobalt ocean... the soft rhythm of the boat on the water...the timeless sound of wind in the sails and rigging...endless sky...salty breeze...healing warmth of the summer sun.

It was past noon by the time we sailed into a small cove on the McNab's Island leeward side and tied up to a battered old wooden wharf. The island, a few miles long and about half a mile wide, was in the middle of the mouth to Halifax Harbour. It was home to a huge park, crumbling fortresses, gun batteries from World War II, an old graveyard and a historic lighthouse. It also had a ton of hiking trails. I had only been there a few times, and I always thought of the island as a time capsule, a throwback to another era that tweaked my interest in history. It would take hours to hike around the island, but it was a gorgeous summer afternoon, and I was up for a chance to breathe in some fresh air and stretch my legs.

"So what's the plan?" I asked as we all stood on the pier.

"I've got a map," Janet replied.

Dropping her backpack on the pier, she zipped open the front pocket, pulled the map out and pointed at it.

"That's Maugher's Beach," she said before turning the map sideways and reading something.

"Hangman's Beach is there, too," she continued. "It says here it was used by the Navy during the Napoleonic wars to hang the bodies of executed mutineers as a warning to crews entering the harbour that this was a port where they better not cause any trouble."

Her face screwed up.

"Gross!"

"Better behave yourself, Molli," Ricky joked.

We pulled on our backpacks and started off toward Maugher's Beach...consulting Janet's map to make sure we were on the right trail. I was watching Molli…trying to determine her mood…state of mind. Walking slightly in front of me…she looked like any other member of our group. Grief and despair don't show themselves like a disease or illness. God, I wish they did! If only you could take someone's temperature and determine the depth of their grief. How much easier would that be than trying to read their expression, mood or mind? Whenever anyone asked Molli how she was doing, they got a simple one-word answer: "okay." She was the queen of one-word answers. Of course "okay" would be her reply. How else was she going to answer? "I'm devastated. I want to die." After countless tears have been shed, grief still lurks under the surface like a sea monster.

"This place is haunted," Phil said as we walked down a narrow path. "Legend has it there are ghosts of people hanged here. Sea serpents and buried treasure, too."

Janet stopped walking and swatted at a mosquito.

"Buried treasure?" she asked, her eyes wide. "Where?"

Ricky smirked.

"If anyone knew where it was, it wouldn't be there any more, would it?"

"Birders love this place," I said. I looked around, taking in the splendor of the natural world. "There's been like two hundred different species of birds spotted here over the years."

Molli turned toward me, her thin eyebrows arched.

"You're a birdwatcher?"

"Yeah." I reached into my backpack, pulled out my Audubon birders guide book and passed it to her.

"I brought binoculars too, just in case I see anything interesting and want to have a closer look."

Molli stopped walking and started leafing through the book.

"Interesting."

She held the book up.

"Can I borrow this?"

"Sure."

We continued strolling on the path toward Hangman's Beach and then stopped at a picnic table beside a salt water lagoon...a warm breeze murmuring in the trees...broken sunlight dancing over the ground.

"I'm going to look at that old graveyard," Phil said. "Anyone want to come?"

Molli stood.

"I'll go with you."

I felt as if I should tag along, but I was hung over and was relaxing at the picnic table.

"Be careful," I said.

That was the beginning of something between Molli and Phil. It was subtle but real. After that I'd get calls from Phil.

"Hey, what's up? Can I stop by?"

-28-

Y ou never forget the foggy June afternoon that death…gazes down on you from the deck of a mountainous ghost ship.

We hung out at the picnic table for a while, then went to find Phil and Molli so that we could eat the lunches each of us had packed. The rest of the afternoon we explored and hiked, stopping to look at ruins, and lazed on the beach.

By the time we got back to the sailboat, a low fog was rolling in. Chen pulled up the sails, and we started toward home. But within 20 minutes the fog had gotten so thick it was impossible to see more than thirty meters in any direction. We were near the middle of the harbour when the sailboat gently rolled to a stop. The sails were completely devoid of wind like deflated balloons. It was an otherworldly and eerie feeling.

"Shit," Chen moaned. "No wind. We're in a dead calm."

"Dead calm?" Ricky replied nervously. "Shit! Stalled in the middle of the harbour? Come on man. Fuck the sails. Start the motor."

"The wind will pick up," Chen muttered.

"Fuck the wind," Ricky blurted nervously. "We're in the middle of the harbour. There's cargo ships, man, ocean liners. There's…"

Before he could finish, a ship horn, so thunderous that it felt as if it had weight, blared through the fog. It was impossible to see through the murkiness, but the ship must have been nearby and huge.

"Come on, Chen," I blurted. "Forget the sails! Start the motor!"

The ship's horn blared again. We jumped in our seats. It was impossible to tell where the ship was coming from...but it was close...and bearing down on us. Chen disappeared into the cabin and starting hitting the engine's start button...the motor only sputtered. I looked around again...desperately trying...to see through the thick blanket of fog...impenetrable to sight.

"Don't worry," Chen yelled nervously from the cabin. "He can probably see us on radar. He'll probably veer off."

"Probably?" Phil blurted. "That's reassuring!"

The ship's horn boomed again...a deep low shutter getting closer in the fog...a wild dog...at the base of the chebucto head foghorn...the dull sound of the ship's powerful engines...pounding...massive propellers churning...as it...closed in on us...suddenly the ship's black hull...seventy feet high...looked me in the eye...breaking through the fog...oh my God...fifty meters away... we were the kids it would slay...bearing down on us...an awesome thing of horrible beauty...death itself...coming...to devour us.

Molli gripped my arm so tightly her nails seared into my skin.

Salt water hissed in the ship's horrendous wake. Screams...a high pitched wail...forget the sail...brace for impact...a loud splash...ricky frantically trying to get away...then...the ship glided past us...missing our boat by a mere ten feet...a dark and ghostly leviathan...glancing down at us like we were insects...totally indifferent to our mortality...morality.

Even in the dense fog I could see rivet heads the size of baseballs in its enormous black hull. I felt as if I could have reached out and touched that awful ship. It took six lifetimes to pass. We all stared up at it in horrendous awe...mouths agape...unable to escape as the sailboat swayed in the ship's tacit wake. SPIRIT was painted on the bow in twenty-foot white letters. It disappeared back into the vapor, like a phantom, the fog closing in behind it.

The sailboat's motor sputtered to life, and Chen stuck his head out of the cabin.

"Did a ship pass?"

"Pass?" Phil said, shaking his head. "It almost cut us in two!"

Chen looked around, trying to see the ship.

"We had the right of way," he said smugly. "Good for him that he veered off."

"Shit," Janet scoffed. "You make sure to tell him that, Chen!"

He shrugged.

"I'm just saying, it's the rules of ocean navigation. A ship has to yield or veer off to a sailing vessel."

I must have been holding my breath because I suddenly exhaled. Molli's eyes were wide and filled with a distant gaze as I touched her arm. She was shaking.

"You okay?"

"Uuuhh."

"Come get me!"

It was Ricky, treading water twenty feet away, waving his arms in the air. The ocean around him was the color of deep jade, its watery arms gently releasing him as we pulled him onboard. He coughed violently as seawater poured from his pockets and sneakers. His black hair was plastered to his head. I pointed at him then turned to Chen.

"He abandoned ship!"

"Damn right," Ricky laughed. "It was coming right at us. Each man for himself."

"Thanks," Molli said flatly. "That's comforting."

"If it makes you feel better, I probably would have been killed anyway," Ricky continued. "I would have been caught in the ship's undertow and cut to pieces by the props."

He flashed a smile.

"And I almost drowned."

"We should have left you in the water," I said, only half-joking.

He poured water out of his ball cap, pulled it on and glanced at Molli.

"See you on the other side, right Molli?"

He leaned back.

"Now you got a story to tell everyone in the states!"

"God," Molli muttered. "Are you trying to be thickheaded?"

Ricky laughed spitefully.

"So tell me, Molli," he asked. "What's the difference between someone in Colorado and someone in Nova Scotia?"

I was waiting for him to follow up his question with some sort of lame punch line. But before he could do that, Molli looked him up and down and with a sly smile quipped: "There's no difference, Ricky. If you're a shithead in Nova Scotia, you're going to be a shithead in Colorado."

Ricky looked indignant. I laughed so hard I almost fell overboard.

The water was flat as a plate as we puttered through the fog to Ketch Harbour. We tied up to the pier below Chen's house, and the boat rocked and creaked softly as we climbed out of it. Phil pulled off his lifejacket and dropped it in the boat.

"That's enough excitement for one day," he said, with a shake of his head. "I'm going home."

"I'll drop you off," Ricky said.

"Thanks for taking us to McNab's, Chen," Janet grinned. "It was a day to remember."

"No problem," Chen smiled. "Good thing that ship didn't hit us. He would have been in big trouble."

"Yep, good thing for him," Janet replied mockingly.

Ricky, Janet and Phil walked up the grassy embankment, got into Ricky's Camaro and drove off through the fog as Chen, Molli and I made our way to Chen's house. When we crested the embankment I saw Hua's red Honda parked in the driveway.

"Can I grab a glass of water?" I asked. "I'm parched."

"Sure."

Hua was in the kitchen helping her mother make dinner. Her hair, tied in a long ponytail, flowed down her back. Tight denim shorts accentuated her long legs. She was wearing a green t-shirt with Fritz the Cat on the front.

"How was your sail?" she smiled. "We were starting to worry. The fog came in pretty quickly."

"No problems," Chen smirked. "We hit a dead calm in the harbour, though. And a ship nearly killed us, but besides that, it was great!"

"What?" Hua said, her dark eyes wide.

"We had a close call," I said.

"Are you okay?" Hua asked.

"We're not dead," Chen answered, then turned to Molli. "You want some water?"

"Okay, thanks."

Chen crossed the kitchen, filled two glasses with water and passed one to me and one to Molli.

Hua took Molli's hand.

"Are you okay?" she asked softly. "It must have been terrifying."

Molli lowered the glass.

"I've seen mountains smaller than that ship."

"Jeez," Hua muttered.

Chen's mother said something to Hua in Chinese, and Hua replied in Chinese. She must have told her mother what had happened because she raised her hand to her mouth.

"Terrible!" she said.

"You will stay for dinner?" Chen's mother asked, or demanded. It was hard to tell.

I was glad for the invitation. Any chance to spend time near Hua was welcome. I glanced at Molli.

"Sure," she shrugged.

I called my parents to tell them we made it back okay and that we were staying at Chen's for dinner. When I went back to the kitchen Molli and Chen were sitting at the table. Hua and her mother chatted softly in Chinese while tending to steaming pots and a wok on the stove. Chen's father had come into the kitchen and started rooting around in the refrigerator. I'm not sure what they were cooking, but it smelled terrible, like fermenting cabbage.

Maybe staying for dinner wasn't such a good idea after all.

"Molli plays chess," Chen said as I slid onto a seat.

I looked at Molli.

"You play chess?"

She nodded.

"I was the team captain on my school's chess team."

"Team captain, really?"

"Yep, really."

"She's going to play my father after dinner," Chen smiled.

"I'm really not that good," Molli frowned.

Chen's father turned from the fridge.

"I'm not that good."

Chen balked.

"Don't listen to him! He just wants you to think he can't play, and then he'll go straight for the jugular."

His father chuckled.

"My son exaggerates."

"How many times have you beaten me?" Chen asked.

His father seemed to be thinking.

"Hhhmm. two hundred and thirty-five times, including the other night."

"See what I mean?" Chen grinned. "He's ruthless."

"Do you want me to let you win?" his father asked coyly.

"No way!" Chen blurted. "Never! I want to beat you fair and square."

He paused.

"And I will someday."

His father smiled.

"I know you will...someday."

We sat down for dinner and thankfully Hua sat beside me. I don't think anyone can really truly understand Chinese culture until they eat "real" Chinese food, not the stuff sold in restaurants. We started off with soup and followed that with a main course of a fish that still had its head and tail, a dish with kale, yellow vegetables, steamed dumplings and rice. Was it delicious? No. Did I enjoy every second of it? Yes, because Hua had her hand on my knee under the table.

We finished eating at around eight, then Molli and Chen's father started their chess game in the living room. Hua had to study and had gone upstairs. Chen and I pulled up chairs to watch the game, but after almost two hours the players were seemingly deadlocked. If I was surprised the game had lasted so long, Chen was absolutely shocked.

Molli moved her pieces...Chen's father did the same...she took a rook...a surprised look...pawns...gone...a bishop and knight...a good fight!

They were concentrating so hard they didn't even notice Chen and me anymore.

It was almost ten o'clock when Hua came into the room and knelt beside me.

"Wow," she said softly. "Looks like a tough match."

I turned to her. Her clean scrubbed face was only inches from mine. She smelled like fresh flowers...as if she had just stepped from the shower. I desperately wanted to kiss her, but obviously that wasn't an option.

"I thought it would be over in twenty minutes," I whispered.

She stood.

"Does anyone want a Coke?"

Molli and Chen's dad were so focused on the game they didn't respond.

"I'll take one," Chen replied.

"Me, too," I said.

I watched Hua go into the kitchen and then tapped Chen on the arm and stood.

"I forgot to tell her I don't want ice."

He nodded, and I crossed the living room into the kitchen. Hua was at the counter, and she turned as I entered. She smiled widely and gently kissed my cheek.

"I've got more studying to do," she said, handing me the Cokes.

"Let's get together," I whispered.

"Soon. I promise."

Back in the living room, Molli's expression was stern and extremely focused as she reached for her queen and took Mr. Lee's other bishop. He didn't seem to notice, or at least didn't let on that it bothered him. He took another one of her pawns with one of his knights. Molli immediately responded by taking his knight with her queen.

Chen elbowed me lightly.

"He had no choice," he whispered. "Either lose the knight or his queen."

Molli inhaled deeply...her gaze on the chessboard...she pushed her hair back behind her ears...two hours in...Molli had a slight lead...chen's dad moved his remaining knight and rook...it was her bishop he took...Molli nodded silently as if someone had said something...only she could hear...moved her queen back six spaces...she was in trouble...chen's dad put her in check...took her remaining knight....leaned back...folded arms across his chest…Molli suddenly on the defensive…reacting instead of playing aggressively…he took her second bishop and a rook…put her in check…attacking her king…as chen covered his eyes with his hands…it was over.

"Checkmate," Chen's father said softly.

He reached across the board and smiled as he shook Molli's hand.

"You are a talented player."

"I'm an okay player," Molli responded. "You're the 'talented player.'"

Chen's dad smiled slightly.

"Thank you."

Molli leaned back in her chair, tilted her head to the side and looked across the board.

"Two out of three?" she asked.

I looked at my watch. It was already past eleven.

"We've got to get going," I said. "We're late."

Chen's dad stood and stretched.

"Not tonight, but another time, okay?"

I was hoping that Hua would make another appearance before we left, but she didn't. Chen walked us out to our bikes, which were learning against the side of the house. It was a dark night, the only light coming from a dim porch light that had attracted a dozen moths, which fluttered and danced around it.

"My father respects your ability," Chen said to Molli. "I'd love to play you sometime."

"Sure," Molli quipped as she grabbed the handlebars of her bike. "I'll beat you, then your father."

Chen looked dumfounded. But Molli didn't incite people to anger. She moved them to toleration.

I climbed on my bike and turned to Chen.

"Thanks for taking us sailing."

He grinned.

"We'll go out again, and try to avoid ships."

"Bye," Molli smiled. "Tell Hua we said goodnight."

"I will," he waved. "Careful on the road."

-29-

Pedaling silently through a cool mist…darkness…Molli stopped. "Look at that," she said motioning to a church close to the road.

"What, the church?"

"Yeah, look at it."

"What about it?"

"It looks like it's hovering there, sitting on the fog."

She was right. Saint Peter's Church appeared to be resting on the fog, which was concealing the small hill under it.

"Have you ever been there?" Molli asked.

"A few times," I replied, gripping my handlebars.

In reality I'd been there once…Kevin's funeral.

"Dad has a thing against churches, religion in general. The only time we go is for weddings and, you know, funerals."

"I'd like to go," Molli said, still staring at the church.

"Go?"

"Yeah, go to church."

"Why?"

She turned toward me, her gaze thoughtful.

"I just want to."

"Because?"

I really didn't have to ask. Her family had been wiped out…she was looking…for some kind of meaning in it…in life.

"I owe it to myself to check out God," she replied thoughtfully, "to try and figure out what it's all about. Is it bull or real? I need to know."

"How do you find that out, determine if Jesus was around two thousand years ago and if he's who he said he is, 'God' and all that?"

She smiled faintly.

"I'm not sure, but church seems like a good place to start."

We continued pedaling, the few streetlights along the Ketch Harbour Road creating an undeniably gloomy atmosphere in the dense fog. But there weren't many cars, so we were able to ride side-by-side most of the way.

"I could have beaten Mr. Lee," Molli quipped as we climbed a slight incline in the road. "I made three bad moves, and he pounced on me."

"Really? He's pretty good and..."

She cut me off.

"I had him."

"He said he'd give you a rematch."

"I'll be ready."

I was glad she took the match seriously and was annoyed by her loss. It was as if her total absorption in the chess match allowed her to, at least briefly, shed some of her grief. But it was still very much present, almost as discernable as the fog we were pedaling through.

We leaned our bikes up against the side of the house and went inside. My mother was upstairs in bed, but my father was reading in the living room. He looked up at us over the rim of his glasses.

"I was starting to worry."

I slipped off my windbreaker and draped it over the back of a chair.

"Molli and Mr. Lee got into a three-hour chess match."

My father's eyes widened.

"You play chess, Molli?"

"I don't know what that's such a *big* surprise to everyone," Molli smirked.

"It's not a... I mean, not everyone plays."

He exhaled sharply.

"I'm glad you play. That's all."

She folded her arms defiantly across her chest.

"Everyone thinks I'm useless! Nobody thinks I can do anything!"

My father and I exchanged worried glances. There was a half bottle of red wine on the table and he looked like he had been drinking, his eyes crimson and tired.

"Nobody thinks that you can't do anything, okay?"

He sensed that what he said made no sense.

"I mean nobody, we all think, you can't do anything, okay? We all think you can't do nothing, something, everything, anything."

Exasperated, he turned to me for support.

"Right, Max?"

"Right."

"I'm beyond exhausted," Molli yawned. "Nobody thinks that we all think that you guys can't do anything."

Once again my father and I looked at each other.

Was that an insult?

She started toward the stairs.

"I'm going to crash."

-30-

Molli huffed off to bed, and I wondered into the kitchen to see if there was anything to eat. I was rooting around in the fridge when my father came in and slid onto a seat.

"How did it go today?"

"It was a great day for a sail. We hiked the island."

I didn't mention our "near death experience" with the ship. It would have alarmed him.

"How's Molli?"

"Like she always is, quiet. I think she enjoyed herself."

Pulling pizza from the fridge, I dropped into a chair across from my father. He seemed tinged by melancholy...a coat he always wore.

"I didn't know her middle name is, 'Jude,'"

His face screwed up.

"'Jude?' Her middle name's not Jude. It's Lynn. Why would you think it's Jude?"

"She said it was."

"She told you that?"

"Yeah, the other night."

He frowned.

"She tells tall tales. She knows what her middle name is, and it's not 'Jude' it's Lynn."

"If you say so."

He was right about that. She was prone to making things up... exaggerating like crazy. My father complained that she was lying. My mother countered that Molli had a vivid imagination. They were both right.

"Max, we got big news from Colorado today."

I stopped eating.

"Did their house sell?"

"No. Molli's Aunt Abby, just found out what happened. She's retained an attorney. She says she's Molli's legal guardian. She wants Molli to move back to the States with her."

I was stunned. I thought the aunt was completely out of the picture. A lost soul and druggie with no interest in Molli.

"She's bad news?"

He inhaled deeply.

"Yep. Real bad."

"I thought *you* were her legal guardian?"

"So did I. It's a bit murky in a strict legal sense."

He rubbed his temples

"The law may see it differently. She's got a lawyer. He's pushing this."

"What are you going to do?"

He leaned back in his chair, his expression defiant.

"She's totally unfit to be Molli's guardian. I'm talking to my attorney tomorrow. I'll know more then. What our options are."

"This woman can come out of nowhere and try to grab Molli?"

He nodded.

"She's more interested in Harry's money. Adding up the sale of Harry's house and his assets…insurance…it's close to two million dollars."

He threw his hands up.

"Abby sees a chance for a big payday. Whoever's Molli's guardian has control over the money until Molli turns eighteen. That's what it's about."

"Two million bucks!"

"It's Molli's inheritance. Her college tuition. Something to give her a start in life. To travel. Buy a house someday. Harry and Beth would have wanted that for her. If Abby gets her hands on it, it'll be gone by the time Molli turns eighteen."

"Did you ever meet Abby?"

He folded his arms across his chest.

"A couple of times. She was loaded."

He paused, his expression turning dark.

"She's coming here to see Molli. To stake her claim."

"When?"

"Soon."

"Soon?"

"A week."

"Why didn't you tell Molli?"

"It's late. I'll tell her in the morning."

He stood and looked down at me.

"I'm going to bed. Turn off the lights before you hit the sack."

I will dad...alone in the darkened kitchen...shadows...battles...changes...coming...lights off...thinking...washed up...went to bed...the mournful foghorn at chebucto head...close to sleep... inaudible singing...from molli's room...like a lullaby...hey jude... was singing herself to sleep.

-31-

When I went down for breakfast the next morning, my father, mother and Molli were already in the kitchen. Obviously my parents had told Molli about the "latest developments" because she was asking questions about her aunt.

"My mom loved her, but she complained that Abby was selfish, dumb and greedy," Molli moaned. "The only time we ever heard from her was when she wanted something, usually money."

"She wants something again," my mother replied. "You."

I poured a bowl of Cheerios and milk and took a seat at the table.

"Can't Molli decide where she wants to live?"

I was kind of...maybe...sort of hoping she wanted to stay with us...or.

She looked down.

"It's a legal thing," my father said holding up his fingers like quotation marks. "I'm talking to the attorney later today."

"I'm moving back to Colorado," Molli muttered, "I'll live by myself in a cabin in the mountains."

My mother crossed the room and sat beside Molli.

"It's difficult. We're all surprised by this. No one expected her to..."

Molli jumped to her feet.

"I need to get out of here, get some air, go for a walk."

"I'll go with you," I said, standing.

Homer got up and led us to the door. The fog from the previous night had lifted, but it was still overcast, the sky a dull and familiar shade of battleship gray.

"Let's go to Chebucto Head," I said.

She stopped.

"Where's that?"

I pointed down the broken asphalt road.

"This way."

"What's there?"

"A lighthouse, foghorn, a great look-off."

"How far?"

"Twenty minutes."

We started walking and I casually asked her about her middle name.

"You said it's 'Jude,' right?"

She nodded.

"Right."

"Really? Because when I asked Dad about it he said your middle name is Lynn."

She stopped and stared at me in disbelief, her eyes wide and angry.

"It wasn't official," she snapped. "Mom and I joked we had the same middle name, 'Jude,' after the song. It was something we did. It wasn't a big deal. It was between her and me. I told you and your friends."

She started walking, then over her shoulder quipped: "Bad idea, I guess."

God she was so moody! I changed the subject.

"How weird for your aunt to show up."

"She smells money," she replied, her gaze straight ahead.

I was tempted to ask her what she would do if she had a choice...who would she chose? I didn't ask. I was afraid she'd turn her back on me...my parents...that she'd chose her aunt... afraid I'd be relieved if she left....afraid she'd stay with us... afraid!

"What did you think of McNab's Island and our sail yesterday?"
I asked.

"I'd like to go back, do some sketching."

"I'll ask Chen about a return trip."

We walked a little further and I brought up our close call with
the ship.

"That was pretty scary."

She stopped walking, her expression flat.

"I wasn't scared. I wish it had hit us, or at least me. It would
make everything *so* much easier."

Not scared? Really? I was tempted to show her the gouge marks
she left on my arm when the ship was bearing down on us.

"Everyone was freaked out."

She shrugged.

"Not me."

So...she still didn't care if she lived or died. She probably
wanted to die, or wished she were dead! I had no answer for
that...except...*so do I!* Nothing my family or I could do or say
would make a difference. My "we love you" plea didn't lessen her
grief. I felt like someone who had thrown a life preserver to a
drowning person who refused to take it. What do you do...let
them drown...jump in...try to save them? I was at a loss. Still, I
figured getting her to talk about her feelings might help in some
way.

"My father loved your father. You're still grieving, but your
whole life is ahead of you. Someday you'll find balance again.
Happiness? I don't know, but you'll get through this. People do."

I was surprised by my pleading tone. At the same time I was
beyond glad that we weren't in the store where Molli had smashed
the vase.

She stopped walking again and stared at me.

"You don't understand, and that's okay. How could you?"

She rubbed her eyes, then stepped toward me until we were only a foot apart.

"I eat. Drink. Shit. Suck in air. I'm not alive. I'm a robot, pre-programmed, detached from myself, from my body. I'm watching myself eat. Drink. Shit. Breathe. And you know something? I don't want to do that anymore! What's the point?

Her hands were clenched into fists so tight, her knuckles were white.

"This is never going to end!"

She glared at me, waiting for a response. I had never felt more put on the spot in my life. I wanted to answer her in a hopeful way, to say something to help her see past the imme-diacy of her grief.

"The point?" I replied, "is that you will find happiness someday, or happiness will find you. You're like a person who was badly hurt in a car wreck. You have to take the time to heal, and you will heal. I promise."

She rubbed her temples.

"Oh my God," she muttered. "Please, shut up."

"Listen to me. I'm not diminishing your pain, your grief by say-ing 'time heals all wounds,' but you know what? It can. You have the strength to get through this. I know you do."

"The point is I don't have any strength left!"

"You said you don't care if you live or die. Are you thinking of hurting yourself?"

She met my gaze.

"'Hurting myself?'" she answered, her blue eyes bloodshot and tired. "You sound like my grief counselor."

She paused for a few seconds before continuing.

"No, I'm not going to hurt myself. I'm not going to do a header off a cliff."

Then to my surprise she flashed a half grin.

"But if another ship comes at me, that's fine, too."

Do a header off the cliff! Was she referring to Kevin?

I grabbed her arm and turned her toward me.

"Owww, let go!" she winced. "That hurts!"

"What do you mean 'header off a cliff?'"

"I'm not going to hurl myself off a cliff, all right?"

"Yeah, well it sounded like you talking about Kevin. I never should have told you!"

She stared at me.

"I wasn't talking about Kevin!"

"Good! And you promised not to tell anyone!"

"I'm not going to tell anyone," she said, then turned on her heel and stated walking. "You have to tell them."

We walked in silence, each of us deep in our own thoughts, the warm summer breeze ushering us down the road.

"Max, if we're going to get along, there's something you should know."

I glanced at her.

"What?"

She stopped and gazed at me…her expression serious.

"Let me have the last word once in a while."

"What?"

"When we were talking, you kept going on about how people love me and all that crap and I didn't want to hear anymore."

I was flabbergasted!

"I didn't keep going. I said my parents want what's best for you. You have a future. My father loved your father. We can make it work. There is life beyond this. Hang in there. We are family. I didn't keep going."

She shook her head.

"Yes, you did, and there you go again."

"I'm not doing anything! I'm just saying…there's a way forward…don't give up."

"God!"

She stomped her feet.

"There you go again! Please let me have the last word on this. I know what you're saying. I understand. You don't have to drill it into my head. I know you guys love me and Abby doesn't. I get it! I'm welcome here. I understand, okay?"

"Good. I'm glad you understand. Go ahead have the last word!"

"Shut up!"

We walked on eggshells. I was afraid to speak.

"Molli," I finally said, "you can have the last word, I promise. But I want us to be able to talk about stuff. You can tell me when you're down, when it's too much."

"Thanks, Max," she replied wearily. "And since we're such good buddies, I know you'll take my advice...you'll tell your parents, Kevin's parents what really happened?"

I scoffed.

"You're not going to start in on that again? I can't do that! I'm too ashamed, too scared to face them."

"So," she said, slowly holding up her hand to shield her eyes from the sun, "you're one of those people who's really good at giving advice but not good at taking it?"

She stared at me waiting for a reply. She had me and she knew it.

"I can take advice. It's just..."

She continued walking and once again said flatly: "Tell them."

-32-

When we got back from our hike, there was a lot of activity around the house. My father had spent hours on the phone arguing with Molli's aunt. She was making it clear she intended to be declared Molli's legal guardian and had hired a big-shot Halifax lawyer to represent her. My father had had to retain an attorney, too. A nasty custody battle was brewing and blowing its way towards us. It would be Hurricane Abby.

Mum and Molli went up to the Superstore and my father was on the phone with his attorney.

"That woman!" he seethed. "Harry would boil if knew what she was up to. Harry's intentions were clear!"

He stopped pacing mid-step and seemed to be listening intently.

"She doesn't give a rat's ass about Molli! She's a gold digger. She was the road manager for a reggae band for God's sake!"

"Dad," I whispered, "it was a country band, not a reggae band."

He turned to me.

"What?"

"Abby was a manager for a country band, not a reggae band."

A meanness filled his eyes. He hated country music, so this information must have made things worse.

"My son just told me that she was in a country band, not a reggae band. A country band!"

The way he said it sounded as if that little detail were enough to indict the aunt. I could imagine the lawyer on the other end of the phone rolling his eyes. But this whole thing had enraged my father unlike anything I had ever seen before. He was going crazy.

"That damned woman!" he yelled into the phone. "I don't care what it costs or if we have to litigate this. I don't care. I cannot in good conscience let her even try to take Molli. My brother would turn in his grave if he knew what she's trying. This is not right!"

He stopped talking and listened for a few more moments but then continued his verbal barrage.

"Molli's starting to get acclimated to living here. Uprooting her now would be disastrous. Do you understand? Disastrous!"

His face was red with anger and the tendons on his neck were sticking out like rope. He couldn't cope. None of us could.

"I am calm!" he yelled, pounding the table with his fist. "This is as calm as I can get when that woman's name comes up. She'll destroy Molli."

He rubbed his eyes.

"Okay. Let me know as soon as possible."

He dropped the phone on the kitchen table and collapsed into a chair.

"What's up, Dad?"

He slowly shook his head. Dark half-circles had formed under his eyes in the last few days. He looked flushed.

"Abby's really making a show of this. She's determined to get custody of Molli and has pulled out all the stops to do exactly that."

"What are you going to do?"

He looked across the table at me, his expression stern.

"I'm going to fight her at every turn."

"What does that mean?"

"It means I have to pay my attorney a twenty-thousand-dollar retainer to fight that woman in court. It means I'll move heaven and earth to keep Molli here."

"When's Abby coming?"

He exhaled heavily.

"She'll be here on Tuesday."

In five days!

To make matters worse...Molli wasn't saying anything about who she wanted to live with. Her connection to her home in Denver was powerful. She loved it there and probably saw Chandler's Cove as some kind of backwater shithole.

That night my mother rapped lightly on Molli's door, went in and softly closed the door behind her. I was in bed and couldn't hear what they were saying, only muffled words now and then. After half an hour, my mother left as quietly as she had arrived.

• • •

The following morning my mother, Molli and me were coming back from town when a dog strayed into the road.

"Watch out!" Molli shrieked.

My mother had to swerve violently to avoid hitting it.

"Stop the car!" Molli yelled.

"I can't stop," my mother blurted. "We'll get hit."

"Stop the car!" Molli yelled again, her face a mask of panic.

My mother hit the brakes...pulled onto the thin gravel shoulder. Before we could come to a full stop, Molli jumped out and sprinted toward the dog!

"Max," my mother blurted. "Help her!"

Leaping from the car...I ran toward Molli...frantically chasing the dog down the middle of the road...a truck rounded the corner...swerved to avoid hitting her...the driver laying hard on his horn...as the truck passed...i heard him cursing.

"Molli!" I yelled breathlessly. "Be careful!"

The dog...a german sheppard mix...crisscrossing the two lane road...in an attempt to elude Molli...as she lunged and grabbed the dog's collar.

"You could have been killed!" I blurted as I reached her side. "Didn't you see that truck?"

"I wasn't going to watch him get hit," she replied between gasps for breath.

Gripping the dog's collar, she led it to the car. I opened the back door, but it squirmed violently trying to get away.

"In!" Molli commanded as she practically threw the dog in the backseat.

One thing I can honestly say about Molli, you were never bored in her presence.

My mother carefully pulled back onto the road.

"Thank God we weren't hit."

The dog…panting heavily…its pink tongue hanging out like a flag…as Molli checked its tattered collar. It didn't seem the least bit vicious…just scared…thin. Molli found a medallion on the collar with the dog's name, "Brutus," and a phone number.

"Hey there, Brutus," she said softly, stroking the dog's side. "Are you lost? How did you get out on the road, boy?"

My mother pinched her nose.

"He stinks to high heaven."

When we got home my mother called the phone number on the medallion. It turned out that Brutus belonged to a guy a few miles down the road in Sambro. He told her he'd come and pick up the dog.

Molli gave it a dish of water, which it greedily drank.

"Look how thin he is," Molli sighed as the dog grunted and lay in the grass.

She was right. The dog's ribs were visible under its black and brown coat. I gave it a can of Homer's food, that it downed in two gulps.

We were still outside with the dog when its owner pulled into our driveway up in a beat-up navy blue truck. He looked to be in his 20s, tall and wiry, with an untrimmed moustache, wearing faded jeans, a tattered red sweatshirt and ball cap on backwards.

"You're here for the dog?" Molli asked sharply.

He nodded.

"I am."

"You live close by?" she asked.

"In Sambro."

"How did you lose your dog?" Molli asked, her voice rising.

He shrugged.

"I keep him tied in the yard. The other day when I went out he was gone."

Molli's eyes narrowed.

"Did you look for him?"

"Hell no," the guy chuckled. "I figured he'd come back when he got hungry. He does it all the time."

"That's a crime!" Molli screamed, her words like a blast from a double-barrel shotgun. "We almost killed him today. He was in the road!"

I couldn't believe how outraged she was.

"Molli, take it easy..."

"You take it easy!" she yelled at me, before turning her attention back to the dog's owner. She knelt beside the dog and stroked its side.

"This is a beautiful animal! You don't deserve to have a beautiful animal like this!"

The guy snapped his fingers.

"Come here, Brutus...Brutus! Come here, dog!"

"He's not going with you!"

The dog didn't budge from Molli's side. It lay there happily panting as if it knew her.

"Molli," I protested, "it's his dog!"

She pulled the dog close.

My father came out in a panic, obviously alerted by Molli's screaming.

"Molli," he said firmly. "Settle down."

"Look how skinny he is!" she shouted. "He hasn't had a good meal in weeks."

She pointed at the dog's owner, her finger shaking.

"Either this guy is lying about when the dog got away or he doesn't feed it!"

"I'm sorry," my father apologized to the guy. "She's been through a lot..."

Molli grabbed the dog's collar.

"You' re not taking this dog. I'm keeping it!"

"Molli, please," my father said. "It's his dog."

"If you don't give me my dog right now I'm calling the cops and telling them you stole it," the guy said smugly. "And you can forget about the five-dollar reward!"

He snapped his fingers.

"Come here, Brutus!"

The dog ignored him and continued laying beside Molli.

"Brutus, come here!"

It was getting tense.

My father strode over, grabbed Brutus by the collar and walked him to the guy's side.

"Take the dog!"

Molli stepped forward and looked the guy square in the eye, her face red and stern.

"If I ever see this dog loose again I'm giving it to a shelter!" she seethed. "I know you live in Sambro, and it can't be that hard to find your place. All I have to do is find your beat-to-shit truck. I'm coming down there. If I see that this dog isn't being fed and taken care of, I'm taking it. Do you understand me? I'm taking it!"

The dog's owner scowled at my father.

"Mister, your daughter's crazy. You better keep her away from my house."

"She's not my...she's not going to your house, okay?" my father replied in exasperation.

Molli's eyes filled with rage as she stormed into the house and slammed the door behind her.

My father wearily rubbed his forehead.

"Shit."

The asshole loaded Brutus into his truck, and then my father went back inside. I followed him in a few minutes later and found him in the kitchen gulping down painkillers.

"Dad, are you okay?"

His face was drawn.

"It's not a good day Max. My back is killing me."

"Mum said you've got to be careful with those pills, that they could..."

He cut me off.

"Your mother's not a doctor, and neither are you. I need these for my back!"

He slipped the bottle into his pocket and went upstairs.

I went up to my bedroom a few minutes later. Molli was in her room sobbing with the door closed. Her uncontrollable weeping filling the house...like the howl of a Nor'easter. She probably shed just as many tears. The dam of her grief had cracked...a little... releasing her tears in an awful torrent. It was the first time I'd heard her really crying since she arrived weeks earlier.

My mother rapped lightly on her door.

"Molli, can I come in?"

No answer, just more crying.

"Molli?" my mother repeated. "Can I come in?"

She gently pushed open the door, went inside and closed it behind her.

• • •

Out by the garden the next morning I asked my mother if Molli had said anything about where she would live if she had a choice. She peeled off her gardening gloves and dropped them in the grass.

"She said she's tired and doesn't have enough energy to discuss it," she said, wiping sweat from her brow with the back of her hand.

"She said she'd live by herself in a one-room cabin in the mountains, which everyone knows is ridiculous."

She rolled onto her side, took off her hat and fanned herself with it.

"The baby's restless."

"You want anything?"

She smiled faintly.

"A glass of iced tea?"

"You got it."

I went into the kitchen and found Molli at the table eating half a grapefruit. Sun was gushing in through the windows painting the room in a soft yellow hue.

"I didn't know you were up."

"Hua's taking me to get my hair cut."

I pulled a glass from the cupboard and filled it with iced tea from the fridge.

"You're going to want to talk to Dad today. He's been on the phone with a lawyer. Your aunt is raising shit."

She looked up at me and smirked.

"I'm being pulled to pieces. I'm moving to a shack in the mountains and leaving everything behind."

I smiled sarcastically

"So I hear."

She knew that wasn't an option no matter how appealing it may have seemed.

"I've got to get ready," she said before turning back toward me. "Know what your problem is?"

I turned my palms upward.

"I'm not sure what 'my problem is,' but I bet you're going to tell me."

"You're an optimist."

She turned on her heel, climbed the stairs and disappeared into her bedroom.

I was at a loss...her tone suggested an insult...what did that mean...*you're an optimist*...since when was that a bad thing...how could that be a bad thing...who could think that was a bad thing!? As usual...Molli was a total mystery...like she didn't have any history. In the morning she'd be one way "This is great. I love it here!" and by the afternoon she had changed completely "I miss Colorado so much. There's nothing to do here. I'm bored out of my mind." You never knew which Molli you were going to get. It was as if there were two Mollis, or five Mollis is more like it. There was absolutely no logic in her thinking. None! One day Ricky was okay and a nice guy, according to Molli. By the next day he was a total jerk loser. It drove me crazy. My father and I were beyond confused, but my mother seemed to know how to handle her, at least a little.

I went outside and handed my mother the iced tea, which she chugged down.

"Molli's up," I said, sitting cross-legged in the cool grass beside the garden. "Hua's taking her into town to get her hair cut."

"I know."

"Do you think I'm 'optimistic?'"

She stopped weeding and looked at me, her head tilted slightly to the right.

"I certainly hope so. Why?"

"I don't know. I was just thinking about what it means, *optimistic*."

The sun on her face really showed how tired she was. The pregnancy and everything with Molli had taken a lot out of her, a lot out of all of us.

"It means you have a healthy attitude, that you see the good in things," she smiled, "that you're hopeful."

"What are you saying? I'm naive?"

She looked perplexed.

"'Naïve?' God no! Why would you say that?"

I shrugged. She reached over and placed her hand on mine.

"Max, pessimists don't change the world for the better, optimists do. Pessimism is a disease I hope you never catch. Optimists see the world as it is. They're not naive. They see past the gloom and doom. It's like they have extra vision."

She squeezed my hand.

"I hope you're an optimist. That's the way your father and me raised you. It's easy to complain and be pessimistic."

"Yeah, but…"

She cut me off.

"Do you know what a pessimist's three favorite words are?"

"No."

"'What's the point?'"

"What do you mean?"

"The worlds sucks, so 'what's the point' of doing anything? That's their attitude. But an optimist says, 'Let's give it a try.'"

What she said made me feel a bit better and took away some of the sting of Molli's insult.

"What's up with you? Why are you so down on yourself?"

"I'm tired," I sighed.

There was a toot of a car horn. We turned to see Hua pulling into the driveway in her red Honda, gravel crunching under its tires. She got out of the car looking like a dream…a coin in a stream…a faded denim jacket…tight jeans and a red halter-top.

"Wow," she said. "This garden looks great!"

"Thanks," my mother replied. "But my tomatoes are looking grim."

She motioned toward the tomatoes climbing slender sticks.

"I'll be lucky to get three pounds from those duds."

"Molli's inside," I said, standing. "Come on in. I'll tell her you're here."

In the kitchen, I pulled Hua close and was enveloped in the fresh scent of her perfume. She wrapped her arms around my neck and kissed me firmly on the mouth.

"You're a boy," she chuckled. "But I like it."

I ran my hands over her slight hips.

"Can we get together soon…like tonight?"

"Not tonight," she whispered. "I've got work at the library."

"When then?"

She pouted in a very sexy way.

"I'll have a break in the next few days. I promise."

I sat at the table, peered toward the stairs to see if Molli was coming, and then turned back to Hua and motioned for her to sit.

"A storm's coming," I whispered.

She leaned in.

"A storm?"

"A custody battle between my father and Molli's Aunt Abby over who's Molli's legal guardian."

She looked perplexed.

"I thought that was all worked out. Your father is her only living relative."

I shrugged.

"We all thought that, but apparently Molli's parents' estate is worth a couple of million, and whoever gets custody of Molli controls the money until she turns eighteen. The aunt's after the money."

"Can't Molli decide where she wants to live?"

"She's too young," I said, leaning back in my chair. "The court decides."

"What's Molli say about all this?"

"That's the problem. She's not saying much, except that she doesn't want to talk about it."

"That sucks."

"See if she'll tell you anything, where she wants to live," I said softly. "What she wants to do."

Hua got up and leaned against the counter.

"I don't know if I should, Max. It's not my place. I'm not a spy. Haven't you or your parents asked her?"

"Yes, but she's non-committal. She says she's going to live in a cabin in the mountains."

She threw her hands up.

"Sounds like fun!"

"Hua, seriously. Dad's spending big bucks on a lawyer to fight Molli's aunt, and Molli may not even want to stay here."

"What can I tell you," she frowned. "You can't force this. She'll tell you when she's ready."

"When's that going to be?"

"I'm not sure, soon, maybe…"

"What?"

I heard Molli's door open and she descended the stairs into the kitchen, a canvas purse slung over her shoulder, aviator sunglasses shielding her eyes against inquiry.

"Hi, Hua," she said. "I didn't hear your car pull up."

"We were just chatting," Hua said, taking a step forward. "Are you ready to go?"

"Can you drop me off at the yacht squadron?" I asked. "Ricky asked me to come by."

Hua waved her keys through the air.

"No problema."

My mother was still working in the garden, her trusty wide-brimmed light blue gardening hat shielding her face from the sun climbing the eastern sky.

"Bye," she waved. "Have fun."

Molli climbed into the back of the Honda, and I hopped into the passenger's seat, the car door hinges squeaking loudly as I closed it. It was a gorgeous summer day. All the windows were down as we pulled onto the Ketch Harbour Road and started toward the city.

"Thanks for this, Hua," Molli said, running her hands through her hair. "The salt air and sun are turning my hair into straw. Maybe I'll get my head shaved!"

I figured she was kidding, or not.

"Dad will love that," I smirked.

We continue driving for a while, and then Hua asked Molli about her aunt.

"She's showing up out of the blue?"

I turned toward Molli, who was gazing out the window.

"She wants the money," she responded flatly.

"I'm really sorry, Molli," Hua said kindly, "and after all you've been through."

"I'm moving back to Denver to live in a ski shack in the mountains," Molli replied grumpily. "I'll snowboard and hike all day."

I sensed a chance to ask her what she would do, where she would choose to live, if she had a choice.

Resting my elbow on the back of the seat, I turned to look at her. "Just stay here."

She stared back as if I had said something incredibly stupid.

"Your mother is pregnant up to here," she said, raising her hand to her chest. "You're living in the baby's room, and I'm living in your room."

"That's not..." I protested.

She cut me off.

"Your father's a pill-popper, and the closest decent mountain's in Quebec, for God's sake! You don't have room for me. Admit it!"

She was right, I guess, but I also believed we could make it work if we tried.

"I'm not admitting anything."

"Right. Mister Optimist."

I glanced over at Hua...hoping for support. Her gaze was set on the road. Obviously she didn't want to get involved. We drove in silence then pulled over by the gate in front of the yacht squadron. I jumped out and Molli got in the passenger's seat.

"Thanks for the ride," I said, leaning in the window.

"No problem," Hua smiled, "and I'll be in touch to give you an update on that thing we talked about."

"Huh?"

"You know, what we talked about in the kitchen? Getting together to talk about 'that thing,' remember?"

"Oh yeah," I grinned. "I really feel like I need it. Let me know."

Molli shot me a curious look then they drove off toward the city. I started toward the boathouse to look for Ricky. I was about to find out he was making plans to become an arsonist.

-33-

A breeze blowing in from the south seemed to ease my endless anxiety as I strolled through the boatyard under a clear blue sky, checking out some of the yachts and sailboats up on wooden slips. Most of the boats were expensive…owned by big spenders… bankers…lenders…lawyers…doctors… financiers…people like that. Ricky made fun of the members all the time, usually dismissing them as "shithead snobs."

One time some guy tossed Ricky his keys and told him to park his car.

"I was going to steal it, but instead I told the shithead snob off," Ricky had said. "I was like, 'Hey mister, I'm not a valet. Park your own car!'"

He had a solid working class hatred for the rich and privileged. He sneered at them. His job consisted of pumping gas and fresh drinking water into boats, painting as needed, helping to launch boats at the start of the season and taking them out in the fall, cleaning the boat yard and goofing off. I thought I'd like to have a sailboat one day, but something smaller, like Chen's boat. Or a small boat and motor for puttering around Chandler's Cove. But, well, you know…

I found Ricky sitting in a small cluttered office in the boathouse.

"Hey, man," he said getting to his feet. "How you doing, man?"

"Not bad."

"Why do people say that?"

"Say what?"

"'Not bad.' It's kind of negative, 'not bad.' What you're saying is things are usually bad, but right now they're 'not bad?'"

"What?"

"I'm just saying a better response would be "things are great. I'm good.' Something like that."

"Whatever."

"How's Moll?"

I threw up my hands.

"Who knows? She's the queen of one-word answers. It's hard as hell to get her to talk about anything."

"Right. She's keeping it all bottled up."

I nodded in agreement

"She said she wants to go to church."

His face screwed up.

"Church?"

"That's what she said. I guess she's looking for answers, in you know, what happened…her family. All that. Is God real?"

"I bet."

We were silent for a moment then I asked him what he believed in? I guess I never really knew.

"What do you think?"

He raised his hand to his chin and seemed to be thinking.

"Nah," he shrugged. "I don't believe it. My grandma Bea was in serious pain when she died. Serious. She believed though. It was always Jesus this and Jesus that with her. She prayed up to the end. They all prayed for it to stop but it didn't. Nothing helped."

He shook his head.

"There's no God."

I wasn't as sure…it struck me that he was using his grandmother's pain…death as a way to deny there's something at work…a grand design…something omnipotent…God. His grandmother was the one who died in pain…yet she believed. It's kind of intellectually lazy using other people's experiences to justify our own disbeliefs. Still…you have to be willfully naive not to see that there's a lot of pain, suffering and injustice in the world. But that's not all there is.

Ricky slipped on his sunglasses and moved toward the door.

"Come on, I want to show you something."

I followed him through the boatyard to a gorgeous sailboat up on a wooden slip beside several other nice boats.

"Look at this boat," Ricky grinned. "This is a beautiful sailboat."

I nodded. It was fifty feet long and absolutely magnificent.

"I'm scraping the hull on this baby, then painting it."

"Big job."

"Yes, it is," he replied matter-of-factly.

"Look at what this boat is named," he scoffed, motioning to the name, "Deserving, "written in gold leaf lettering on the stern.

He pushed his sunglasses up on his nose.

"Do you like this boat?"

"It's sweet."

"Yes, it is *sweet*." he smiled. "The teak on this boat cost fifteen grand."

He pointed to a shiny wench up on the deck.

"The wenches on this boat cost ten grand each, and there's four of them."

"Wow!"

"You're damned right, wow."

He stepped back, his arms folded across his chest.

"The sails on this baby, forty grand," he continued. "The galley, fifty grand. This boat probably cost a quarter of a mil."

"No shit?"

"Yeah, man, no shit."

He frowned.

"But, Max my friend, this is an unlucky boat."

"Really?"

"Oh yeah. A guy died on this boat and a year later the mainsail broke."

"Shit. Not good."

"There should be three a's in a boat's name," he said thoughtfully. "That's good luck. My dad's lobster boat is named, *Anna Gail.* Notice the three a's. But there's not a single 'a' in this boat's name."

He shook his head.

"Very bad."

"If you say so."

He stepped back and looked at the boat.

"Who names their boat 'Deserving?'"

"Some rich person I bet."

He nodded.

It seemed like our conversation was leading somewhere, but I wasn't sure where.

"It seems arrogant doesn't it?" Ricky continued. "They're saying 'I'm rich and I'm deserving of owning this boat. I'm deserving of the rich life, the good life. And by the way, the fact that I'm deserving also means you're undeserving. You're not good enough. I'm better than you. You'll never be a good as me because I'm deserving!' Shitheads!"

I had to chuckle.

"I'd like to be deserving enough to have a boat half this size someday."

He took off his ball cap, pulled a green bandana from his pocket and wiped his sweaty brow.

"Do you know who owns this boat?"

I shrugged.

"I have no idea."

He smiled wickedly.

"This boat belongs to your neighbors, man. That shithead in the castle. John 'asshole' King!"

"Really?"

"Yep"

"Asshole."

He took a step toward me and lowered his voice.

"I just wanted to let you know...I'm going to burn his boat down."

I couldn't believe what I had just heard.

"What?" I scoffed. "Don't be ridiculous."

"It's not ridiculous," he replied with indignity. "It's a service to the community."

I stared at him, trying to read his expression.

"You're kidding right?"

He shook his head.

"Nope."

"You'll go to jail."

"I'm not stupid," he whispered. "I'll make it look like an accident. It's happened before. It's a wooden hull, man. I'm using the blowtorch to loosen the old paint. But it's tricky. I've got to be careful not to start a fire. Paint thinner is like jet fuel, man, highly flammable, and once it starts, God oh God, it just takes off. This boat would be gone by the time the fire department got here...especially if I had accidently left a quart of paint thinner on the deck."

"This isn't funny."

He chuckled.

"It's better than burning his house down, right? The way I see it this boat here is 'deserving' of being torched."

I knew he was just about crazy enough to do it.

"Forget it. Bad idea!"

He looked at me for a moment and then playfully pushed my shoulder.

"Yeah, you're right," he smirked. "I'm just yanking your chain, man."

-34-

Awful things happen within the walls of a seemingly normal household. Godless things. Violence. Abuse. Rape. Lies. Murder. Terrible secrets. Cruelty...every other kind of sin. It doesn't matter where you live or how much money and power you have. No one is immune. People try to keep it quiet...but everyone knows the truth.

I hung out at the yacht squadron for the next few hours, kicking around, catching rays and gazing out over the Northwest Arm. When Ricky got off we walked through the boatyard to his Camaro.

He tossed me the keys.

"You drive."

I slid into the driver's seat and turned the ignition, but the car only sputtered.

"Shit," he muttered. "Pop the hood."

He jumped out, leaving the door open, stuck his head under the hood, made some adjustments and then told me to try it. The car still wouldn't start. I heard him swearing as he continued working on something.

"Try it again," he said, emerging from under the hood. "Give it some gas."

I did and it chugged to life.

"I gotta do some work on that fuel filter," he said as he climbed in.

The trees along the road cast long shadows as we drove through Purcell's Cove. That section of road is a bid winding and I was watching my speed because cops often laid in wait ready to give out speeding tickets even if you're only going five miles over the limit.

Ricky pulled a joint from his pocket and lit it. I shot him "a look," but he just grinned.

"Don't worry," he laughed. "Keep your eyes on the road."

"So," he said taking a big hit off the joint, "when's your driving test, man?"

"I haven't scheduled it yet."

"Yeah, whose car you using?"

"My dad's"

"His Toyota?"

"Yep."

He flicked ash from the joint onto the floor.

"You can use this if you want. This is the car you did most practice driving in, right?"

"Thanks," I said glancing at him, "but my dad will probably drive me there, and you know, I've driven that car too, so I feel okay about it."

"You're right. They'd probably fail you for just showing up for the test in this piece of shit."

He was right about one thing. I certainly didn't want anything to impede my chances of passing that test. Having a driver's license and access to a car is exquisite freedom. Every teenager knows that. When you get your driver's license the world suddenly become bigger...or smaller...I guess...depending on how you look at it. There are new exciting frontiers to explore. You can drive to the store or to McDonald's and just hang out. A trip like that on a bike was too far but takes but mere minutes in a car.

"So what's up with your cousin, man?" Ricky asked.

"Her aunt's coming from the states to lay claim to her."

He looked puzzled.

"I thought Molli didn't have any family. That's why she's with you."

I explained everything to him and how the aunt was just after the money.

"Molli's worth two million buckaroos?"

"Yeah, technically, but she can't touch the money until she's eighteen."

"How old is she?"

"Fifteen."

He pounded his thigh with his fist.

"Two million bucks! Shit!"

We were passing through Herring Cove when we saw a friend of ours, Bryan Grant, walking on the shoulder.

"Where you headed?" Ricky asked as we slowed beside him.

He turned to look at us.

"Home."

"Get in," Ricky replied. "We'll drop you."

Bryan climbed into the back seat. Ricky knew him better than I did, but I always thought he was a good head. Bryan's father was a real mean guy...a dark glint in his eye...a lobsterman drunk... his heart had sunk....he beat Bryan and his two brothers...their mother...Bryan often seemed to be fuming...like a disaster was looming.

Domestic violence wasn't rare around there. It's not rare anywhere. Lots of families within a few miles of us were living on the edge financially...spiritually. That combined with bad fishing, booze, drugs, and a lousy economy had caused a slew of domestic problems. Sure, some people had built nice and expensive houses in the area within the last 15 years, but it was a safe bet that a lot of families between Sambro and Halifax were living in quiet poverty and desperation. As I pulled back onto the road Ricky turned to look at Bryan.

"Big party coming up," he said, his elbow resting on the back of the seat.

"Great," Bryan replied.

"What happened to your lip?" Ricky asked.

I looked in the rearview mirror and could see that Bryan's top lip was swollen and cut.

"I fell."

"You fell?" Ricky asked.

He reached out and pulled off Bryan's sunglasses.

"Holy shit," Ricky asked, "how did you get that?"

I glanced again in the rearview. Bryan's eye was a purplish oozing black and was swollen shut.

"I walked into a door," he muttered, his gaze cast down.

Ricky scoffed.

"Yeah right," he scoffed, "more like you walked into your old man's fist."

He grabbed his sunglasses from Ricky and slipped them back on.

"I deserved it," Bryan replied. "The old man's real stressed out. Fishing has been shit for years. The price of fuel for the boat is going up like crazy."

"And that's your fault?" Ricky smirked.

"I'm quitting school," Bryan said. "I'm not going back to Isley for grade twelve in September. I'm going to work on the *Alice Barbara*."

The *Alice Barbara* was his father's lobster boat. I could not imagine a more hellish scenario than being out on the ocean in rough seas with his mean-as-shit father who beat and berated him...no escape from it. He'd have a grade eleven education, probably end up marrying a Herring Cover or Spryfielder, have a few kids and never travel more than 50 miles from home. I'd see them up at the SuperStore every once in a while. And that could be a good life, I guess. That was the choice of a lot of guys I went to school with. In some ways I had the same choices but more prospects. Yeah, some guys went on to university and lived broader lives, drove nicer cars and lived in nicer houses. Then there were guys like Tom Densmore from Spryfield. He was a few years older than me, a fantastic hockey player that everyone said was going to be drafted into the NHL by the Chicago Blackhawks. But the summer before that, he crashed his motorbike and mangled his hand. That ended any chance at a hockey career. Last I heard he was wearing an orange apron and working at Home Depot.

Ricky stared at Bryan in disbelief.

"Are you nuts? Out there with your old man trapped on a lobster boat?"

He shook his head.

"Screw that. Shoot him. Yeah, just shoot him and make it look like an accident."

I glanced over at Ricky to see if he was kidding, because with Ricky, it wasn't always easy to tell.

He winked.

"Max and I will back you up one hundred percent," he grinned. "'Oh yes officer. Mr. Grant was careless as shit with guns, ehhh. I'm not the least bit surprised it went off. Poor guy, ehhh, Bryan's devastated.'"

He let out a loud howl.

"You can pay me off with the insurance money!"

We all laughed…but a year later…the father beat one of Bryan's brothers so badly…he lost the sight in his left eye. An awful thing.

-35-

It was around that time that events started speeding up. If we had been on a rollercoaster climbing to the top…we were now catapulting down the backside like breakneck greed.

Ricky dropped me off and drove Bryan home. My father's Toyota and Hua's red Honda were parked in the gravel driveway and another car I didn't recognize was parked near them. When I went inside, my father was sitting at the kitchen table, a newspaper spread out in front of him. He peered up from the paper, a look of concern on his face.

"Where were you?"

"At the squadron, Ricky just dropped me off."

"Your mother's sick. When Hua and Molli got back they called me, and I called the doctor."

Anger crossed his face.

"I've been trying to reach you."

"Mum's sick?"

"Yes. The doctor's with her now. She thinks your mother's just worn out, but we all got a scare."

I started toward the stairs.

"I'm going to check on her."

"Not now, Max," he said sternly. "The doctor's with her. You can see her later."

"Where are Hua and Molli?"

He motioned outside.

"In the A-frame."

I started for the backdoor, but he pointed at a chair and told me to sit.

"Max, I need you here when I'm not here. What if your mother had to go to the hospital?"

"I was only gone for a few hours," I protested. "She was fine when I left, and she told me to go. I knew Molli and Hua would be back in a few hours. I didn't…"

"Excuses are like assholes," he said crossly, "everybody has one."

He flipped the newspaper closed.

"I need you to give me your word that you'll be here with your very pregnant mother when I'm out, or when Molli and I are out. She can't be here alone. Can you do that?"

"Yes, of course."

He shook his head wearily and waved toward the door.

"Good. Now get outta here."

I knew I'd be on a short leash until the baby arrived. I loved my mother, but having to be home to look after her would be a major drag during the peak of summer.

I found Molli and Hua sitting in the A-frame. The summer sun high in western sky flowing in through the door and skylights brought out the rich detail in the wood, like abstract waves flowing across the walls.

Molli and Hua stopped talking and looked at me as I approached the door.

Molli had been transformed…her hair…completely different…shorter…she looked older.

"Your hair looks nice," I smiled.

She blushed.

"It was Hua's idea for me to get it cut like this."

Hua leaned forward.

"Yeah, but you had the guts for a big style change."

Molli cracked a half-smile, slipped her phone into her pocket and grabbed two shopping bags by her knee.

"I'm going to check my email."

She turned to Hua.

"Thanks, I really appreciate all you've done. But I'm still going to beat your father in chess."

Hua laughed and then got up to hug Molli.

"Remember what we talked about, okay?" she said, then let go and looked at Molli. "A lot of people here care for you."

"I know."

She went inside, and Hua and I sat beside each other.

"What was in the bags?" I asked.

She stretched out and laid her long slim legs across my thighs.

"We did some shopping."

"You don't have to buy her clothes. Mum's taking her shopping."

"Your Mum asked me to do it, and said she'd pay me later."

"How was Molli?" I whispered. "Did she say anything?"

She tilted her head to one side, her long jet-black hair shimmering in the sunlight.

"She said she was tired and missed Denver. I didn't push it."

So, the mystery continued.

I glanced over Hua's shoulder to the back of our house. No one was coming. I closed the door...kissed Hua firmly on the mouth...as she wrapped her long thin arms...around my neck...pulled her on top...tugged at her denim jacket...as she pushed me away...jumped to her feet.

"I can do this faster than you," she giggled sexily. "It'll have to be a quickie."

She tore off her clothes off in ten seconds flat...God I was happy with that...off came my clothes...my back onto the bench...my lusty thirst she would quench...hard as a rock...she was on top... don't stop...she was a thrilling combination of passion...elation...

going at it…completely lost in it…sweat pouring from our heaving bodies…three distinct loud knocks…glanced over Hua's shoulder…the door was open…Molli was standing there!

"Shit!"

Hua turned to look, jumped to her feet and grabbed her clothes from the floor.

Molli stepped to the side of the doorway out of view.

"Sorry," she said, "but your father asked me to get you…"

"It's okay, Molli," Hua blurted as she pulled on her clothes.

I was still frantically getting dressed as she went outside.

"I'm *so* embarrassed," I heard her say to Molli. "Max and I are, we're ummm, you know we're…have you ever heard that term 'friends with benefits?' Well, that's what we are. We really like each other."

"It's okay," Molli replied softly, "you don't have to…"

"It's just that if anybody found out, if my parents found out, they wouldn't understand."

Hastily pulling on my T-shirt and cutoffs, I pulled up my zipper and stepped out to join them. Molli was looking at the ground.

"Hua's right. Our relationship is a secret. It's easier that way. I didn't know you were coming back out."

She looked up.

"Your father said to get you."

I wasn't sure what to say, and I sure as hell didn't want Molli to mention anything to anyone about what she had just seen.

"Don't say anything," I said, half pleading. "No one's supposed to know, and…"

She cut me off.

"It's okay. I'm not going to say anything."

She paused.

"I already knew, anyway."

Hua's eyes widened.

"You did?"

Molli nodded.

"I could tell."

Smiling widely, Hua hugged her.

"Of course you could!"

-36-

A fifteen-year-old girl who knows your deepest...darkest secrets is a dangerous person. They can wield power over you. You've given her a bomb with your name on it. I'm not talking about about Hua and me, I'm talking about Kevin.

Hua jumped into her Honda and headed home as Molli and I went inside. My father and the doctor were up in my parents' bedroom talking in hushed voices to my mother. She was as pale as the bed sheets and looked beyond exhausted.

"Doctor Adams says your mother has to stay off her feet for a few days," my father said grimly.

"No gardening for at least a week," the doctor added.

"Max, Molli and I will be her devoted servants," my father smiled.

"I'm not that bad," my mother protested, sitting up in bed. "Just a little tired."

"It's more than that," the doctor replied sharply. "You and the baby need some serious rest, and if you can't get it here, I'll have you admitted. I mean it."

"Okay," my mother replied sheepishly.

My father walked the doctor to her car, and Molli and I sat on the edge of the bed.

My mother placed her hand on Molli's.

"I absolutely love your haircut," she said softly, her brown eyes filled with affection. "It's perfect for you."

"Thanks."

"Has Hua left?" my mother asked weakly.

Molli's eyes met mine.

"She had to go home," I replied.

"That girl is a gem," my mother smiled. "What a sweetheart."

I glanced at Molli. She was suppressing a grin.

"Mum, do you want anything?"

She shook her head.

"I'm fine. But what are you guys going to have for dinner?"

Molli smiled.

"I can make something."

"No, honey, you don't have to make dinner. Your uncle Geoff can make dinner or order something."

"I'm going to make dinner," Molli insisted.

"No need, Molli," I said, "we'll order pizza."

Her face turned red, and it looked like she was on the verge of tears.

"You don't want me to cook? Does everyone think I'm useless?"

"I didn't know you cooked," my mother replied softly, "that's all."

"I can and I will."

Down in the kitchen Molli started rummaging through the fridge.

"There's eggs and cheese, milk and green onions. I'm making you guys omelets!"

My father and I exchanged worried glances.

"I didn't know you cooked," he said.

"There are a lot of things about me that you don't know."

Yeah right, I thought, like where you want to live for one thing.

Molli stopped for a moment and pointed to a wedding invitation that my mother had stuck to the fridge months earlier. The daughter of someone my father knew through the symphony was getting married, and we had been invited.

"This wedding is in a few days," she said.

"That's right," my father replied. "We'll all go together as a family."

Molli shrugged and continued cooking...a blur of activity... stirring...mixing...making toast. As she was cooking the omelets, my father talked to her about her aunt and the pending court case.

"You may have a choice, you know," he said, "about where you prefer to live."

We both looked at her...waiting for a reply. She stopped what she was doing and turned to us, her face stern.

"A choice?" she scoffed. "My choice is to be in my house in Denver."

"I know," my father said, "but..."

She cut him off.

"Do I want to be here? No. I want to be in my house in Denver. Is that possible? No. Do I want to live with Abby?"

She paused.

"No...maybe, I don't know. I miss my family *so* much. I miss Denver *so* much. I miss my friends *so* much. It doesn't matter anyway. The court will decide where I live."

Obviously it wasn't a good idea to press her on it.

After twenty minutes she slid two omelets with toast onto the table in front of us. There was something about that omelet and toast...how they looked on the plates...in a word...unappetizing. I didn't think it was possible to make an omelet...burned to a crisp on the edges but raw in the middle. But she did it. My father cut into his and a watery slime flowed onto his plate. I got the same result. I glanced at my father and grimaced.

"Molli, sit down and join us," he said.

"I'm making Aunt Karen's omelet. I'll eat in a while."

She was puttering around, making Mum's omelet, but at the same time she was watching us like a hawk out of the corner of her eye to make sure we ate every bite.

So, that's what love is, eating a raw omelet and greasy toast to the last disgusting bite because you don't want to fight and hurt the feelings of the person who made it.

"I'm bringing this up to Aunt Karen," Molli said, holding a plate in one hand.

"Dad," I said after she had left, "I can't eat this. It's, it's…"

I pushed my plate away.

"I know, but you're got to finish it," he whispered urgently, "or she'll be very upset."

"Yeah but…"

Before I could finish, Molli came back downstairs. I managed to eat everything on my plate, as did my father.

"Thanks, Molli," my father said standing, "that was great."

He went upstairs…tried to quietly puke in the bathroom…who can puke quietly…i've tried it…it's impossible…doesn't work…an involuntary reaction…a spasm…no control…but he did it!

Maybe that's what love is? Puking quietly so as not to offend the person who made you puke.

Later that night I asked my mother how she liked her omelet?

"It was delicious! Molli really can cook."

"Ours were a bit runny, soggy or something."

"Mine was perfect."

Hmmm…did she make my omelet…my father's omelet…crappy on purpose?

-37-

Love and prayer…two good things for chasing away the devil. That's what we did at "the society wedding" of summer. No one wanted to go to the wedding. My mother moaned she was too pregnant. My father said he was too tired. Molli was sulking and wasn't saying anything, and I knew it would be a beyond a major drag…a chore for my father.

The only reason we went…the bride's parents…big shot patrons of the symphony…successful society types…halifax's upper crust…heart surgeon…architect…rich…living in the south end…a gorgeous house…overlooking the Northwest Arm.

I had never met their daughter, Gail…twenty five…a big disappointment to her parents…marrying a black guy from preston…mostly poor…mostly african canadian community outside of Dartmout. Her parents were beyond horrified…having expected her to marry a white doctor or lawyer…someone exactly like them.

"Her parents think she has an infatuation with black men, or at least this one black man," my father had laughed. "They think it's like the 'ultimate bad boy' and their daughter is going through a phase."

"A phase? Sounds racist."

"Sure does. They tried to talk her out of it, begged her to change her mind."

He stopped for a moment and shook his head in disbelief.

"They finally said they thought she was doing it to piss them off."

I chuckled.

"I guess it worked."

He shrugged.

"The daughter screamed she loved him and stormed out of the house."

My thoughts: It should be an interesting wedding.

My mother had given Hua money to buy Molli a dress for the occasion. I was forced into a two-piece navy blue suit tight as a sausage casing...two inches too short in the sleeves. I had grown a lot in a year, and the suit had already been let out as much as possible.

It was a beautiful July day for a wedding as we drove into Halifax.

"Molli, I love that dress!" my mother said. "It's so you."

She turned to my father.

"That dress is perfect for her."

My father glanced into the rearview mirror.

"You look like a million, Molli."

Molli was gazing out the window.

"Thanks."

"I've got to tell Hua how good it looks," my mother gushed. "She and Molli went to a used clothing boutique in Halifax."

Reaching over the backseat...my mother patted down a row of wrinkles on my shoulder.

"Max, you need a new suit."

"I've needed one for the past year."

We sped past two crows eating something by the side of the road...reminding me of a finch that had slammed into the living room window a few days earlier and died.

"Another bird hit the window and broke its neck," I said to no one in particular. "That's ten so far this summer. Dad, we have to do something."

My father exhaled heavily.

"Nothing else we can do, Max."

215

"We could cut the trees down."

He examined me in the rearview mirror.

"That's not really an option, is it?"

"We've got to do something!"

By the time we got to the church it was packed. Despite all the drama over the bride and groom…the bride's family dropped serious cash on that ceremony and reception. It was first-class all the way…Saint Mary's Basilica at the foot of Spring Garden Road…halifax's premier catholic church…with free valet parking…which my father loved.

An usher in a tux escorted us to a pew…creaking as we settled in….hushed voices echoing through the church…the smell of incense…a feeling of expectation…hung in the air…like sunlight spilling in through the tall stained glass windows…everything painted in a pleasant soft light.

I had never been in that church before. I was impressed with how…it was…a grand old Halifax lady. Looking around…the left side was pretty much all black…the right side…was mostly white. There were a few whites sitting on the black side and some black people on the white side…it was split right down the middle for the most part. Halifax's upper crust…all there…judges… doctors…professors…actors…business   people…lawyers…the mayor and a life-size wooden carving of Jesus Christ…his gaze cast down.

A black pastor from Preston…a white priest from St. Mary's performed the ceremony. At one point everyone was invited to come up and take communion. When it was our row's turn we moved aside to let people out. There was a long line of people… black…white…together…who took the sacraments before returning to their seats.

The bride's mother wept…tears…echoing through the church… not happy tears…more like…bawling…sobbing…genuinely upset…

her husband...comforting her...his arm around her shoulder. In that way it was more like a funeral than a wedding. After the ceremony the bride...smiling widely...standing on the steps of the church...threw her flowery bouquet into a crowd of eager young women...diving over each other to get it...one girl emerging with it for everyone to see.

The reception...the swankiest...most high-class hotel on the Halifax waterfront. "The plan," my father explained as we drove there, was to stay for an hour so he could "have face time" with the orchestra supporters in the crowd. It was work for him.

It was packed and due to a seating mixup...Molli and I ended up at a table with a bunch of people from Preston...we'd didn't know. We were the only white people at the table...a first for me. I didn't cross paths with many black people...everyone was nice... a guy introduced himself and the entire table. He pointed to the right.

"That's the groom's uncle in from Alabama. He came up for this."

A guy in his twenties, sitting next to me, tapped me on the arm.

"This is a big deal," he grinned. "Half of Preston is here!"

"Half is here, and the second half is on the way here," a man on the other side of the table chuckled.

There were ten people at our table, all drinking...except of course for me and Molli. I decided to steal a drink. When you're underage...stealing drinks in a social situation...a wedding... there's a routine you must follow...walking around casually look for...new drinks left unattended by people up dancing... social-izing...steal a rum and coke...whiskey or rum and anything...its looks like you're drinking soda. When you spy an unattended drink...walk up and grab it as if it was your drink in the first place. If anyone gets in your face and says anything like "that's my drink" or that's so and so's drink...apologize and move on.

"I'm going to find Mum and Dad, to tell them where we are," I said to Molli.

She looked up at me.

"Want me to come?"

"No. I'll be right back."

The crowd was big and getting bigger as the bride and groom flowed into the room. It had to be the largest party room in the hotel. On one side, glass doors opened up onto an expansive patio that offered a spectacular view of the waterfront. It was getting dark, and the lights from Dartmouth across the harbour sparkled.

I found my parents' table and crouched down beside my mother.

"Where's Molli?" she asked over the din of the crowd.

"At our table."

I motioned to the other side of the room.

"We're way over there."

"Max, we're not staying long," my father said. "Your mother's tired."

I stood.

"Okay."

A tall black guy in a tux with red trim...the master of ceremonies...made an announcement from the front of the room.

"We have a lot of nice gifts to give away tonight," he smiled. "We have two-hundred-dollar gift certificates from Sobey's, SuperStore and those nice shops along Spring Garden Road."

People applauded emphatically. It was the first wedding I ever attended where they gave away nice door prizes!

"We have a lot of other beautiful thing to help you remember this special day, including a fantastic family vacation give away, a week in Montreal!"

My mother's eyes almost popped out of her head. She really wanted to win something.

"I'm going back to our table," I said.

"Don't forget," my father repeated, pointing at his watch. "We're not staying long."

On the way back to Molli I saw a thick black wallet sitting unattended on a table...glancing around...i grabbed it...stuffing it into my front pocket. Inside a bathroom stall I pulled out...$137... dropped the wallet on the floor and hurried out. I desperately needed money to pay Mister D. On the way back to the table I stole a drink. As soon as I sat Molli eyed me suspiciously.

"What are you drinking, Max?"

"Coke."

"Coke?" she snorted. "Right. If your parents find out you're drinking 'Coke,' you're going to get busted big time."

I shrugged.

"Don't worry about it."

We sat there without saying much, but after a while I noticed Molli was staring at a kid sitting at the next table. It was as if she was in a trance.

"Molli, are you okay?"

She didn't hear or was ignoring me.

"Molli," I asked loudly. "What's up?"

She turned toward me, her eyes wide, the blood seemingly drained from her face.

"That little boy at the next table. My God, he looks just like my little brother, Tim. It's unbelievable!"

I glanced at the boy. He was with his parents. Eight or nine, dressed in a brown suit and tie, he looked bored to death. What could I say to Molli? I sensed she wanted to talk about her brother.

"What was he like?"

She smiled slightly.

"He was a pest. But I'd give anything for him to still be here. He was always bugging me to take him snowboarding, but I'd blow him off. He was just learning and couldn't do much except go down the hill. On the rare occasions when I did take him, I was with my friends, and he'd slow us up. I'd get so aggravated."

Tears welled in her eyes.

"I wish I had been nicer, more patient, a better big sister."

I very much wanted to say something comforting.

"He probably thought you were the best sister in the world. The fact that you took him snowboarding with you at all is a big deal."

She seemed to be thinking, taking in my words the same way you breathe.

"Of course you'd say that," she muttered.

A band…the best in the land…a dozen players including a horn section…set up on stage…a gorgeous black woman…a singer…in her thirties…grabbed a mic…welcoming everyone.

"We're going to chase the devil away tonight!" she said glee-fully. "I don't care if you're black or white. I want everyone up on the dance floor tonight. Let's raise the roof on this place. We're going to chase the devil away. I mean it!"

People cheered and clapped.

"Come on, people, on your feet!"

The band broke into a rousing version of, Soul Man. If there had been a race to the dance floor the black side would have won, but it quickly filled with people of all ages and races. A guy across the table said something to me, but I couldn't hear him above the music, so I went over and sat beside him.

"You from Halifax?" he shouted.

"No, from outside of Halifax. Chandler's Cove."

He nodded.

"You from Halifax?" I asked.

"Preston."

A well-dressed black guy came over to our table and asked Molli something. I couldn't hear what it was, but she smiled and shook her head, and he left.

"Is that your sister?" the guy next to me asked.

I leaned in so he could hear me.

"My cousin, from the states."

He nodded.

A few moments later another black guy around my age approached Molli, said something and offered her his hand. Obviously he had just asked her to dance. She shook her head politely and said no thanks.

When the band finished the song another black guy, in his late teens, sat down beside Molli and started talking to her. The band was between songs, so I could actually hear most of what he was saying. He was dressed sharply in a black and pink tux. His cologne wafted in the air, and he was smiling in a sheepish way.

"Do you hate black people?" he asked Molli.

She looked perplexed.

"No!"

He smiled.

"I just watched two brothers come up and ask you to dance, and you blew them off like a hurricane to a candle."

Molli frowned.

"It's not them, it's me. I'm sorry, but I don't dance."

It was his turn to look perplexed.

"You don't dance? What do you mean you don't dance?"

He glanced over at me.

"Everyone dances right?"

I nodded.

"If you say so."

He smiled a little sarcastically.

"Nice suit!"

"Thanks" I replied flatly.

"Is this your girlfriend?"

"No, she's my cousin."

"I just wanted to be sure," he grinned, "because I would never birddog another guy's girl."

He turned back to Molli.

"If everyone dances that means you can dance. Trust me, if you can inhale, you can dance."

Molli smiled, a little. Obviously the guy was nice and was kidding around, trying to break the ice.

"I'm with the groom's side of the family," he grinned. "He's my cousin. I'm respectable, not like those other two guys."

He moved in a little closer to Molli.

"If everyone can dance, that means you can dance," he repeated," and if you don't dance one dance with me, I'm going to cry."

He pouted, pretended to cry then offered her his hand.

"One dance?"

She looked at me.

"It's up to you."

They made their way to the dance floor...crowded with people dancing under pastel lights...so many...bright colored suits...fancy boots...long dresses...where lust confesses...cufflinks...stickpins...catching light...a wonderful sight...flashy rings...and other things...painted nails...men in tails...fancy hats...splats...new shoes...lots of booze...heels...backroom deals...stunning women...miles of smiles...and...more curves than a roller coaster.

"I want to take you to church now," the singer said, sweat forming on her forehead. "I want to take you down the road...over the bridge...to first baptist congregational church in preston...i learned to sing there...i got my wings there..."

The band broke into a rousing version of Three Dog Night's "Joy to the World." Everyone danced. My parents danced on the far side of the room...Molli danced...I danced with some woman I had never seen before...she dragged me onto the dance floor...on a spectacular july night...framed by an amazing sunset chasing the devil away...thanks to that band...that took us to church...a better world...the only colors from the lights on the dance floor...good times joy...laughter...love...a fight broke out...that was quickly extinguished and everyone continued the celebration.

I lost track of Molli and had just successfully stolen my third drink when I heard someone call my name. Greg Turner was approaching. I knew him from high school. He was a popular hockey player.

"What are you doing here?" he asked.

"My parents know the bride's family."

"Same with me."

That made sense. His father...a beyond rich...bond broker... living in an amazing old mansion on the arm...back...in the woods off the Purcell's Cove Road.

"How's your summer going?" he asked.

"Not bad."

He motioned to the cup in my hand.

"What's that?"

"Soda."

He looked at me.

"I heard what happened with Kevin."

He shook his head.

"That was crazy!"

I nodded.

"It was sad." *Even here I can't escape him.*

There was a tug on my sleeve and I turned to see Molli standing there.

"I can't dance anymore," she frowned. "My feet are killing me."

I introduced her to Greg, and they shook hands.

"We've got to find my parents," I said.

We waded through the crowd to where my parents were sitting. My father stood and slipped on his suit coat.

"I've been looking for you two. It's time to go."

My mother pouted and got to her feet.

"I didn't win a single thing."

On the drive home I felt the warm afterglow of the party, as if somehow it had stayed with me the way a dream sometimes stays with you. My mother and Molli were asleep in the backseat within fifteen minutes. I was in the front with my father, my window down to let in the soft summer night breeze.

"That was some party," I said, slurring my words slightly.

My father glanced at me...then back at the road...headlights cutting a swath through me...through the summer night.

"I lost track of you and Molli. Did you have fun?"

"Oh yeah. We danced. It was a ball! We chased the devil away!"

He looked at me again.

"Did you have anything to drink at that reception?"

"Drink? No, nothing. Some Coke, that was it. I'm just tired," I lied, happy with my quick response.

-38-

I desperately wanted to retreat back into the naive innocence I had known. Before Kevin died I was just another teenager... navigating the deep...treacherous currents of adolescent life. His death...added deeply to my strife...catapulting me into a world of secrets...culpability...morality...mortality. Normality...a distant land...a distant planet. There was no way to un-ring the bell that was Kevin's death. Why not just surrender to my fate? Inevitable. What could save me from my actions? Nothing.

On Wednesday afternoon I went to Crystal Crescent Beach to meet Mister D and give him a hundred bucks from the wallet I'd stolen at the wedding. He had not yet arrived so I sat on a rock... gazing out over the ocean...a sheet of molten gray stretching to the horizon.

A car pulled up and a couple in their twenties got out, sauntered down to the beach hand-in-hand, rolled up their jeans and waded in up to their knees. They were laughing and having a good time, which somehow added to my deep sense of dread. I was watching them when Mister D pulled up, honked, reached out the window and waved me over. He seemed in a better mood than the last time I saw him. As soon as I climbed into the car, he tossed a bag of chips at me.

"A box of these fell off the back of a truck," he grinned, bits of chips stuck in his moustache.

Thanks."

"You got my money?"

I pulled five twenty-dollar bills from my pocket and handed them to him. He counted it and smiled.

"Nice job, kid."

I started to mumble a reply, but he cut me off. A half-smile crossed his unshaven face.

"I like you, kid."

"Thanks."

"I don't want to have to burn your house down, you know."

"Then don't!" I protested. "I gave you the money and the extra money. There's…"

"Shut up, dickwad!" he sneered…his mood suddenly black. "I like you, and I don't want to burn your house down. But if you don't have another hundred bucks here this time next week, that's what I'm going to do."

"I don't have any more money," I pleaded.

I pointed to the bills in his hand.

"That's it, and I had to steal that. I don't…"

He chortled and flashed a fiendish grin.

"Hell, I don't have to burn down your house. I'll pick up the phone and tell the cops what you done. I'll call your parents and Kevin's old man and tell them what you done. You get me? You'll go to jail. Your life will be over."

"I don't have a job! I don't have any money!"

"Kid, that's your problem, not my problem."

He leaned in until his disgusting face was only inches from mine. His breath was rank.

"Get that money. Steal your old man's watch, steal his phone. I don't care, just get me that money."

"Okay."

He left and I went down to the beach, sat cross-legged in the sand and gazed out over the ocean. Someone had built a sand castle and the incoming tide was slowly destroying it.

-39-

Death was once again swept into our cove...this time in the form of Nike sneakers...thousands of them.

Kevin lost his sneaker when he went off the bluffs. Now, it was being returned by the ocean ten thousand fold by a Nor'easter that blew in and howled like a banshee for the whole day...like a demon was loose in the rafters of our house...sheets of hard rain lashing the windows...the roof...an otherworldly clatter. The leaves on the trees turned their backs to it, and we all hunkered down to wait it out.

That evening, after it had died down a bit, my father went outside to check our TV antenna. He came back dripping with rain and said the storm had swept something into the cove.

"What is it?" I asked.

"I can't tell. Come on, let's take a closer look."

Coves and inlets offer randomness a voice in the ocean, especially after storms. Over the years many things, living and dead, found their way into Chandler's Cove. A baby beluga got caught...its mum was fraught...an empty casket...a picnic basket...numerous hats...a few drowned bats...deflated balloons...loons...dead fish...a bottle and wish...driftwood...a headless doll...bouncy ball...beach chairs...fish snares...plastic...oil slicks...beach toys...lost by boys.

The drowned birds tended to be seagulls...but once in a while I'd see a Baltimore Oriole...a Yellow-headed Blackbird...drowned during a storm...wings spread open...trying to make one last desperate attempt at flight. That's the way the ocean is; haphazard and deeply spiritual...with all the time in the world to make a point.

My father grabbed his heavy-duty flashlight as I tugged on my raingear and followed him back outside. Incredibly dark and still raining heavily. Carefully making our way down the slippery slope behind our house...my father pointed the flashlight out across the cove.

What are those?

What was bobbing around out there like someone had taken flecks of brightly colored paint and spilled it on the tops of the black waves.

"What is it?" I yelled.

He pointed the flashlight into an area closer to us...its beam landing on a pair of new blue sneakers. A monster wave washed a container filled with Nike sneakers from the deck of a ship on the way to Halifax. It smashed into the rocks and cracked open like a piñata, spilling out hundreds of pairs of green...blue...yellow... red...pink...orange sneakers bobbing around the cove like psychedelic seaweed.

One of Kevin's Nike's was missing when they found him...now he was bellowing from the grave...demanding justice.

Yet another insidious reminder of what I had done. Thank you...death!

"What a mess," my father groaned.

A pair of green sneakers washed up near us. The rocks were slippery with seaweed, but I carefully navigated them, grabbed the sneakers and held them up for my father to see. They were soaked but in perfect condition.

"These look like they're my size."

"Max, you can't keep those," he said, rain dripping from the bill of his hat.

"Why?"

"It's not your property. It's stealing."

Those sneakers would easily retail for a hundred bucks, and I knew my mother would never drop that kind of money on them. It would be against everything she believed in. And besides, if Kevin was bringing them to our doorstep, who was I to refuse?

"But Dad..." I protested.

He glared at me.

"Max, put them back."

"I found these! No one's going to miss them. It's the law of the sea, 'finders keepers.'"

"Max I don't care about any 'law of the sea!'" he replied impatiently. "Put them back!"

"I'm keeping them!"

I trudged through the rain up to the house, rinsed the salt water off the sneakers in the bathtub and left them by the radiator to dry. Molli plucked a pink pair from the cove the following day. My father didn't say anything else to us about taking them. I knew he was disappointed...not just for disobeying him. He thought we were stealing...honesty...integrity were paramount to him...a foundation of some kind. He harped on it all the time, his favorite saying..."being honest is like being a little pregnant. You are or you aren't." He was honest to a fault.

He called the coast guard to report the container, but it took a few days for someone from the government to come out. Meanwhile word of the sneakers spread faster than gossip. Within two days it seemed like everyone from Spryfield to Sambro had fished a new pair of Nikes from the cove. At one point cars lined the Ketch Harbour Road as people waited for a chance to get in and snatch up a pair of sneakers. My mother and I were coming back from the SuperStore when we saw Ricky in the middle of the road directing traffic.

"What are you doing?" I asked.

He motioned around.

"It's all backed up. They're all trying to get in."

"So you're playing traffic cop?"

He waved a car in and they honked thanks.

"Yeah. Otherwise it would be a free-for-all."

I shook my head.

"I guess."

"Any sneakers left?"

"Hundreds."

He grinned.

"Good. I've got five different colors, all like new. But I don't have any red ones yet."

He motioned to the cars lined up to get into the road.

"I've got to direct this traffic, man. Can you grab me a red pair, size eleven?"

"My old man will kill me."

"Grab them if you can. I'll be down in a while."

My father would stand in the backyard watching the "scavengers," as he called them, and shake his head in disgust. For months afterwards whenever I saw anyone wearing a new pair of Nikes... i'd smile.

-40-

Nothing in this world makes sense. Otherwise how could an arsonist be hailed as a hero?

I was sitting on the deck with my binoculars one afternoon looking for birds. Molli and Hua had gone for a hike. Hurricanes sweep birds wildly off course and I was hoping to see a few specimens that typically never make their to Nova Scotia. The storm had scrubbed the air clean...a beautiful summer afternoon...new sky amazingly clear and blue...a soft southern breeze sweeping the ocean.

I heard a car in the driveway, and after a few moments my father rounded the corner of the house.

"Hey, Max."

I put down the binoculars and turned to look at him.

"Hey, Dad."

He pulled up a chair beside me and looked out over the cove.

"There's a big fire at the yacht squadron. Fire trucks everywhere, lots of smoke."

"Really? What was on fire?"

He shrugged.

"I have no idea."

I didn't think much of it until the next day until I heard it was the kings' boat...*Deserving*...the same boat Ricky said was "deserving of being torched" a few weeks earlier.

That night when I confronted Ricky about it, he shook his head calling it a weird coincidence.

"I would never burn down a beautiful boat like that."

He threw his hands up.

"The universe did it."

I balked.

"The universe did it? No way. You did it!"

He glared at me.

"I did not. But I feel guilty as hell because I said it."

He rubbed his eyes.

"I feel like shit, man. I never should have said he deserved for his boat to burn."

"Bullshit! There's no way that was a coincidence. You're an arsonist!"

He just shrugged and took a long, slow drink of beer. I never told anyone what he had said. He got away with it... credited as a hero for stopping the fire from spreading to nearby boats up on slips. "Slick Ricky." Unbelievable! The universe protects scoundrels like that.

The next morning...stretched out on the living room sofa... nursing another hangover...something smacked into the window. I knew what it was...hurrying outside...a dead Blue Jay in the grass.

At first I thought it was Ziggy. But its wing tips were tinged with white...an older bird...I was so pissed off...at meaningless death... if I had had a shovel or baseball bat...i would have smashed out the windows. What would that accomplish? Nothing. Unlike dead birds...shattered windows can be replaced.

-41-

Black Friday was the day an angry ocean tried to claim Molli… gleefully smashing her in the eye leaving a deep laceration on her cheek. My father had gone to rehearsal and my mother was up in bed resting. The weather…foul…gusty…raining…sky dull… ominous gray.

I was eating cereal when Molli came into the kitchen wearing my mother's raincoat and her black rubber boots with orange tips.

""Where are you going?"

"To Champayne Dam."

I put down my spoon and scoffed.

"In this? No! Are you crazy? You'll be blown across the ocean." She pulled up her hood.

"Good," she grinned. "I've always wanted to see Europe."

"There's no way you can go out in this."

"I'm going," she replied matter-of-factly. "I want to be out in it, to feel its energy."

"'Its energy?' Are you crazy? Its energy is dangerous. What if a tree falls on your head?"

"That's not going to happen."

"How do you know that?"

She shrugged.

"I just know. And if it does, you can tell everyone you warned me."

"Man alive," I muttered, "aren't you afraid of anything?"

She sat down across from me…her blue-eyed gaze harsh under her hood.

"You know what your problem is?" she asked...then answered herself: "You live in fear."

"Fear? That's ridiculous. I don't live in fear."

"Yeah, you do!"

"So, not only am I an 'optimist,' I also live in fear. Is that what you're saying? Wow! How can someone be both? It doesn't make sense!"

Her grin turned fiendish.

"I know, but you're both!"

As usual, there was no use arguing.

I couldn't let her walk in the storm by herself. Who knows what could happen to her.

"If you're really going, then I'm coming with you."

She stood.

"Fine, let's go."

Fuming...i went to the closet...pulled out my heaviest raincoat with a hood...best boots...montreal canadiens hat with a bill...to help keep the rain out of my eyes.

It didn't help much. As soon as we stepped outside we were pelted by rain so hard it stung my face. The wind...a schoolyard bully shoving us around. I pulled the ties on my hood tight...Molli did the same. It was like trying to walk in a hurricane. Who knows...maybe they were hurricane strength winds? Skirting the few buildings near our house we made our way to an unpaved road, that led to the path that would take us through the woods to the dam. The wind...so fierce...rain so unforgiving we had to yell to be heard above the storm. Drenched...I might as well have been swimming.

"Have you felt its energy enough?" I yelled after we had walked for ten minutes. "Can we go back now, please? It's dangerous out here."

"Don't be a chicken."

A sudden gust almost knocked me off my feet.

"What?"

She waved toward home.

"Go back if you want."

"Come on," I hollered, "let's keep going."

Heads down against the storm...we walked...stumbled...staggered...as if...through a carwash...fought our way...struggled... wind...rain...it was insane...lurching blindly forward...the road ends...turning into a path...winding through the woods...more sheltered...be careful...the path is narrow...water soaked... uneven...strewn with half-buried boulders...tricky trees roots.

I led the way, with Molli trudging a few feet behind me.

"Remember what I said before about going to church?" she asked.

I stopped and turned to her.

"Yeah."

She stared at me, rain dripping from her nose.

"Will you come?"

I shook my head.

"I don't know. We're really not a church family. It's not something..."

She cut me off.

"Please, Max, would you come with me?"

I wasn't going to argue.

"Okay. Do you know which one, which church?"

"That one in Ketch Harbour, what was it, Saint Peter's? That one looked all right. Let's go to that one."

We walked a little further, and finally...thankfully, came to the short rocky path that leads down to the dam. That path is treacherous at the best of times. Boulders stick out at bad angles and you practically have to be a mountain goat to navigate it, let alone in a storm! The wind and rain were battering me as I carefully inched my way toward the dam as I pulled my hat down and reached back and gave Molli my hand.

We sheltered below the dam's cement lip...the wind...storm conjuring immense waves...crashing into the inlet...rushing in...a foaming sprint up onto the rocks...as rain fell on the surface of the water in the reservoir...expanding circles....a huge relief being out of the wind...even if we were still getting rained on a little.

"I love the feeling of the storm," Molli smiled, rain dripping from the bill of her hat. "The pure energy in it? Don't you love it?"

I shook my head.

"No."

"I wish I could bottle it."

She pulled her phone from her pocket.

"I'm going to take a picture."

She made her way down the right side of the inlet, carefully navigating over boulders, some the size of lobster traps, as I cupped my hands to my mouth.

"Molli, be careful!"

She waved me off and continuing down the inlet...getting close to the water...five feet high on the rocks...as i yelled to her again.

"Molli, you're too close to the water! Come back!"

She turned...held up her phone...took a picture. I thought she was coming back but instead she ventured out a little further.

"Molli!" I yelled. "Get back here!"

She must have heard me yelling above the din of the storm... she stopped and turned toward me.

A lethal mistake. Never turn your back on an angry ocean!

An enormous black wave swept in and dragged her into the inlet.

"Molli!"

I couldn't see her anywhere. Suddenly she came to the surface...flailing...gasping for breath.

"Molli!"

I scampered over the rocks as quickly as I could but fell and banged my knee...a nauseating fire like pain...staggering to my feet I frantically looked out over the inlet just in time to see a massive wave crash over Molli...getting tossed around like a ragdoll in a washing machine. The pain in my leg...intense...I pushed it aside...limping as fast as a limper can...wading into the heavy surf...only to be driven back by two waves that crashed into my thighs...struggling to maintain my balance, I frantically looked out over the inlet. Molli was gone.

"Molli!"

A scream...to my left...25 feet away...i drove forward through a wave...within seconds I was only ten feet from her with water up to my chest...kelp and seaweed dragging me down.

"Take my hand!" I yelled.

She just looked at me, a blank expression on her face. My boots were filled with ocean water. I had to struggle to keep from being pulled under.

"Take my..."

Before I could finish...a hideous black...a widow maker... rogue wave...a seaman's curse...slammed into me. Struggling to the surface...gasping for air as I tried to find footing on the slimy seaweed-covered rocks. Molli was still being knocked about like a cork. The ocean was trying to claim her...its black eyes in the waves...its evil smirk. I'd seen it before.

"No!" I screamed. "You can't have her...you witch!"

"Molli," I yelled. "Take my hand!"

She was stricken with fear.

"Molli, take my hand!"

A monstrous gray wave crashed down on us...under water again...tumbling...legs and arms taking a horrible battering...on the rocks...like being pummeled with a baseball bat. I fought for the surface with everything I had. Molli was twelve feet away... exhausted...on the verge of passing out.

"God save us!"

You may not believe this...there was a lull...for just a few seconds. I lunged for Molli...snagged her collar...violently yanked her toward me.

Did she just push me away?

Summoning the very last bit of strength in my body...I pulled her toward shore. A wave lifted us up and threw us onto a huge pile of slimy seaweed, a much softer landing than the rocks would have provided. With a death grip on her collar, I pulled her over to safety as a thunderous wave crashed down in a last vain attempt to claim us. I felt like turning to the ocean and yelling, "Screw you!"

Molli and I slumped on the rocks...gasping for air...spitting up salt water...the ocean pouring unapologetically from our pockets and boots. We were both shivering, more out of fear than from the cold water. Molli was weeping.

"We could have been killed!"

"You should have left me," she cried. "It was my fault. I got too close."

She had hit her face on something...blood gushing from a gash on her right cheek. Her eye was swelling shut.

"Let me look at you," I said, turning her face toward me. *Shit, when Dad sees this...*

She pulled away.

"I'll be okay."

I leaned back and looked out over the stormy inlet where we had almost drowned.

"What do you think, Molli?" I asked sarcastically. "Have you had enough of the storm's energy? Let's get out of here."

Soaked…battered, defeated and shivering we staggered through the woods toward home. When we reached our house Molli grabbed my arm.

"Get out of your wet things, then go up and talk to your mother," she said, her teeth chattering. "I don't want her to freak when she sees my face."

"She *will* freak, and so will my father."

"Listen," she said. "Tell her that I made you go out, that I slipped on the rocks and hit my face. Spare her the details about us almost drowning. I'll get cleaned up and then come up and show her that I'm all right. That way she'll be prepared and won't get too worked up. Okay?"

I did as she asked.

"Where is she?" my mother gasped when I told her what happened.

"She's in the kitchen."

I called down to Molli. She came up to the bedroom, the stairs creaking under her weight. She had changed out of her wet clothing and had put Band-Aids on her cheek.

"My God, Molli, are you okay?" my mother asked.

She started to sit up, but Molli sat on the side of the bed.

"It's just a scratch," Molli replied.

"Let me see," my mother said.

Molli moved a little closer, and my mother carefully examined her bandaged cheek and the area around her eye, which was turning purple.

"How bad is the cut?" she asked.

"It's not that bad."

"Let me take a look under the Band-Aids."

Molli pulled back.

"I'm fine."

"Your eye is swelling shut."

"I'm going to put some ice on it," she said reassuringly. "The swelling will go down."

My mother turned to me, her face red with anger.

"What in the world were you thinking going out for a hike on a day like this?"

The wind rattled the windows as if to indict me.

"It didn't look that bad out," I stammered. "You know we…"

Molli cut me off.

"I talked him into going. It's not his fault. I wanted to feel the storm's energy."

My mother looked bewildered.

"The storm's energy?"

"That's right. I like walking in storms."

My mother laid back in bed.

"When your uncle hears about this and sees you…"

"I'm fine," Molli repeated.

My father hit the roof when he got home that evening.

"Max, I expected better from you," he said angrily. "You left your mother alone after I specifically told you not to. What would have happened if she needed help or someone to call the doctor?"

"We were only gone for a little while. Mum was sleeping and…"

"You and your lame excuses!" he said.

"I made him go out," Molli said.

"You didn't *make* him do anything! He can make his own decisions, for God's sake."

He sat at the kitchen table, shaking with anger. I rarely saw him that mad.

He turned toward Molli.

"And what's your aunt going to say when she gets here in a few days and sees your face like that?"

He pounded his fist on the table.

"She going to have a shit fit!"

"I'll tell her the truth," Molli replied calmly, "that I slipped and fell."

He glared at her.

"And you think that's going to make a difference?"

"It was an accident," she pouted. "It's not like somebody hit me."

"I can't talk about this right now," my father said standing. "I'm too angry."

His mood was as dark and foul as the weather.

"I've got to make some calls."

He crossed the kitchen, then stopped and turned back toward us.

"Max, you and I will talk about this later."

Oh Great!

• • •

That night I was slouched on the sofa watching TV when Molli came in and dropped down beside me.

"I was just looking at my face in the mirror."

I turned toward her.

"Oh yeah?"

"Yeah, and you know what?"

"What?"

"I'm hideous."

I scoffed.

"You're not hideous."

She grinned slightly.

"Yes I am. I'm hideous, and I like that. I like being hideous. I embrace my hideousness."

She pointed at her face.

"My cheek is gashed, swollen. My eye is purple. There's puss. Blood. Some kind of orange fluid in there. It's squishy all around my eye. Go ahead, look."

She leaned in so I could see get a closer look. It was disgusting. I gently pushed her away.

"No thanks."

"Come on Max, look at it! This is real! I'm hideous. I am. Admit it! I don't mind."

I hit the mute button on the remote and turned toward her.

"You're not hideous. Some meth-mouthed hooker is hideous. You're not."

She pouted.

"Okay, if you don't think my eye is hideous, what about my nose? It's always been hideous."

She leaned forward again.

"Look at it. It looks like a half grapefruit on a plate. And what about my mouth? It doesn't fit my face and my eyes are way too far apart."

She paused.

"And I'm fat."

"That's nothing," I said, trying to conceal a smile. "Look at *my* face. Look at my acne. I look like a goalie for a dart team! Plus, I have buckteeth. You have nice teeth, but look at mine! And look at my ears! I'm a taxi with the doors open. That's hideous!"

She folded her arms across her chest.

"I'm way more hideous than you. It's not even close."

I laughed.

"You're not hideous, Molli. You're ugly, and you'll still be ugly when your eye gets better. There's a big difference between hideous and ugly. Who knows, maybe you're a bit of both!"

She cracked a half-smile.

"Sorry for getting you in trouble," she said...sheepishly. "You saved my life today. Thanks."

"No worries. I would have gotten grounded forever if I let you drown."

She pulled her knees up to her chest.

"I want to drown...not die...to know what comes after drowning...where my family is."

"They're in a better place," I replied. I don't know why I said that. It was a reaction more than anything. Isn't that what everyone says to someone who has lost a loved one?

Molli rolled her eyes.

"God," she moaned. "People keep telling me, 'They're in a better place. They're with God now.' As if that's supposed to help."

"People want to comfort you," I offered.

She threw her hands up.

"You know what? I hope they're not 'with God.' That they're just gone. Because if God is real, He could have stopped that crash."

She paused and stared at me, her eyes wide.

"Yeah, I guess. If He's real and all-powerful and all that, He could have stopped it."

She leaned back on the sofa.

"There are no explanation for tragedies like Kevin's death or my family getting wiped out because there can be no explanation other than there is no 'God,'" she continued. "Hit and miss. Life is a roulette ball that drops at random. Life. Death. Nothing is preordained. If God loves us *so* much, why does He allow shit to happen all the time?"

Good question.

She started counting off on her fingers.

"Ebola...sick babies...endless wars...pain...suffering...injustice...corruption...cancer...AIDS...the slaughter of innocents...

families killed…orphans! If He's so all-powerful and all-seeing and a loving father and all that, why doesn't He just stop all that shit? There are little kids living and dying in squalor! Put an end to it, God! Why does He allow all this shit to keep happening over and over and over?"

I shrugged.

"And what about the endless greed?" she said, spitting out the word "greed" live venom. "It's like a virus. And people literally getting away with murder. There's actually genocide happening, and ethnic cleansing…endless misery…"

People literally getting away with murder. Was she saying something about Kevin?

"The world sure is a mess," I mumbled.

"I know what it is," she continued. "Either God isn't real, He isn't all-powerful or He's completely abandoned us and we're orphans left to our own devices. That's the way I see it. It's obvious. Anything else is simply wishful thinking or mass delusion. How can anyone believe in God? How? Why didn't He stop Kevin from falling over the edge? Huh. Why? It should have been simple for Him to do, right? I mean, He parted the Red Sea and all that, right? He raised Jesus, His son, from the dead, right?"

Once again I shrugged.

"That's what they say."

"He created the universe!" she blurted, her voice rising. "So why didn't He stop Kevin from falling? Why? If He's half as powerful as religious people say He is, it should have been easy for Him to do, right?"

"Right."

"Why didn't He give my father's plane engine trouble so he couldn't take off the day they were killed?"

Her voice was labored and throbbing with pain.

"Why didn't He at least give my mother a mild case of the flu so she would have stayed home that day? Why? They would still be here if He just stepped in."

I had absolutely no answer for that.

Her blue eyes widened.

"I know what it is!" she exclaimed sarcastically. "God hates me. That's what it is. For some reason He hates me!"

"I'm not sure if…"

She cut me off.

"Yeah, okay, the church has done some good things, I guess. Feed and shelter people, build hospitals and schools in Africa and places like that and sell them their story of redemption. Yes, that helps, I guess. The minister at my family's funeral was nice. She took me aside and we prayed together. That was nice."

"Good."

"It doesn't matter, anyway."

She motioned around the room.

"Look at the world, Max. It's an evil mess. Religion is a scam. Everyone knows that. The world could sure use an all-powerful, loving God, and maybe that's why people created Him. God didn't create people. People created God because they needed one, something to give life some sort of meaning and a higher purpose."

She folded her arms across her chest.

"I'll admit that. But that's all I'll admit."

I was at a loss as how to respond. She was so cynical. I desperately wanted to help her see that there was hope for her.

"People do love you, you know?" I said softly.

She shot me a dismissive glare.

"Maybe love isn't for everyone," she scoffed. "Maybe some people aren't allowed to experience it. Maybe they're not engineered for it."

She smirked.

"They don't have the 'love gene,'" she said, holding her fingers up like quote marks. "Or maybe some people hate love. Maybe some people see love as an illness as a weakness. Did you ever think of that?"

Before I could respond she continued in a cold and deliberate tone.

"Love is just another four-letter word to make people feel better. How many insanely jealous men have told their scared-to-shit wives 'I love you' before they blow their heads off with a shotgun or stabbed them a hundred times? I love you. Bam!"

She slowly shook her head.

"You can keep love. I'm not interested in it."

I didn't for a second believe she actually thought that, and there was no way I was going to let it go unchallenged.

"What are you interested in? Hate? Suffering?"

Her expression turned hard.

"At least those are real! Things you feel. You see them every day. Just open your eyes, Max!"

Her rant was beyond depressing.

"You're not answering my question. What do you believe in?"

She paused, thinking, and then turned her cold gaze back on me.

"I believe in five feet of the softest powder snow you'll ever see. I believe in strapping on my snowboard and throwing up ten-foot rooster tails and dropping into a half pipe. I believe in the Rocky Mountains. That's what I believe in."

She stared at me, unblinking, expecting a reply. I didn't have one. Who could blame her for ranting? Not me. No way. Considering what had happened to her family, she had every right to ask "God" for an explanation.

"Know what?" she asked smugly. "All human failure is a failure to love, and from what I can see, there's a lot of failure in the world!"

Once again she looked at me waiting for a reply. I stared back at her in silent disbelief. Then it occurred to me. Take the "l" out of love and replace it with a "d" and you get...

The fallout from our hike in the storm that day was swift and ruthless. My father forbade me from any driving practice. Of course Molli didn't really get any punishment. She had assured me that she was sorry, but that didn't take away the sting. I spent the next few days sulking around the house...reading...watching TV...to make matters worse...the specter of Molli's aunt's arrival hung over us...a heavy and suffocating weight.

Something in Molli changed after that day...a little. She had been at death's front door. We both had. I couldn't really put my finger on exactly what changed...she seemed more alive...more vibrant...more present? But real transformation...real healing... real growth...come one step at a time. It's heartbreakingly naive too expect too much from one solitary experience.

-42-

A few days later "Hurricane Eddie" slammed into Nova Scotia. Every person...every storm has a unique personality...like the first snowfall...or hurricane eddie...a crazed heavyweight fighter... gusts like mighty hammer fists...malevolent sustained winds of 120 kph...howling straight into halifax harbour...downing power lines...smashing phone poles...trees...lives.

Storms are born blind. People are not.

Our cove is sheltered and small...but...we felt that hurricane big time...a two-foot storm surge...dirty rain and evil winds that swelled the ocean to well above high-tide marks...howling and wailing at our windows...ripping away roof tiles.

We even had an evacuation plan in case things got really bad. We didn't get many hurricanes like that, a direct hit. "Eddie" knocked out power to half the province, including us. My father's a real "boy scout," so we were ready for it with lamps, candles, batteries, a gas stove, food and water. Shortly after our lights blinked out, my father came into the kitchen and slid a sheet of paper across the table.

"Max, have you read this?"

It was a map of the area and a printout of an evacuation plan. I glanced at it, then up at him.

"I haven't read it, but I know what to do. Make a beeline for Halifax."

"I know, but if the roads are blocked or there's flooding, I've marked areas where there's high ground. Take a look at it, son."

You'll never forget the frightful sounds and sights of a hurricane after you've ridden one out. The sky...ominous gray... black...we were under attack...howling undisciplined wind...like a wounded thing...moans...groans...screams...hard rain ripping at seams.

It's frightening and exhilarating like a monster rollercoaster.

I was looking out the kitchen window when I noticed a thin gold ring of my mother's sitting on the sill. My father was always admonishing my mother to be careful with her jewelry because she'd leave earrings, bracelets and other items by the sink or in places where they could easily be lost. I picked up the ring and slipped it into my pocket.

"This storm is bad," Molli said at one point. "This is scary."

"Really?" I replied in a slightly mocking tone. "I thought you might go for a walk, you know, to check out its *energy* and all that. Take a few pictures at Champayne Dam?"

She flipped me the bird and turned on her heels.

"Jerk!"

An eerie calm settled over our cove as the center of the hurricane passed...right over us. My father and I donned our rain gear and went outside to look around and check on the roof. After twenty minutes the wind and rain picked up as fiercely as they had been. We trudged back inside. I peeled off my rain gear, went upstairs...flopped onto my bed and listened to the howling wind and rain pelting the roof. Molli was in her room reading...three candles flickering on her bedside table.

"I couldn't wake you this morning!" I heard my mother say angrily to my father, in the kitchen. "I was scared to death. I thought you were dead!"

He scoffed.

"Obviously, I wasn't dead."

She crossed the room and pull open a cupboard.

"My God, Geoff," she exclaimed, "this is half empty!"

I figured she was talking about my father's bottle of painkillers.

"That's impossible," my father scoffed. "I just refilled it last week."

"How many pills did you take last night?"

"I can't remember. I need the pills. I'm not…"

She cut him off.

"We're having a baby in a few months! For God's sake, you have to be careful. Geoff, you have to get help."

"I take them for my pain, to get through the damned day."

He climbed the stairs to their bedroom and slammed the door shut behind him. I rolled onto my side and stared at the wall.

"Hey, Max, want to see my board?"

I turned to see Molli standing in my doorway.

"Your snowboard?"

She nodded. I sat up in bed.

"Okay, sure."

She held it out.

"I got it for Christmas last year," she smiled. "I was stoked. It's a 'Never Summer Proto HD board.' This baby is made for powder. It's the board I'd wanted forever."

"It's a good one?"

"Oh yeah."

"Cool."

It was four feet long…black…yellow…with an awesome green psychedelic paint job.

She sat on the edge of the bed…passed it to me and pointed at the bindings.

"The bindings on powder boards determine your stance. They're usually set back to help you float the tip of the board through deep snow."

"Awesome."

She pointed to the front end of the board.

"The rise of the tip and tail starts farther back on powder boards."

I nodded.

"It's designed like that to help maintain tip-float through powder."

I passed the board back to her.

"It must be a blast!"

"There's nothing like it."

I was going to say something about taking a trip to the valley in the winter to snowboard, but I stopped. Who knew where Molli would be living in a few months?

She lowered her voice to a whisper.

"Your mom's real upset with your dad."

"You heard that?"

"Yup."

-43-

The following afternoon I rode to Crystal Crescent to meet Mister D. When I handed him my mother's gold ring, his face screwed up in anger.

"What am I going to do with this?" he said, holding the ring up between two fingers.

"It's gotta be worth at least two hundred bucks. You can sell it, get drugs."

He grumbled something inaudible and then slipped the ring into his jeans pocket.

"Okay, dickwad, but next week you better have cash. You understand? I like you and I don't want to have to burn your house down."

He flashed a kind of sincere look.

"You're leaving me no choice here."

I swear to God, if I had had a gun I would have shot him! I got out, and he sped off, his tires kicking up rocks and dust. That's when I knew what I had to do…which had nothing to do with telling anyone what I had done or giving him one more thing.

-44-

Just as she had confided in me earlier…Molli told my parents that she felt compelled…to go to church.

The following Sunday morning we dutifully piled into the car and drove to Saint Peter's Church in Ketch Harbour. My father didn't want to be there. The previous day he had tried to finagle his way out of it by offering an excuse about having to practice violin. My mother got angry, saying we all had to "support Molli," and he sheepishly agreed to go.

It was a nice enough church…pretty standard…white on the outside with a steeple. It was the same church where Kevin's funeral had been, so I *really* didn't want to go.

"Churches are always after money," my father grumbled. "When the offering plate comes around, I'll put in a donation for the whole family."

If I knew him…that would be one dollar. He was "cheap."

We sheepishly filed in and slid onto creaky pews on the right side about halfway up. Wads of gum…some thirty years old…were stuck under the pews. I casually looked around to see if I knew anyone. I didn't. The morning light…cascading in through large stained glass windows. Just like the church where the wedding had been a few weeks earlier…a faint scent of incense and expectation…hung in the air. The church…about half-filled. The service started…I watched what everyone else did and tried to follow along with the working class congregation.

You can tell a lobstermen, a fishermen from across the room… their shoulders…huge…like wrestlers' from the heavy lifting…

hard work on the boats...wharfs...brawny arms...granite upper bodies...deeply tanned faces...sunburned during fishing season... often squinting...even when it's dark.

I wanted to be respectful and also didn't want anyone to know we were interlopers. I mumbled responses with the rest of the congregation, pulled a Bible from the pew for a reading, looked at it with Molli and tried to kneel and stand with everyone else at the right times. My father gave up halfway through. By the time the priest got up to deliver his sermon, I was totally confused and glad that I'd be able to sit still and listen.

The priest...in his forties...slightly stooped...slim...religious... bald with a gray goatee...wire-framed glasses that hung from the end of his nose. His vestments made him look a little like a glorified doorman...which if you stop to think about it. He strode up to the podium and smiled widely.

"Do you know what I did last week?" he asked the worshippers. "I went fishing with George Clancy. He took me out on his lobster boat, *Anna's Dream*. Now, don't worry, we weren't looking for lobster out of season. We had a couple of poles and had hoped to catch some mackerel."

There was a murmur of understanding among the congregation.

"It was the first time I've ever gone fishing on the ocean, and I've been here for what, almost six years? I used to fish for lake trout in New Brunswick when I was a kid, but I've never been fishing on the ocean before."

He paused and grinned.

"We didn't have a lot of luck, but it was a wonderful day on the ocean. That was the blessing of it. Nature is God's general revelation. You can see His handiwork there. He reveals himself there. It is *His* creation. Sometimes you'll hear people say that they don't need or believe in God, but that they feel some kind of divinity in nature. While I'm sure that's true, I'd caution them not to confuse the gift with the Giver."

Once again the congregation murmured in agreement.

"I enjoyed every moment of our fishing trip," he continued after a moment. "To be out there on the vast expanse of the ocean, land nowhere in sight, just the endless sea and the sky. To feel the current and waves gently rocking the boat, the nurturing warmth of the sun on our backs. To inhale the ocean's fresh and briny scent. To hear the gentle sound of the waves lapping against the hull. You know, I think that's become my favorite sound. There's something soothing about it."

He paused…thinking.

"We were on the boat, casting our lines and reeling them in. I started thinking about the significance of fish and fishing in the Bible. Fish are the first creatures to appear in the Book of Genesis. They are the only creature not taken into the ark, moving some theologians to believe fish are self-supporting. And if you were to open your Bibles to Leviticus, you'll see laws regarding which fish are kosher and which are not. Very important to Jews of the day!"

I glanced over at Molli. She was listening intently. I leaned forward a little and looked at my parents. My mother was paying attention. My father had slipped his phone from his pocket and was secretly checking the time or his voicemail.

"In the *Book of Habakkuk*, in the Hebrew Bible, descriptions of fishing are given," the priest continued. "Job jokingly asks if a leviathan can be caught with a hook! In *Kings* One fish are directly associated with the wisdom of Solomon. In the *Book of Tobit*, Tobiah is told to cut a fish open and take out its liver, gall and heart and to make remedies from them. He uses fish gall to remove cataracts from his father's eyes. And did you know that when Jerusalem was rebuilt by Nehemiah after the Babylonian captivity, a Fish Gate was built into its wall. Yes, it was! And Jeremiah speaks of fishermen when talking about bringing the Israelites back from Babylon."

Once again he paused, then cast his gaze out over the congregation.

"Do you know who else in the Bible talks a lot about fishermen and fishing?"

Silence.

"I know you know this."

He paused.

"Come on. I know you know this!"

"Jesus?" an uncertain voice echoed through the church.

"That's right, Jesus!" the priest smiled. "He preached in terms of fishing, like Jeremiah in *Luke* Five, when he says to Peter and the other fishermen: 'From now on, you will be fishers of men.' Miraculous catches of fish are related in *Luke* Five and *John* Twenty-one. All of the gospel writers say that Jesus fed thousands with a few fish and half-loaves of bread. It was a miracle! In *Matthew* Thirteen, Jesus compares the kingdom of heaven to a dragnet. He paid taxes with a coin, and He told the disciples they would find it in the mouth of a fish! If you don't believe me, look it up yourself in *Matthew* Seventeen."

He stopped again, as if recharging, then gripping the pulpit with both hands, continued.

"This church carries the name of a fisherman, our good friend, Saint Peter," he said. "Peter was one of twelve apostles chosen by Jesus. Peter was a fisherman, and he later played a critical leadership role in the early church. He was with Jesus during events witnessed by only a few apostles, including the Transfiguration. Peter confessed Jesus as the Messiah. Our Lord is often depicted as preaching from fishing boats and sailing in fishing boats. In *Mark* Six you'll see crowds following Him carrying bread and fish.

Jesus was given fish to eat after His resurrection in Jerusalem, and He cooked fish for his disciples on the shore of the Sea of Galilee. He traveled to and from places in the company of fishermen. And, most importantly, Jesus chose fishermen for the world-changing job of spreading His Word and building His church!"

He paused and seemed to be thinking.

"Jesus was a carpenter before He became a fisher of men. He went into the family business. I bet He was a fantastic carpenter, don't you think? He understood it, the precision and patience it takes."

He looked down at his Bible, flipped the page, then turned his gaze back over the congregation.

"I could talk all day about what a good carpenter Jesus was, but I'd be getting off-topic."

He grinned.

"I was talking about fishing. Today there are factory trawlers, and all the boats have fish-finding sonar and modern technology. Two thousand years ago several methods of fishing were common on the Sea of Galilee. Some fishermen caught fish with their bare hands, their bare hands! Others used wicker baskets or fish traps made of nets or rope. Some used spears, arrows or harpoons. The last method, still used today, is the familiar hook and line. The same method George and I used last week. Peter and Andrew were said to be fishing with a line and hook when they caught the fish with the coin in its mouth."

He gripped the podium and leaned forward.

"Friends, Jesus entrusted fishermen from Bethsaida with spreading his life-changing message. He commissioned them to be 'fishers of men' and to teach all nations. Fishermen were then, and are still, smart businessmen. Their native tongue was Aramaic, but they were multilingual and knew Hebrew, a little Latin. And understanding Greek would have been essential for Peter and others in the business of fishing. Fishermen had to develop attributes others did not have. They had to be very skilled at their trade, knowing the when, where and whys of fishing. They had to be patient, and that, my friends, is a virtue! They're not easily discouraged; they're strong, hardworking and community-minded. As businessmen they had to be good judges of character and intelligent about the marketplace. They had to be respectful of the law and to function within its limitations. All of these things were essential in their enterprise. They brought the skills of their trade to Jesus, and these ordinary fisherman helped change the world!"

He pushed his glasses up on his nose and gazed at the parishioners.

"Some of you know that my mother was a high school English teacher."

I glanced at my mother. Her ears seemed to perk up and a slight smile formed on her lips as the priest continued.

"She loved to write and she always talked about writing the 'perfect sentence.' She'd write all the time, trying to come up with, the perfect sentence. I don't know if she ever wrote the perfect sentence, but when George and I were fishing last week, I started thinking about what would the perfect sentence could be, and I came up with what I believe is a contender."

He paused.

"Do you want to hear it?"

Silence.

"Come on," he continued, a little sternly. "I know you want to hear it, right?"

"Let's hear it," someone replied loudly, their voice echoing through the church.

"Okay ready?" the priest grinned. "This is my contender for 'the perfect sentence.'"

He cleared his throat, then leaned forward and belted out: "God loves you very much!"

It was quiet for a moment as if everyone was taking it in...followed by a murmur of satisfied agreement from the worshippers.

The only sentence that I thought would be perfect that morning was: "The service is over. Thanks for coming." That's two sentences, but you get my drift. I wasn't sure what we were doing there?

"Okay," the priest said. "Since we're taking about perfect sentences, how many of you have read the novel, *Moby Dick?*"

My mother put her hand up and then grabbed my father's hand to hold it up. The priest pointed toward us and smiled widely.

"You'll probably remember the sermon in that story?"

My mother nodded.

"I loved it," he continued. "There is a vivid passage in which a preacher, Father Mapple, stands boldly in front of the congregation in a church that resembles a sailing ship, and he preaches about Jonah and the whale."

My mother kept smiling, but my father sank a little lower into the pew.

"You'll all remember that story from your Sunday school days. I'm not going to relate the whole story, but suffice to say Jonah is the central character. God commands him to go to the city of Nineveh to prophesy against it, 'for their great wickedness is come up before me.' God says He will destroy the city unless they repent. Instead of doing what God has told him to do, Jonah takes off because he doesn't think anyone will listen to him and that they'll probably kill him. The Lord said, 'tell them,' but Jonah didn't want that job! He fled from the presence of the Lord to Jaffa and to Tarshish, in the opposite direction of where God told him to go. In a big storm, Jonah is thrown overboard and ends up in the belly of a whale. But a loving and all-powerful God delivers him from his terrible plight, and Jonah finally goes to Nineveh, and the people there actually begin to believe his word. They proclaim a fast. Even the king comes off his throne in repentance. God sees all this, and in a great act of mercy spares the city."

He threw up his hands.

"We are like Jonah. We flee from God and what He wants us to do. Wind and waves go where God commands them to go. If He commands them to sink a ship, they do it without question. If He commands them to drag a soul to the bottom, they do it. If He commands a whale to cough up Jonah, it does it."

He paused and seemed to be thinking.

"Friends, God knew what Jonah, a Holy man, didn't! God sees into our hearts. We cannot escape God. We cannot hide from God, nor should we want to. Ask Him to come into your life and He will. I promise. Jesus knocks on the door of your life. Will you answer it? Jonah was disobedient to God, but God delivered him from the belly of a whale! The same eternal, omnipotent, loving God will deliver you from your deepest sorrows, from the thickest wood, from the deepest pit. He will give true meaning to your life. Friends, call on Him. Trust in Him. Jesus shares in our suffering. He came here from heaven and died a horrible death on the cross so that we may live. Friends, there has always been one 'fisher of men' above all fishermen and fisherwomen. Jesus Christ! His net is made from enduring love, grace and truth. The greatest of these is love. Who wouldn't gratefully swim into that net?"

He sat down...the service continued...as i glanced at Molli... her head slightly lowered...eyes tightly closed as if in deep in thought or maybe...praying?

My father was looking impatiently around the church... my mother...watching the rest of service. I wasn't sure what to think. I had heard the story of Jonah and the whale before but wasn't sure where I had heard it. My mother taught *Moby Dick*, and chances were that I'd be assigned to read it in grade twelve. I'd seen it around the house. It was as thick as a Bible...just as intimidating. I'd never really thought about how closely related fishing...fishermen and the Bible are. I also wondered why God was so active two thousand years ago but seemed pretty quiet... since then? That church was nice...the priest seemed like an okay guy...but how...how could you tell if God was real? Going to church that day raised more questions than it answered.

When the service ended, we made our way to the door where the priest was saying goodbye to people. The morning sun was shining on his face, forcing him to squint.

"I'm Father Jake Morris," he said, gripping my father's hand. "Are you visiting the area?"

"We live nearby."

A soft grin formed on the priest's face.

"Then you'll have to come to our Saturday bingo!"

"I'll keep that in mind."

The priest turned to Molli.

"Is this your daughter?"

"My niece."

"Hello, miss. What's your name?"

"Molli."

"Molli! I love that name. That's my mother's name!"

"Thanks," Molli replied shyly.

He motioned to her face.

"It looks like you had an accident?"

"I fell," she shrugged. "It looks worse than it is."

He turned to me.

"And who is this young man?"

"I'm Max. These are my parents."

"Do you ever go fishing, Max?"

"Sometimes."

"I need fishing tips. George and I couldn't catch a single fish the other day. The fish were avoiding our lines!"

"Try dry oatmeal."

A fisherman in Herring Cove had told me about this.

"Throw it out on the water. Fish are attracted to it as it sinks, kind of like fish food in a fish tank, I guess."

"Oatmeal? Really?" he grinned. "I'm trying that next time."

He took my mother's hand and held it.

"I know I've seen you somewhere. But I can't for the life of me remember where."

"I teach at Isley," my mother smiled.

"At the high school?"

"Yes. Grade twelve English. And I used to sell my bread at your Saturday market."

"Was that the bread in flower pots?"

My mother smiled.

"Yes, it was."

"We love that bread!" he beamed. "Catholics are all about our daily bread! I wondered what happened to you, why you stopped coming?"

My mother ran her hand over her stomach.

"With the baby on the way, I can't spend as much time on my feet. I can only make enough for the family right now."

"Of course. You're welcome back anytime, okay?"

"Thank you."

"See you next Sunday!" the priest said.

My father mumbled a reply...i couldn't make out what it was.

"I never knew so much about fishing in ancient times," my mother said as we drove home. "I found that very interesting. Choosing fishermen to build the church was a smart move."

She was a teacher so her "read" on everything made sense.

Molli was gazing out the window…million of miles away in her thoughts. I wanted to ask her what she was thinking. Had the service answered any of her "God questions" or helped her in any way? But I sensed she wasn't ready to talk about it yet.

We had just turned down the road toward home when Molli looked over at me.

"I'm like a fish," she said flatly. "I know what it's like to live underwater."

My father looked at her in the rearview mirror…forehead creased in concern.

"It's lonely as hell," Molli continued. "It's depressing. You're always wet and cold…a million years old. All you want to do is to crawl up on some shore and feel the sun on your body, to feel its healing warmth."

My mother and father exchanged worried glances.

"I live underwater now, and I can't escape it," Molli said. "But I can breathe under water."

"How do you do that?" I asked sarcastically.

"You just do it. All you do is breath, eat and shit," she smirked. "There's no joy there. No love. You just exist. That's all you do."

"Molli," my mother said in a comforting tone, "you do more than that."

Molli turned back toward the window.

"No, I don't."

There was an awkward silence…then Molli continued.

"Do you know why the first ever sea creature crawled out of the ocean onto dry land a zillion years ago?" she asked to no one in particular.

Silence.

"It just couldn't stand being underwater anymore. It would have rather died than spend one more minute under water. It's like being buried alive."

"How do you know that?"
She turned toward me, her expression drained.
"It makes sense. It's all about wanting something better."

-45-

We pulled into our driveway…Hua's red Honda was sitting there. *Yes!* She was on the deck waiting for us.

"Where are you guys coming from?" she smiled. Her denim cutoffs gave an extra flair to her tanned legs. Dressed in a sleeveless white blouse…she looked like…a watery dream.

"We were at church," my mother replied cheerfully.

Hua looked surprised.

"Church? I didn't know you guys went to church."

"I made them go," Molli replied gruffly.

Awkward silence.

"I've got to practice," my father said.

"Geoff," my mother asked, her eyebrows raised. "Have you seen my wedding ring? I can't find it."

My gaze fell to the ground…guilt sweeping over me.

"I've haven't seen it," my father replied. "I've asked you a thousand times to be careful with things like that."

"It'll turn up," my mother smiled.

No it won't.

Hua held out her keys, catching the sun's rays.

"Chen said your driving test is coming up. Do you wanna practice with my car?"

"Great!"

"Why don't you take Molli with you?" my mother said.

No!

"That's okay," Molli said. "I'm going to hang here. Take a walk, get some air."

"Are you sure?" Hua asked.

"Yep."

Hua and I rounded the corner of the house. Out of the corner of my eye I saw something flopping around in the grass. An adult sparrow had smashed into the living room window...it was mortally wounded. We watched it die.

"Those trees!" I blurted. "They're the antechamber of death for birds. This is number twelve...I swear to God there's not going to be a number thirteen!"

"What can you do?"

"I'm not sure."

I jumped into the driver's seat next to Hua. My "driving practice" only lasted the few lustful endless minutes it took us to reach a concealed spot in nearby Bear's Cove. Hua had all her clothes off in like 20 seconds flat. She was nimble and amazing.

"Let me tell you about something," she whispered lustfully as she climbed on top of me. "This may sound stereotypical since I'm Chinese, but you've heard of 'yin and yang,' right?"

Her pale skin...like silk...milk...as i leaned forward and slowly ran my tongue over her nipples...small and hard.

"Yes," I murmured, "a little."

She pushed me back into the seat...kissing me firmly.

"It describes how seemingly opposite...contrary forces are complementary, interdependent in the natural world."

"Really?"

She laid a wet passionate kiss on my neck, arousing every cell in my body.

"Yes," she whispered lustfully. "'Yin and yang' give rise to each other. They interrelate to one another."

"'Give rise?' I moaned. "You're not kidding,"

She started riding me a bit harder.

"Tangible dualities like light and dark, water and fire..."

She gently grabbed my chin and turned my face toward hers.

"Male and female are thought of as physical manifestations of the duality of yin and yang. Duality lies at the origins of classical Chinese science and philosophy...guidelines to traditional Chinese remedies."

Her breathing picked up as she rode me in a steady rhythm.

"It's balance, Max. You and I are good," she murmured, her breath hot and labored. "We match each other. Sometimes one person has too much yin and the other person too much yang. Not us. We're a good match."

I lustily ran my hands down her slim hips.

"Tell me more..."

She wrapped her hands round my neck. Our eyes met.

"Yin and yang...complementary instead of opposing forces... interacting Max...you're a man...understand...a very dynamic system...the whole greater than the assembled parts."

I tried to match her rhythm.

"Yes, assembled parts. I believe that."

She threw hear head back.

"Yin and yang are in everything," she moaned passionately. "Aspects manifesting strongly... depending on the criterion of the observation...shadow can't exist without light...day without night..."

It was beyond extraordinary. I had never experienced anything like it. I've never been able to look at a circular yin-yang symbol without thinking of Hua. Sex with her wasn't a metaphor for anything except...carnal pleasure...the female body...hard sensory satisfaction...universal balance.

When we finished, Hua turned to me, her expression serious.

"Max, I need to tell you something, but please don't freak out, okay?" she said as she struggled to pull on her cutoffs.

I glanced at her as I yanked on my jeans.

"Freak out? Why, what is it?"

"My period is late, and I'm worried, you know, that I could be...pregnant."

She stared at me, waiting for a response. I was beyond shocked.

"You use a diaphragm. How could you be pregnant?"

"I do use a diaphragm and very carefully."

She turned her palms up.

"Who knows what could happen when we're bouncing around in here. Maybe it got knocked loose. It's not one hundred percent protection."

She threw her hands up.

"I'm late..."

I felt as if I had been kicked in the head.

"How late?"

She looked at me sharply.

"A month."

"What if..."

She cut me off.

"Don't worry. I shouldn't have told you. I've got a doctor's appointment on Wednesday...I'll find out for sure."

I was stunned. I had never even considered the possibility that...

"What are you going to do if you're..."

She cut me off again.

"I don't know if I'm pregnant. I'm not sure. I'm sorry. I won't know until Wednesday."

She placed her hand on top of mine.

"I'm just as freaked as you are. If my father ever found out we're having sex..."

She slowly shook her head.

"Not good!"

She'd know Wednesday! It was Sunday afternoon. We'd have to wait three days to find out!

"Where you wearing your diaphragm just now?"

She kissed me lightly and smiled.

"Of course."

We drove home without saying much. It was only a mile, but it took forever. When we reached our house, I jumped out of the car and leaned in the window.

"Thanks for the 'driving lesson.'"

She smiled sheepishly.

"I'm going to be busy for a few days, but let's talk Wednesday after my doctor's appointment, okay?"

"Okay."

"Max," she said quietly, "there's one more thing."

God, now what?

She leaned over and opened her hand...revealing two of my father's painkillers.

"These were in my car the other day. They fell out of Molli's pocket."

I gazed down at the pills and then looked up at Hua.

"Are you sure?

"Yeah. Do you know what they are? Is she taking a prescription?"

"No," I muttered. "They're my father's pills, for his back. Heavy duty pain killers."

Hua winced.

"That's not good."

I grabbed the pills and slipped them into my pocket.

"She must be stealing them."

"This is serious," Hua frowned. "You've got to say something to your parents."

• • •

Standing there, I watched Hua drive away…a cloud of dust, worry and sky trailing her car.

I found my mother weeding in the garden, beads of sweat on her brow.

"You're back already?"

"Hua had to work."

She looked up at me.

"I hope you thanked her for taking you driving?"

"Driving?"

Obviously my thoughts were elsewhere.

"Did you thank Hua for taking you driving?"

I fought back a grin.

"I thanked her big time."

"Where's Molli?"

"She went for a hike to the dam."

I made a peanut and butter sandwich and sat at the kitchen table thinking…*what if Hua's pregnant*…i could barely contemplate the possibility.

And what about the painkillers Molli was stealing?

When Molli got back I was slouched on the sofa watching TV. I was going to confront her about stealing my father's pills, but my parents were around. I didn't want them to overhear me grilling Molli. Things were already stressful enough. She came into the room and flopped down beside me.

"How was your walk?"

"Nice."

She paused then turned toward me.

"You missed seeing a cool bird."

"A bird?

"Yeah, a dove I think. It perched on the chimney for like thirty minutes."

"Could you see its markings?"

"Kind of. Red feet and legs. Its wings were dark gray with white stripes."

"Hmmmm. Sounds like a white winged dove."

It was quiet for a moment, then I asked her if she saw anyone on her walk. I was just making small talk.

"Yep," she replied without looking at me.

I waited for her to continue and tell me who it was. She didn't. But then again, Molli was the queen of one-word answers.

"Anyone I know?"

She looked at me.

"Nope."

I had no idea who it could be, and she was being evasive.

"Well who was it?"

"I'm not going to tell you."

"Why?"

"Because you'll laugh."

"Why would I laugh? Who was it?"

She leaned forward and lowered her voice.

"Do you promise not to laugh and not to tell anyone who it was?"

I wasn't sure what to think.

"Cross my heart and hope to die. Who was it?"

She stared at me, her gaze unwavering.

"You promise?"

"I promise."

She sat back.

"It was Jesus. I met Jesus."

"Jesus who?"

I didn't get it for a second.

"What other 'Jesus' is there?" she scoffed. "I met Jesus Christ."

I was beyond shocked...unsure what to think.

"What happened?" I finally asked.

She sighed and our eyes met.

"We wept."

• • •

What is real? God...guilt...mourning...pain...death...lust...hate...love...the ocean...ideas...thought...the spirit...the soul...emotions...experience? They're all real...clashing together on a mystical canvas...every person committed to painting...a singular masterpiece...over their lifetime telling the story of who they are...and aren't. No two spiritual worlds...realities are alike...each painting holding a truthful and unique story...brushstrokes added in good and bad shades of truth.

What's undeniable is that something happened to Molli during her hike that summer afternoon. Something real was added to her masterpiece, something genuine and good. She changed after that. She wasn't nearly better, but we all noticed a transformation in her, as if a tiny particle of light had been added to her grief darkened canvas.

The only other person who ever told me that they "met Jesus" was a girl from school a few years earlier. We were at a beach party, and someone had asked her about her mother, who was battling cancer. She smiled and said she had met Jesus, and that he told her everything was going to be okay. But after she had left, someone rolled their eyes and said the girl had moved to the area from "California," which was supposed to mean she was a bit nutty.

I stared at Molli in disbelief.

"You met Jesus? The same Jesus that was on the cross at church today? Jesus...son of God? That's who you met?"

She looked down and muttered.

"I knew you wouldn't believe me."

I balked.

"Who would? You're saying you met Jesus on the path to the dam today and you cried together?"

"Keep your voice down," she whispered urgently, then shook her head.

"It wasn't on the path. It was in the inlet below the dam."

"Below the dam?"

"Right," she replied somewhat sarcastically, "you know the inlet where we almost drowned?"

I sat back.

"Continue."

She leaned forward and lowered her voice.

"I heard someone on the path above me. A guy was standing there looking out over the inlet. I was startled. But after that initial shock I kind of sensed he was all right, that I didn't have to worry. He waved, 'Hi.' He came down, offered me his hand and introduced himself. He knew my name. He said, 'Hi, Molli, I'm Jesus.'"

Her eyes were wide.

"I was like you," she continued, her voice still hushed. "Thinking to myself, 'Jesus' who? But before I could say anything, he said, 'You know, Jesus Christ. The guy Father Morris was talking about in church this morning?' I was stunned. I thought it was some guy who had seen us at church and was putting me on. 'You're Jesus?' I asked. He smiled. 'Yes, I am.' I apologized as politely as I could but told him I found that a little hard to believe. 'I know you do,' he said. 'But you asked me to come, and I'm here.'"

I stared at Molli, desperately trying to read her expression. Was she putting me on? Had she lost her mind? Had she experienced some kind of dream or hallucination born out of her immense grief and stress? Was this another one of her "tall tales?"

"He was right," Molli continued softly. "I asked him to come. At the end of the sermon I prayed. I asked him to make himself real to me. I said I was at the end...I needed help real bad...or I was going to…I prayed that if He was real, He could take me so I could be with my family."

"Really?"

She nodded.

"Yes. He said my parents and brother are in heaven."

"Your father, the atheist, is in heaven?"

She exhaled heavily.

"Max, I was skeptical, too. He said I'd be surprised by who's in heaven."

She stopped, and seemed deep in thought.

"I told Him I can't go on!"

She began trembling…her voice suddenly overcome with emotion. I wanted to say something comforting…words were suddenly elusive. I could only watch helplessly as she shook with spasms of grief.

"I told Him," she cried. "It's too much. There's no way to go one more day."

An awful silwnce.

"I'm too weak," she continued after a moment, choking on her words, her face red and twisted in pain, as fat tears rolled down her plump cheeks.

"I'm not strong enough to go on. I told Him. I don't want to go on. Everything's been taken from me. Everything!"

What a terrible insight I was given into her state of mind. She had been so good at hiding her pain. I had thought she was doing better…now it was as if she had dropped a mask. Her unexpected and raw heartache showed the real and awful truth.

"I asked Him why I was left alone?"

"Molli, you're not alone, we…"

She was deaf to me.

"He said I was given a strong heart because His Father knew I'd need it."

"Yeah you…"

Still ignoring me, she continued.

"He said 'love God first, with everything you have. Everything. Love others as you love yourself. Do this with all your heart, all your soul, all your mind.'"

"Yeah but…"

A faint smile crossed her face as if a particle of luminosity had passed through the woe and darkness in her smoky blue eyes.

"There were tears in his eyes. He promised that God would carry me through this."

She paused, then held my gaze.

"He put his hand on my shoulder and asked if I wanted to be friends?"

"He touched you?"

She shook her head.

"Not really. He just put his hand on my shoulder."

"But he touched you, right?"

She must have sensed my alarm.

"It was fine, Max. He wasn't the least bit creepy."

"If you say so."

"But then, then I started thinking that if he had stepped in and used his so-called great authority, my family would be okay, you know? He could have prevented my dad from flying into those power lines, right?"

I nodded.

"I was mad, and I knocked his hand away."

"You did?"

"Yeah! I demanded to know why he took my whole family and left me alone."

"Molli, you're not alone," I replied softly. "We…"

She cut me off.

"I wanted to smash him in the face! I really did! Why does he allow all this terrible shit to happen, right? I was getting steamed!"

"I bet."

"Know what he said?"

I shrugged.

"He said, 'I didn't take your family. I welcomed them.'"

"Huh?"

"That's what he said. 'I welcomed them.' He said I'd have troubles in this world and that with Him life is also filled with love, joy and peace. He said the greatest of these is love."

"Love?"

She turned her palms skyward.

"That's what he said."

I found that hard to believe. I guess "love" is good and all that...is it really a cure for all the horrible...unjust...painful and evil things in the world?

"And you know what?" Molli asked.

"What?"

"Looking at him, the anger kind of drained from me."

"It did?"

She smiled faintly.

"Yeah."

"Did he say anything else?"

"Yeah. He told me to come to Him when I'm downhearted, miserable or lonely, like I did in church this morning. He said he'd be there."

I was completely astounded. She might as well have said she had been abducted by aliens!

"Then what happened?"

"He asked me what I thought of the sermon and all the talk of fishermen. I told Him I enjoyed it and found it interesting that fishermen are so prevalent in the Bible. He smiled and said he chose them very carefully."

I was pretty much speechless.

"He did?"

She wiped her tears away with her hand.

"Yeah, he told me that thousands of years ago certain laws were written just for fishermen and fishing. He said there are still laws on the books pertaining to fishermen."

"What laws?"

She shrugged.

"I don't know, Max."

I suppressed a grin.

"Did he walk on water?"

She slapped me on the arm.

"No! But he baptized me with water."

"What? How?"

"He asked me if I wanted to be baptized. I said okay. Then he did it."

"Did what, exactly?"

"Dipped his hand into the water from the dam, said something about converting the water from a common to a Godly use, said some more things then poured the water cupped in his hand over my head."

I was still shocked…unsure what to say to her…how to respond.

"What did he look like? Did he have long hair and a beard like in the pictures? Was he wearing a robe?"

I cracked a half-smile.

"Did he have a halo?"

"No," she sighed. "He looked like a guy, just like a guy. He had on jeans. A blue sweater and hiking boots. His hair was down to his shoulders. He had a short beard, like he hadn't shaved in a few weeks."

"How old was he? Did he look two thousand years old?"

I couldn't help but to tease her a little. It was such an outrageous story.

"I couldn't tell. Thirty something?"

She waved her hand through the air.

"That's not important! He helped me up over the rocks to the main path and pointed in the direction of the ocean. 'I'm going this way,' he said and hugged me. 'Remember, I'll always be with you, even if you think you can't feel me there. I promise, Molli, I love you.' He looked me in the eye and smiled. 'You did not choose me, but I chose you.' Then he asked me again about being friends."

"And you said?"

Once again she shrugged.

"I told him I'd be his 'friend,'" she said, holding her fingers up like quote marks.

"You did?"

She exhaled heavily.

"Yeah, why not? I have no friends anymore, so you know…and besides, if you're going to have just one friend in your whole life, He seems like He'd be the best choice."

She grinned slightly.

"I was okay with that."

"You were okay with that?'"

"Yeah, he didn't seem dangerous or anything."

She paused as if thinking.

"He had kind brown eyes."

"Then what happened?" I asked, barely concealing my skepticism. "Did he fly into the clouds?"

She grimaced.

"I shouldn't have told you. I knew you'd make fun of me."

"I'm sorry," I replied ruefully. "It's just hard to…what happened next?"

"I came back here."

She obviously read my look of complete disbelief.

"Remember, you promised not to tell anyone," she whispered urgently. "You promised. That's the only reason I told you. I know it's unbelievable, but you promised."

There was a moment of silence...she placed her hand on mine and looked me squarely in the eye.

"He said one more thing, Max."

"What?" I grinned. "Did he give you the winning lottery numbers?"

She paused as if collecting herself.

"He said, 'tell Max he is forgiven.'"

"I'm forgiven?"

She shrugged.

"That's what he said... and for you to 'tell them.'"

"Bullshit!" I blurted angrily. "None of that happened. You're just..."

She cut me off.

"That's what he said okay? I'm not making this up!"

Arguing was useless.

"Did talking to him help? Do you feel different?"

She met my gaze.

"Yeah, a little. There might actually be life, or something like that, down the road."

We were quiet for a moment, and then my father came in holding his violin.

"How was your walk, Molli?"

"Nice."

She glanced over at me.

"It's beautiful out there."

-46-

The devil knows when you're weak, hungover and vulnerable. He can sense it. That's when that son of a bitch comes after you.

A couple of days later, Molli and I were hiking through the woods toward Champayne Dam when she stopped and pointed to an overgrown trailhead branching off the main path. It was a beautiful summer day, but I was hungover and in a wretched mood.

"Where does this go?" she asked, her dark eyebrows arched.

"Way back in the woods to a pond."

"Let's check it out."

"There's nothing there, Molli. Just more woods, a pond. I hardly ever go back there."

She brushed past me and started down the path.

"Come on, let's take a look."

Inhaling deeply, I fell in behind her. I love the earthy bouquet of the woods...comforting...spiritual...familiar...healing.

The path, it you could even call it that, was overgrown with low-hanging branches.

Walking slightly in front of me, Molli playfully ran her fingers over the tips of the leaves.

"Molli, hold up for a second."

She stopped and turned to me. I pulled the pills from my pocket and held them out for her to see.

"What are these?"

She shrugged.

"I don't know."

I glared at her.

"The hell you don't!"

She stepped forward and brushed her hair from her eyes.

"Are they pills?"

"You're damned right, they're pills. And you know exactly where they came from!"

She stepped back.

"No I don't."

"You stole these from my father!"

Once again I glared at her, waiting for a reply.

Her face screwed up in anxiety.

"I didn't steal anything!"

"Yes you did! You stole them and left them in Hua's car!"

"Let me see them again."

I held them flat in my palm for her to see.

"Oh yeah, right," she finally replied. "They were on the kitchen table. I was afraid Homer might get them, so I pocketed them and forgot to put them back later."

Her face was the very picture of innocence.

"You stole them. Admit it!"

She looked taken aback.

"I didn't steal anything, but I probably saved your dog's life!"

What a liar! Albeit a good liar.

There was no way I could disprove her lie because there was a slim chance that my father may have left the pills out.

"I don't believe you, but there's nothing I can do right now except keep an eye on you and my dad's pills. I don't want to tell my parents because they're already beyond stressed."

She started walking down the path.

"Believe whatever you want."

We navigated the trail in silence for ten minutes and then entered a small clearing. That's when I saw him...Mister D...sitting cross-legged in a bunch of leaves on the ground. He looked as surprised to see us as we were to see him. He jumped to his feet and I immediately noticed a Bowie knife with a black handle tucked into the belt of his denim cutoffs.

"What are you dickwads doing out here?" he asked.

His eyes…bloodshot…clothes filthy as if…he had been living in the woods.

"Nothing," I stammered, "just walking."

He flashed a wolfish smile…disgusting rotting teeth…narrowed eyes…like flies…the hair on the back of my neck prickled. I sensed peril and knew from Molli's pensive expression that she did as well. There were muffled voices and the sound of something going on back in the woods twenty feet away. I figured Russ was standing guard for whoever was back there.

"This is your cousin, right?" he asked.

I eyed him warily.

"Yep."

"What's your name, kid?"

Molli glanced at me before answering.

"Molli."

He held out his hand, but Molli refused it. He was indignant.

"I'm Mister D. You heard of me, right?"

Molli shrugged.

The sharp snap of a beer can opening broke the silence…followed by more hushed voices from back in the woods. What were they doing back there? Making out, drinking, taking drugs? What sounded like a woman cackling wafted through the underbrush. My eyes were drawn to the knife in Russ's belt, its ten-inch blade shimmering in the sun.

"Let's go, Molli."

Mister D stepped forward and grabbed my shoulder.

"What's your hurry, dickwad?"

"No hurry," I answered, trying not to sound half as scared as I was. "We don't want to interrupt anything."

He frowned.

"Interrupt anything? Do you think I'm doing something wrong, illegal?"

"No, I'm just saying…"

My knees turned to rubber…my mouth dry.

He turned toward Molli.

"You're a pretty sight," he sneered. "A virgin, right? A carpenter's dream. Flat as a board and never been nailed."

Molli stepped back as a wave of anger and fear swept over me. I looked at the knife and then up at Russ's contorted face. He was obviously stoned, drunk or both. He grinned maniacally at Molli.

"Old enough to bleed," he snickered, "old enough to butcher."

An appalling silence…then we heard voices…three kids…thirteen or fourteen…came trudging through the undergrowth…diffusing everything.

"Hey guys, what's going on?" I asked, my heart in my throat.

"Nothing," one of them replied.

"You headed back to the main trail?"

"Yep."

"Good! We're lost, so we'll tag along with you."

"Sure, come on."

I grabbed Molli's arm and we started following them.

"I'll see you, Max. And I'll see you again, Molli," Russ chortled. "Carpenter's dream you are."

When we got back to the main path Molli grabbed my arm.

"That's the "Mister D" guy you gave the money to? The guy who's blackmailing you?"

"Yes."

"You can't let a guy like that control you. He'll…"

"He'll what?" I snapped. "Burn our house down? Kill us?"

I slowly shook my head and met Molli's gaze.

"I know he's an evil jerk, but if I don't do what he says…" I exhaled loudly. "Trust me. I know what I'm doing."

By the time we got home the sun was sliding down the backside of the sky…asking why…shadows…crawled across the cove…sky turning mauve…woods…rocky shoreline…low tide…no where to hide…filled   with…perfume…seaweed…rockweed…kelp…and every ancient fragrance the ocean dutiful offers.

Molli went inside, slamming the screen door shut behind her. That's when I saw it. A dead robin below the living room window. I walked over and nudged it with my foot.

-47-

I woke late and stared at the ceiling…an uneasy feeling real as the blankets…encased me…embraced me…i realized what I had to do…something new…my singular purpose that summer day.

Quickly tugging on my cutoffs and a t-shirt, I slipped on my sandals and went downstairs. My father was at rehearsal, and my mother and Molli were gone, probably to the grief counselor, as they had every Friday morning for the last six weeks.

Our neighbor Norm Pinnet (the nickname committee had dubbed him: Norm Pinhead) had a gas-powered chainsaw. Every fall he'd pull it out of a shed in his backyard and take down sickly trees on his property or in the nearby woods and then cut them up for firewood.

Under a faint blue sky I went to the A-frame and chugged down three large gulps from a bottle of tequila. It was warming my blood and filling me with liquid courage as I crossed our yard onto the Pinnets' property. There weren't any cars in their driveway, so I figured no one was home. *Perfect!* The shed door creaked impatiently as I yanked it open. The inside was as dimly lit as a cave and reeked of gas and lawn fertilizer. I left the door open to allow the sunlight in. The chainsaw and an old pair of goggles were sitting on a shelf with a bunch of rusted plumbing supplies. It was almost as if the saw had been left there for me. I carefully picked up the saw and goggles, and everything on the shelf seemed to rattle in protest. I screwed off the gas cap, checked to make sure it had gas (it did), grabbed the goggles and then left the shed, slamming the door behind me.

I had never used a chainsaw before, but I knew what do to. Make sure the trees don't fall on me or on the house! The way you do that is by cutting a six-inch V into the side into the trunk of the tree, facing the direction you want the tree to fall. Then get the hell out of the way. Gravity does the rest. Sounds easy, right?

The tequila had helped calm my nerves. But I was still nervous, so I gave myself a little pep talk.

You've tried everything and nothing worked. This is the right thing to do. It's time to stand up and be counted!

I slipped on the goggles then pulled the chainsaw's starter cord. It chugged but refused to start. *Shit!* I pressed the prime button and then pulled the cord again.

The chainsaw coughed…sputtered to life. It was noisier than I had anticipated. Chainsaws are dangerous. If you hit a knot in a tree, the saw can kick back violently and cut off your hand.

Holding the saw waist-high in front of me…i advanced… toward the three trees…twenty feet high…trunks the diameter of a pie. I slowly pressed the saw's trigger and it answered…revving loudly…unwieldy…trying to take flight. Half crouching, I carefully pressed the blade of the saw into the trunk of the first tree… bits of bark…sawdust spit back at me…i gripped the saw firmly… cutting a V shape in the first tree…inhaling the smell of freshly cut wood.

I stepped back as the tree groaned and crashed to the ground. I was astonished at how easy it was. *Maybe I should become a lumberjack?* The second tree came down just as easily but fell a little close to the house. No problem. All I'd have to do on the third and final tree was to adjust where I cut. I later learned that trees have "a certain way" they want to fall, as if they're predisposed to it.

The breeze picked up as I approached the tree from the right side instead of from the front. I had just finished making the V cut when….a devilish wind…blasted in…from the ocean…slamming into the tree…as it groaned and teetered…deciding which direction to take.

To my complete horror…it crashed into the side of the house… Roof tiles…a section of gutter went flying. *Shit no!* I turned off the chainsaw…dropped it in the grass, and still in shock, inspected the damage. The tree was leaning against the house at a forty-five-degree angle. It may have poked a hole in the roof, but it was impossible to tell from the outside. Flinging open the back door I sprinted inside, expecting to see a branch sticking through a gaping hole in the living room ceiling. *God please no. Please!* I was so relieved to see the ceiling intact that I punched the air.

I carefully put the saw back in the shed and then went inside to watch TV and wait for my father to get home. Obviously there was no way I could hide what I had done. And you know what? Some part of me was happy to own up to it! On Fridays my father usually left work right after lunch, so I figured he'd be home at any minute. I was right. I heard a car in the driveway and went outside. My father was just getting out of his Toyota when I rounded the corner.

"Hey, Dad."

He pulled his violin case from the backseat and smiled.

"Hey, Max."

"I need to tell you something."

Still holding his violin case he walked toward me, gravel crunching under his feet.

"What's up?"

"I want to tell you before you see it yourself."

His eyebrows arched.

"See what?"

I paused, then met his unwavering gaze.

"I cut down the fir trees by the house," I confessed matter-of-factly. "I'm sorry, but I couldn't get the image of the dead birds out of my mind. I had to do something."

He looked puzzled, as if he didn't quite understand what I had just told him.

"What?"

"The fir trees, the bird-killing trees, I cut them down and…one of them hit the house."

"You're kidding?"

"Nope."

He brushed past me, and I followed him. The third tree was still leaning against the house. I had been afraid to try and move it, fearing I could cause more damage. My father just stood there for a few seconds, obviously in shock, looking at the fallen trees and stumps. After a few moments he turned to me, his face crimson with anger.

"I cannot believe you did this! I planted those trees!"

"Dad, I know and I'm sorry, but there's no way I was going to see another bird die. It's too much to take. I'm having nightmares about it."

"A few birds get killed, so you cut the trees down!"

"It was more than a few."

He strode over to the tree leaning against the house and looked up at the roof. He tried to say something but was unable to get it out due to his anger and shock.

"Dad, I'm sorry but nothing else worked. There wasn't any other option. The wind took that tree. I tried…"

His face erupted in anger as his hand formed a tight fist. I instinctively raised my hands, waiting to be hit. But instead he lowered his fist and shook his head in disgust.

"Get out of my sight!"

I went for a long hike past Champayne Dam…walking along the bluffs…past the crack…following the rocky shoreline almost as far as Ketch Harbour. Climbing up on a bolder the size of a car, I gazed out over the ocean's indigo surface. A lone sailboat five miles off slowly inched forward, its triangular sail proudly filled with wind. *I wish I had brought some booze.* A drab gray naval destroyer slowly passed, headed out to sea. Sailors were moving around on its deck as a dozen seagulls flew behind the ship, hoping for a meal.

Maybe I should join the navy...a fantastic way to get the hell out of here and see the world...join the navy...right...who was I kidding? Myself. That wasn't going to happen. Besides, what was the point of going on?

I stayed there for two hours watching the ocean as dark thoughts demanded to be heard. Returning home, I found Molli sitting on the deck, her sunglasses perched on her forehead. She motioned to the fallen trees.

"Nice work," she said sarcastically. "Your dad is pissed!"

I claimed a seat beside her.

"I don't care."

She shook her head in disbelief and smirked "unbelievable!" under her breath. We sat there without saying much, and then I asked her how her grief counseling session went.

"It sucks," she replied before pulling down her sunglasses to shield her eyes.

"Are my parents home?"

"Your mom is. Your dad went out."

I found my mother in the kitchen, peeling potatoes by the sink. She stopped and looked at me, her face a mix of emotion.

"Max, what in God's name were you thinking?"

"I wasn't going to watch one more bird die."

"Your father's livid."

"I know."

She put down the potato she had been peeling and placed her hands flatly on the counter.

"He planted those trees."

"I know."

"Thank God that tree didn't smash through the roof. This is *not* good."

I could feel my anger rising.

"I thought you of all people would understand! You know how I feel about birds and those trees, those trees…"

She cut me off.

"Surely there was another way to solve that problem?"

"We tried everything, and nothing worked. I'm sorry, Mum, but there wasn't any other option."

My punishment…swift and painful. I was forbidden from getting my driver's license that summer. What a bummer…beyond a major drag. It cost two grand to fix the damage to the house…a small price to pay for what I had done. I didn't regret it one bit. How many more birds would have died if I had not taken action?

-48-

The most wicked…bloated…violent…deranged storms can't do nearly as much damage as one human being can do to another. Storms kill at random and smash up the land. The ugliest storms take a human toll and leave paths of random destruction in their wakes. Storms are born blind. Most people are not. The pain people inflict on each other is much more destructive…intentional… lasting lifetimes. And you know what else? Nature will mock us. It did that on the day Molli's aunt arrived. The weather was like something you'd see in a travel brochure. Castle-like clouds danced across a cobalt sky, ushered along by a soft southern breeze.

It was easily the nicest day of the summer. The temperature balmy…summer air spiced with the unsullied scent of fir and pine trees across the cove. Considering what was happening…who was arriving…it should have been storming… a black and brooding sky…thunder crashing…lightning flashing …as if it were the end of humanity.

That afternoon Ricky and Janet had stopped by. Ricky was inside with Molli, and Janet and I were sitting on the deck having iced tea when we heard a car roll up. I went to the driveway just in time to see Abby and some guy get out of a taxi. I had never met them before or even seen a picture of the aunt, but as soon as I saw her, I knew who it was. She was in her thirties. Her eyes were bloodshot and her hair was a bird's nest, like she had just rolled out of bed.

She rushed over and hugged Janet.

"Molli, you poor girl, how are you? It's so good to see you! We got here as quickly as we could."

"I'm not…" Janet tried to reply.

Before she could finish Abby knelt and cupped Janet's face in her hands.

"Oh my God, you look just like your mother."

"I'm not Molli," Janet repeated flatly. "Molli's inside."

"What?"

Janet stepped back.

"I'm not Molli. I'm Janet, a friend of Max's."

The aunt stood and glared at me.

"You're Max?"

"Yep. Molli's inside with my parents. Let's go in."

We had only taken a few steps when Ziggy suddenly dive-bombed Abby, screeching and flapping his wings violently. She shrieked and waved her hands as if her hair was on fire. I grabbed a broom that was leaning against the side of the house and swatted at Ziggy.

"Get outta here!"

He took off toward the other side of the cove, and calm was restored.

"Sorry," I said, placing the broom back where I had found it. "He's got a nest around here and is very protective."

"His attack made me dizzy," the aunt said.

My parents and Molli were sitting in the kitchen, and Ricky was coming down the stairs pulling up his zipper, having just used the bathroom. Abby didn't even acknowledge my parents. Instead she swept past everyone, rushed over and hugged Molli.

"Molli, Molli, you poor girl. We got here as quickly as we could."

She cupped Molli's face in her hands.

"Oh my God, you look just like your mother."

It was the exact same thing she had just said to Janet. She had probably rehearsed it! She started squinting violently as if she was trying to cry but couldn't quite summon up tears.

"Hi, Aunt Abby," Molli replied weakly.

"You poor girl, what happened to your face?"

"I'm okay. I slipped on the rocks and fell."

"Okay? It looks like you were hit with a baseball bat. You poor girl."

She hugged Molli again.

"Don't worry," she muttered, "we're going to work everything out."

Abby stood and reached for my father's hand.

"Geoff, thank you for all you've done. I can never repay you. We're all devastated. I loved Beth, Harry and my little nephew Tom so much."

My father cleared his throat.

"You mean 'Tim,'" he said. "Molli's brother's name is Tim."

Abby looked aghast.

"Did I say 'Tom?' I meant Tim. It must be my exhaustion and grief. I loved Tim like a brother."

It was the first time I'd ever seen anyone "crying" without shedding a single tear. She turned back toward Molli.

"I'm just thankful to God you were able to look after my little niece."

My father wasn't buying her badly acted sympathy routine. I could tell by his look of repugnance. But he went along. He's a nice guy, and I figured he was humoring her, for the time being, anyway.

"We're all devastated," he said. "It's been a tough haul since… you know."

He motioned to my mother.

"You remember my wife, Karen?"

My mother smiled tightly, then crossed the room and lightly embraced the aunt.

"So nice to see you again," my mother said, "but under such tragic circumstances."

"You're having a baby?" Abby asked.

"In a couple of months."

Abby smiled widely.

"Isn't that wonderful!"

"You've met my son, Max," my father said, "and these are his friends, Ricky and Janet."

She smiled at us then turned to the stranger she had arrived with...around her age...in a wrinkled beige blazer...faded jeans...beat-up shoes...sunglasses...over...a ratty handlebar moustache.

She grabbed his hand.

"This is my fiancé, Bruce. He'd never let me come all the way to a place like this by myself."

A place like this?

"Fiancé?" I thought. Really? Ha! No one believed that for a second. Who knows who he was? Probably some guy the aunt had sold on the idea of helping her secure a small fortune. They were just trying to put on a show like a big happy family.

"Nice to meet you all," Bruce nodded.

It sounded like he had an accent of some kind.

"Abby, we didn't know you're engaged," my mother said.

"Yes! We hope to tie the knot next summer."

"You must be starved," my mother said. "I've made some sandwiches."

She motioned to the table.

"Sit down. I'll make tea."

"The taxi's waiting," I said.

"I forgot!" Abby said. "We didn't have time to stop at a cash machine to get money."

She looked at my father.

"If you could take care of it, I'll pay you later. Better still, perhaps you could drive us back to our hotel in the city and we can stop at an ATM on the way there?"

My father's face reddened but he kept his cool.

"How much is it?"

"Seventy or eighty dollars."

My father pulled a handful of bills from his wallet and trust them toward me.

"Max, pay him."

I took the money and started toward the door.

"Can you grab our bags?" Abby asked.

"We better get going," Janet said.

"Yeah," Ricky added. "I gotta pick some things up at the store. They got bananas on sale."

The three of us went outside together.

"That woman is a piece of work," Ricky laughed.

"The nerve of her asking your father to pay for the taxi!" Janet added.

"My father knows what they're up to."

"I'll call you later," Ricky said with a wave.

Janet got in the car, but I grabbed Ricky's arm and pulled him aside.

"You still got your twelve-gauge shotgun?" I whispered.

"Hell yeah. Why?"

"I need to borrow it."

He looked puzzled.

"What for?"

"For something," I muttered.

"What's that?"

I exhaled heavily.

"Can I just borrow it? It's nothing important. I don't want to get into it right now, okay?"

"Okay man. No problem. I'll bring it by."

Janet and Ricky left, and I went to the taxi idling in the driveway. The driver had his elbow hanging out the window and the trunk was open. I pulled out their luggage then asked the driver how much the fare was.

"Ninety-five dollars."

I counted the money my father had given me. Five twenty-dollar bills. I passed it to the driver.

"Keep the change."

It was more than he'd get from my father.

He looked at the money, frowned at me and then drove off, his tires kicking up gravel. I left the luggage on the deck and went back into the kitchen. They were all sitting at the table, chatting politely, eating egg sandwiches and sipping tea. I reached for half a sandwich and took a seat.

"Max, you must be so excited about getting a little sister," Abby said, her mouth half full.

"You bet."

Abby reached over the table and gently pushed Molli's curls off her forehead.

"Your eye is horrible," she said, then turned to my parents. "How could you let this happen?"

My father stirred in his seat, his anger obviously rising.

So much for the pleasantries.

"We didn't let it happen," my father replied curtly. "Molli and Max were hiking. She slipped and fell. It was an accident."

"She could have been seriously injured. This is very disturbing."

"Molli's fine," my mother said softly, "it looks worse than it is."

"Well thank God for that!"

"I'm okay," Molli said.

"You're not okay," Abby continued. "It's very upsetting to me."

"I told you, it was an accident," my father repeated.

"It may have been an accident this time, but what about next time? What if she falls again or is hit by a car on the narrow road we took getting here?"

"That's not going to happen," my father snapped.

Abby looked at Molli, then at my parents.

"I've been told that this village, town or whatever you call it, is unsafe," she said flatly. "My attorney tells me there was a death out here this summer and that a young man fell off a cliff and lost his life."

I was stunned. There was an awful silence. I turned toward Molli. She was looking at me out of the corner of her eye.

"That had nothing to do with us," my father replied, thankfully breaking the silence.

"The point is, it happened," Abby continued, "and it makes me very concerned for Molli's safety. Very concerned."

Bruce the fiancé nodded in agreement.

"How big is your house?" Abby asked.

"How big?" my father replied.

"Yes, how many bedrooms?"

"I don't see how that's relevant to anything."

"We have three bedrooms," my mother said.

Abby smiled smugly.

"You don't have to be a genius to see that this house is not big enough for Molli to live here, especially when the baby comes. It's completely inadequate."

Good for her that you don't have to be a genius!

I glanced at my father. His eyes narrowed. Abby didn't know him well, but she knew how to hit him "below the belt." Saying our house was "inadequate" was an insult to everything my father believed in.

"This house?" he replied, his temper rising. "This house isn't adequate to raise Molli? This house is perfectly adequate. I built this house!"

"I noticed damage to the roof and gutters," Bruce said smugly. "No way that's a…"

My father cut him off, then glared at me for a half second.

"Storm damage," he said matter-of-factly. "None of that matters because we're buying a new larger house."

My mother and Molli both looked as shocked as I was. My father had never mentioned anything about buying a new house. I figured he was bluffing the aunt to up the ante.

"You're buying a new house? Abby asked curtly. "A bigger house?"

"You heard me correctly," my father replied.

Abby stood.

"That doesn't really matter. Molli belongs in Denver with her friends and schoolmates."

She turned to Molli and smiled the most plastic, fake, hideous smile I have ever seen.

"Where she can snowboard and ski, the things she loves."

She turned back to my parents.

"We all want what's best for her."

My father's chair screeched across the floor as he jumped to his feet. Bruce stood and his chair did the same. It was beyond tense.

"What's best for Molli is to be with family who care about her!" my father said angrily.

Abby scowled.

"That would be me."

"We'll see about that!" my father blurted.

"Bruce, let's go!"

My father is a nice guy! Despite the ugly scene, he drove them to town! He probably wanted to talk to them alone.

-49-

We are either drawn to people in deep pain or repulsed by them...sprinting to...or away from them. What makes us the kind of person that has humanity and compassion, or the kind with a hardened heart?

Phil was drawn to Molli.

Later that afternoon he showed up on his bike. I knew he had a crush on Molli, even if he wouldn't admit it. He was always casually asking about her or dropping by to visit, something he never did before Molli arrived.

I was sitting in the sun on the deck "decompressing" after the blowup with Molli's aunt. Molli was in the kitchen talking with my mother.

"Hey Max," Phil said as he laid his bike in the grass. "How you doing?"

"Hi Phil," I replied, holding up my hand to shield my eyes against the sun. "What brings you by?"

I knew very well what brought him by: a chance to see Molli. But I wanted to see how he would react.

"I was out on my bike, and thought I'd drop by to see if you know...if you and Molli, maybe wanted to go for a ride?"

I was in no mood for small talk.

"Molli's inside. I'll ask her." I stood, started toward the backdoor and then turned to Phil.

"If you came by to see Molli, that's okay. You don't have to make up excuses."

Even in the bright sunshine I could tell he was blushing.

"I was just, ahhh, on my bike, you know…and thought I'd drop in, that's…"

I cut him off and pointed at a chair.

"Sit."

He pulled up a chair and I sat across from him.

"It's obvious, to me and everyone, that you like Molli. It's okay to admit it."

He was really squirming.

"I'm not trying to get over on anyone," he finally muttered. "Yeah, I do like her, but I'm not sure how she feels. I just want to be her friend."

I looked at him for a moment without responding. I wanted him to feel uncomfortable.

"I don't have to tell you she's gone through a lot and is still going through a lot. She's really vulnerable. My parents and I are *very* protective of her."

He looked up at me, his eyes filled with emotion.

"I'd never do anything to make the situation worse."

He stopped for a moment and then continued.

"I should have said something to you. I'm sorry. I feel connected with her in some way, that's all. I promise."

Phil was an okay guy, I knew that. He was an honor roll student at Isley, and I don't think I ever once saw him drinking or smoking pot.

"Don't sweat it."

I got up and started toward the door again, but he stopped me, a look of genuine concern crossing his face.

"You're not going to say anything to her, are you?"

"Say anything?"

I knew what he meant, but I guess I wanted to see him squirm a little more.

"Yeah, you're not going to tell her how I feel, are you?"

I waved him off.

"Your secret's safe with me."

"Max, there is one thing."

"What?"

"I was going to invite Molli, I mean you and Molli, to my little brother's Bar Mitzvah."

"When is it?"

"In a couple of weeks."

"You can ask, but it's up to her. I don't care either way."

"Thanks."

Inside the kitchen Molli and my mother were still softly talking.

"Phil's outside," I said looking at Molli. "He wants to know if we want to take a bike ride?"

I've got to admit that I was kind of hoping that Molli would say she wasn't interested. But instead she got to her feet.

"I could use some air."

Outside, Molli greeted Phil and then got on her bike.

"You know what?" I said. "You guys go ahead. Dad doesn't want Mum to be alone."

I looked at Phil.

"Be careful."

He nodded.

"We will," Molli smiled.

My father got back a half hour later. He was fuming, beyond mad.

"That damned woman!" he seethed. "If Bruce is really her fiancé, I'll eat my violin! They're grifters!"

He went to the cupboard, took three of his pain pills and washed them down with a glass of water. My mother and I exchanged worried glances.

"I'll fight her every inch of the way," he growled. "She has absolutely no right to waltz in here and try to take Molli. It's ridiculous!"

"Geoff, calm down," my mother said.

"Did you hear what that woman said?" my father asked no one in particular. "She said this house isn't adequate? Isn't adequate! Can you believe that?"

"She's crazy, Dad."

My mother and I sensed it wasn't a good idea to ask him what he meant when he told Molli's aunt that we were getting a new, larger house. My father sat at the table and buried his head in his hands. He may have been crying.

"This is ridiculous," he murmured.

My mother gently placed her hand on his shoulder.

"Don't worry," she said softly. "We'll get through this."

By the time Molli got back from her bike ride with Phil, it was dinnertime and my mother casually suggested that my father barbeque chicken for dinner. She knew him well. Barbequing relaxed him the same way tying fishing flies did.

-50-

It was Wednesday, and I'd been trying frantically all day to reach Hua to see what the doctor had told her. It was also the night that Molli and Chen's dad were to have their chess rematch.

That afternoon I rode to Crystal Crescent Beach and gave Mister D a watch I had shoplifted in Halifax a few days earlier. He sniffed at it and then tossed it into the back seat.

"That all you got?"

"It's worth at least..."

He cut me off.

"It's not even digital."

I threw my hands up.

"It's better than digital. You can sell it. It's..."

"Shut up, dickwad. I know what it's worth. Next week I want cash. You understand? Cash. No rings, watches or any other shit."

"I don't have a job," I pleaded. "I don't have any money. At least not the amount you want."

"That's your problem. Not mine. Go rob a gas station."

He flashed a menacing grin.

"You're good at that, right?"

"I don't...I can't..."

"Kid, do you like your house?"

"What?"

"Do you like your house?"

"Yes I guess so, but..."

He moved forward until his unshaven face was only inches from mine. His breath foul, his bloodshot eyes wild.

"I've told you before, and I mean it. I'll burn your house down unless you get me that money. And since you're such a little bitch, I think I'll burn it down with everybody in it."

He leaned back and seemed to be waiting for me to react. What a worm! I could tell from his deranged half-grin that he really enjoyed seeing me squirm. I sat there completely and utterly scared to shit. But you know what? There is an upside to fear. When you're cornered like that certain decisions become easy. It's almost as if the circumstances make the decision for you. Everything suddenly became clear, as if the clouds had parted revealing the sun. I knew what I had to do. The thing is…you can't kill a guy in a parking lot in broad daylight and expect to get away with it. I had to get him to agree to meet me at a more secluded location.

"I'll get the money but I'm nervous about meeting you here. People might see us and start asking questions."

He eyed me suspiciously.

"No one's going to see us, dickwad."

"They might. Do you know where that old fire road is on the other side of Halibut Bay?"

"Yeah I used to screw up there."

"Okay, let's meet there. I'm scared to shit meeting here, and no one will see us there."

He shot me a look of disdain.

"I don't give a damn as long as you have my money. Same time next week on the fire road."

I got out, and he sped off, a cloud of depraved dust and smoke trailing behind his car.

-51-

What horny teenager ever thinks sex can lead to pregnancy? Zero. It's a hard fact of life made irrelevant by youthful lust.

By the time we finished dinner I was so anxious to see Hua I was pacing the floor waiting for Molli to get ready. She had spent hours online looking at chess sites. She was taking her rematch with Chen's father beyond seriously. She didn't say much about it, but whenever I brought it up, a look of steely resolve flared in her eyes. She had a competitive streak, and it was starting to show itself in different ways.

Night was crawling in from the east as we rode along the road under a lingering lilac and orange sunset.

"How do you feel about this chess game?" I asked, as Molli rode slightly behind me.

I was in a hurry to get there.

"Chen's dad is really good, and…"

She cut me off.

"I know he's really good, but so am I. I wasn't captain on my school's chess team for no reason."

I glanced over my shoulder.

"You were captain? I didn't know that."

"There's a lot of things about me you don't know," she said as she pedaled past me.

I set myself up for that one. She loved saying *you don't know me, and you don't have any idea what I'm going through, and you don't, etc. etc.* She pulled that line out whenever anyone expressed surprise at something she said she was able to do, like playing chess, cooking or sketching.

We glided into Chen's driveway, and I was confronted with a very confusing scene. Hua was standing beside a car talking to some guy I had never seen before…around her age…driving a new suv…handsome…an expensive suit coat…pressed pants… white shirt open at the neck revealing…a puff of chest hair…he looked like…a freaking movie star.

"These are my friends Max and Molli," Hua said as we coasted to a stop beside them. She motioned to the guy. "And this is my friend Brad."

He shook my hand and then Molli's hand.

"Hey, guys."

I was stunned. *How could she do this? What a betrayal!* She was obviously going on some kind of a date. My heart plunged…blood drained from my face…the first time I really experienced such deep and sickening feelings of jealously…heartbreak. At the same time I desperately wanted to know what the doctor and told Hua.

"We're going to study at the library," Hua said.

My eyes were drawn to hers. She looked nervous. I was speechless. *Was she pregnant? Who was this guy?* There was an awkward silence before Chen came to the front door and yelled for us to come in.

"See you," Brad grinned.

I shot Hua a look of utter dismay.

"Right, see you," I mumbled.

Inside the house I asked if I could get a glass of water.

"You know where it is," Chen replied.

I had just poured it and was standing alone in the kitchen feeling totally ambushed and stressed when Hua came in and pecked me on the cheek.

"I forgot my wallet," she said, holding it up for me to see.

She moved closer to me, and the fresh scent of her perfume hung in the air like an indictment.

"Everything's cool," she whispered.

"Cool?"

She smiled.

"It was a false alarm," she smiled. "I'm not pregnant."

She threw her hands up.

"Everything's fine."

I was immensely relieved but at the same time insanely jealous. I had never experienced so many contradicting emotions as I did that summer.

I looked her in the eye.

"Good," I replied flatly.

I placed the glass on the counter and stared at her.

"Glad to meet your new friend," I said barely controlling my anger.

"Brad?" she grinned. "We're buddies, in some of the same classes together. We have a study group."

My thoughts: *Your "buddy" sure drives a nice car, and I've never seen you wear a tight dress and screw-me shoes and makeup like that before.* She was a totally different woman. Sophisticated…sexy…mature… transformed. I also figured that if Brad had one single drop of lust in him, he thought they were more than "buddies."

"A study group?" I scoffed. "It looks like you're going clubbing."

She playfully pushed my shoulder.

"Clubbing? No way. We're going to the library. These summer courses are kicking my ass."

She kissed me lightly again, then gently wiped away a smudge of lipstick on my cheek.

"I'll talk to you later, okay?"

"Sure."

She left, and I went into the living room where Molli and Chen's father were setting up the chessboard. My mood was going from gray to black.

Chen came into the room and asked if we wanted anything to eat.

"We already ate," I replied, dropping onto the sofa.

"Can you please make us some tea?" Chen's father asked his son.

I didn't want any tea! I wanted to sulk and feel sorry for myself. But over the years I had learned that when a Chinese person offers you tea, it's an insult not to accept it. Besides, I had grabbed a bottle of Gin before we left home and planned to slink off into the bathroom to sneak drinks whenever possible.

I looked around the living room...books in piles...stacks of files...jade figurines...silk screens...paintings of dragons...herons...fountains...mountains...a hundred different things in that living room...a home committed to clutter...which suddenly really annoyed me!

Chen brought out a tray with a small teapot and four tiny cups without handles. He carefully poured us each a cup, then sat down and grabbed the TV remote. He turned on the Blue Jays game. Steam was rising from my cup of tea, which smelled very earthy. It was so hot I could only take small sips.

Chen was really into the ballgame, but I was distracted the whole evening thinking of Hua and Brad. *What are they doing? Where are they?* For the third time I went to the bathroom to take a shot from my bottle. It burned going down, but it was having the desired effect. I was getting quietly drunk, and it was starting to calm me. Meanwhile, Chen's father was ruthless. He thrashed Molli in thirty minutes. It wasn't even close.

"You are a good player," Chen's father smiled at Molli after they finished.

"Thank you," she muttered.

She looked beaten and exhausted as she turned to me.

"We better get going."

"Going?" I slurred. "Really? Why don't we hang out here for a while?"

I was stalling, hoping we'd still be there when Hua got back.

"I'm tired," she said.

Chen saw us to the door.

"Don't forget, we're going sailing again," he said, leaning against the doorframe. "We'll sail to Chester."

"Okay," I replied.

Molli and I got on our bikes and pedaled toward the Ketch Harbour Road under a night sky as black as the asphalt below us. There wasn't a moon or a single star. The Gin was really kicking in. I became completely disoriented in the darkness, lost control of my bike and tumbled into the road. Molli stopped and helped me to my feet.

"You're drunk!" she said accusingly. "I can smell it on you."

"So what?"

"You were drinking at Chen's house!"

"Yeah, big deal. No one knew."

"Can you make it home?"

I could barely see her in the darkness as I carefully climbed onto my bike.

"No problem. Let's go."

The light on the Ketch Harbour Road was better thanks to the streetlights.

"What happened tonight?" I asked as we rode side by side. "That chess game sure didn't last very long."

"I lost my nerve," she replied glumly.

"How does *that* have anything to do with chess?"

"I went on the defensive, and he killed me. It was a stupid mistake, really stupid."

"He beat you in six moves," I scoffed.

I was drunk and still in a foul mood. I guess I was trying to push her buttons a little. Isn't that the way anger is? You have to take it out on everyone around you.

Molli stopped pedaling and glared at me.

"Six moves?" she growled. "That's ridiculous!"

"He pounced on you." I snapped my fingers. "It was over like that."

She shot me a look of utter contempt.

"When you drink you turn into an idiot."

"You're just pissed because you got your ass kicked by Chen's father."

Her eyes widened.

"If that's the case, at least I own it," she smirked. "I am mad that I lost. Real mad. But you, you keep it all inside. Your guilt, your pain, your fear. You drink to dull all of it!"

"That's crazy! I drink because I like it, the way it makes me feel."

"Bullshit! You can lie to yourself, but don't lie to me. I know what's going on. You're a drunk! And you know what? It's going to kill you."

I glared at her hatefully through the darkness.

"You're so smart, aren't you?" I snarled. "You know why everyone does everything. But what you don't know is that we've done everything for you! My parents and I have done everything for you, and what do we get in return? Nothing! No thanks. No appreciation. You walk all over us. You're an ungrateful, self-centered little bitch. That's what *you* are. You should go live with your aunt. Yeah, go back to the states with her. You're both alike anyway. You're both users, takers. Ha! Why don't you go talk to your imaginary friend, Jesus? Yeah, go talk to him. Tell him what you know, how smart you are."

I gripped my handlebars and stared at her, waiting for a reply. My tirade must have cut her deeply because her eyes were heavy with tears. We stood there in the dark, staring at each other for what seemed like an eternity.

"You can go to hell!" Molli yelled, breaking the silence.

She turned and started pedaling toward home...leaving me standing...in a pool of white light. I stood there for a moment, unsure what to do. Where there had been bitter anger only a few moments before, there was now guilt and remorse for the spiteful things I had said. I didn't mean a single word of it, or at least I don't think I meant a word of it. I was just angry over Hua's date, and I was drunk.

"Molli!" I yelled into the night. "I'm sorry. I didn't mean it. Wait for me. Molli!"

She kept pedaling without looking back. By the time I caught up to her, she was turning down the Chebucto Head Road toward home.

"Molli," I said breathlessly as I got to her side. "Please stop."

She gripped her brakes, glided to a stop and glared at me, her eyes filled with pain.

"I'm sorry," I gasped in a pleading voice. "I'm angry. It's not your fault. I shouldn't have said those things. It's not how I feel, and..."

She cut me off.

"Do you know what I *like* about your drinking? When you're drunk you tell the truth, how you really feel. Booze is like a truth serum for you. I really do appreciate that."

"It's not how I feel," I stammered. "I'm angry, not at you, but with Hua. I'm sorry."

She reached into her jacket pocket, pulled out the pint of Gin I had been drinking from and held it up for me to see. A wicked smile formed on her lips.

"I bet you didn't even know you lost this. It was on the sofa. Good thing for you I picked it up."

I reached out to grab it...but she pulled away...then intentionally dropped the bottle onto the pavement...where it shattered. The pungent aroma of alcohol filled the air like a silent indictment. She turned toward the smooth dirt road leading down to Chandler's Cove and our house. Then without looking back, blurted, "Jerk!"

• • •

That night...after the fight...a screaming girl...her face a mask of horror...a primal inhuman wale from the murky depth of her soul...bleeding into a bowl...dying...crying...something evil...unstoppable...cover my ears...my eyes...my lies...make it go away...screaming...please stop...God make it stop...I can't take it...wake it...God make it stop...stop her...stop it...

Waking from my nightmare I gasped for breath...it's death... darkness...screaming through the walls to eat me alive...rip off my skin...announce my sin...its evil smirk...fangs...blood red eyes... rank breath...God make it go away...give me one more day...save me...confusion...darkness...my parents' bedroom door flings open...their muffled voices...in Molli's room...the scream wasn't a dream...it was Molli. She had just woken from a horrendous nightmare.

-52-

The truth is…I don't dream anymore. I don't even know for sure if I sleep. I hover in a brutal no man's land…a sadistic twilight somewhere between sleep and being awake. You never know how important sleep is until it is taken from you.

I tossed and turned restlessly for the whole night and in the morning opened my door to the heavenly aroma of freshly baked bread. That was the aroma of that summer. Or maybe it was Hua's exotic perfume…the brewing Atlantic…cold sweat and panic… hot asphalt…alcohol and vomit…Ricky's skunky pot…the fresh paint in Molli's room.

It was all of the above.

I was hung over, and instead of going downstairs I stumbled to the bathroom and performed my morning ritual. After I threw up, I felt a little better. Down in the kitchen, my mother was making bread, her apron, hands and face covered with flour. She looked like a mime as she peered up from her work and smiled.

"I didn't hear you come in last night."

I grunted, poured myself a large glass of apple juice, drained it, and then dropped into a seat at the table.

"Where's Molli?"

She wiped sweat from her brow with the back of her hand, which left a white smudge on her forehead.

"She said she was walking to Chebucto Head."

I was worried she had told my parents about our argument, my drinking, or worst of all, about Kevin.

"How did she seem?"

She shrugged.

"The same."

"Did she say anything about the chess game with Chen's father?"

"That he beat her and she was going to push for another rematch."

She paused.

"I think the competition with Chen's father is good for her. It's given her a spark."

"She sure doesn't like losing."

She pointed to a post-it note stuck to the fridge.

"Molli put that there last night."

I glanced at the post it. "TELL THEM!" was written on it.

"What's that mean? Tell who what?"

I was speechless, unable to come up with anything.

"Oh yeah, right. Tell Ricky and Phil about a party tonight," I finally replied, happy with my lie.

"A party?"

"Yeah a few of us are getting together. It'll be low-key."

"Are you feeling okay?" she asked, a look of concern forming on her face "You look terrible."

She crossed the room, and as she had done so many times before, lightly pressed her wrist to my forehead.

"You're clammy."

"I'm fine."

I put my glass in the sink and headed for the backdoor.

"I'm going to see if I can meet up with Molli."

"What about breakfast?"

"I'll have something when we get back."

The sun was warm and at its apex as I climbed the short dirt road toward Chebucto Head Road. I caught up with Molli halfway to the lighthouse.

"Are you okay?" I stammered. "Last night…your screaming…It sounded like…I wasn't sure if…"

She turned her sad and tired gaze toward me.

"I had a nightmare. It was so…so real."

Her eyes were somnolent and red as she wearily shook her head.

"I can't talk about it okay?"

"No problem."

We walked in silence for a few moments before I gently grabbed her arm and turned her toward me.

"I'm sorry for what I said last night. I didn't mean it. I was angry with Hua and took it out on you."

"Don't worry," she smiled weakly. "I'm over it. Words said loudly and in anger are usually false."

"Yeah, they were false."

She shot me a half-grin.

"Apology accepted."

We started walking again, but after a few second Molli stopped.

"Max, I do think your drinking is really bad for you."

I shrugged.

"Thanks, but I really don't drink that much, and…"

She cut me off.

"And there's one other thing, Max."

I met her gaze. *God, now what?*

"Okay."

"You said something about my 'imaginary friend Jesus.' Obviously, you don't believe I met him."

I turned my palms skyward.

"It is far-fetched. You admitted that."

Her expression turned somber.

"It's hard to believe, but I want you to know one thing."

Her gaze was unwavering.

"It happened. I wasn't making it up."

I didn't feel like arguing.

"Okay, fine."

We walked a little further, and then I asked her about the "Tell Them!" note she had stuck to the fridge that morning.

"Why did you do that? You promised you wouldn't tell anyone."

"I didn't tell anyone," she replied glumly. "The note was for you. 'Tell Them!' could have meant anything to your parents."

"Mum asked me about it. Thanks a lot! She put me on the spot. Thankfully I was able to come up with a lie."

She exhaled heavily.

"Tell them what happened with Kevin, and you won't have to lie anymore!"

"I'd rather die!"

-53-

We continued home under a pale blue sky without saying much. When we got back to our house, Abby and Bruce were sitting in a rental car in the driveway.

"Molli?" Abby gushed as she jumped from the car. "How are you?"

"Good," Molli replied flatly.

Bruce pulled me aside.

"We need to talk to your parents."

Our car wasn't there, so I figured either my mother or father, or both of them, had gone out.

"Come inside."

My mother had left a note on the counter saying they had gone to the store and would return shortly. Bread she had made was cooling on the counter. We sat in the kitchen, and I offered to make tea.

"I don't drink tea," Bruce replied gruffly, like I had offered him a cup of piss. "Do you have any coffee?"

"Coffee? No, we're tea drinkers around here."

"Can I use your bathroom?" Abby asked.

I motioned to the stairs.

"Upstairs on the left."

"We've been checking out places in Denver for us all to live," Bruce smiled at Molli. "We have a few real good possibilities."

Molli grunted. I was tempted to tell him to shut up. He had absolutely no right to bring that up with Molli without my parents there. Before I could say anything Abby came back down the stairs and reclaimed her seat at the table.

"I feel like I'm on the moon out here," she moaned. "It's so far from everything."

"That's why my parents chose it," I replied. "Besides, it's only thirty minutes from town. It's not like it's the middle of nowhere."

Maggie and Bruce started chatting when Molli gently nudged me with her elbow.

"Check out the white powder under Abby's nose," she whispered.

I casually looked. She was right. Molli grinned slightly.

"It's probably coke or meth."

I was astounded. She turned to her aunt.

"What were you doing in the bathroom, Aunt Abby?" Molli asked. "Eating sugared donuts?"

"What?"

"There's white powder under your nose," Molli continued, brushing the spot under her own nose.

"Were you eating sugared donuts?"

Abby rubbed her nose.

"It's makeup."

"You use white makeup?" Molli asked.

"Sometimes."

"Really?" Molli replied, barely concealing her skepticism.

We sat making small-talk until my parents got home. My father put the groceries on the counter, and then he and my mother sat down with us.

"Bruce and I have been discussing things with my attorney," Abby said. "We want to make a home for Molli in Colorado. What's the point in a custody battle? Molli needs to be near her friends, to be able to snowboard and ski, the things she loves."

"You're right," my father replied. "There's doesn't have to be a custody battle. Molli belongs here with her family, with people who love and care for her."

"That's us!" Abby said.

"Bullshit," my father barked.

"Geoff, please," my mother said, placing her hand on my father's. "Let's keep this civilized."

He pulled away from her.

"Civilized? This woman is unfit to be Molli's guardian."

He sneered at the aunt.

"What are you going to do, take her touring with the latest band you hook up with?"

"I will make her a good home!" Abby blurted.

"That's right," Bruce chimed in.

I glanced at my father and then at Molli...her face scarlet... as she...leveled a defiant stare at her aunt as if she was aiming a double-barreled shotgun right at her.

"My mother loved you, but she said you were ungrateful and immature!" Molli said, her voice deliberate. "She'd say, 'She's my only sibling, and all she has ever done is let me and my family down.'"

Abby looked as if Molli had slapped her!

"My mother, your sister, didn't raise a dumb daughter," Molli continued. "She always told me that I was smart, that I had a good mind and that I should use it."

"Of course you..."

Molli cut her off.

"We all know why you're here," Molli continued, her eyes narrowing. "To cash your lottery ticket."

Bruce started to say something, but Molli ignored him and continued staring at her aunt.

"Remember when my parents sent you ten thousand dollars so you could supposedly buy a car? Mom knew the money wouldn't be used on a car, that you would spend it on drugs and booze. But she was guilt-ridden by her relationship with you."

Molli slowly shook her head.

"You used it, her love, to squeeze money out of her."

Abby sat erect in her chair, her face as red as a humiliated tomato.

"Remember Christmas two years ago?" Molli asked, her eyes locked on her quarry. "Mom was so excited because you were coming to stay with us. Everything had to be perfect. She worked so hard. She hadn't seen you in like forever. When you didn't turn up, I mean you didn't even call to say you weren't coming, I saw how that really hurt her. Her heart was broken."

"I apologized," Abby blurted. "I told her what happened. I was in a car wreck and in a coma for a week. She said it was okay and that she understood."

A lone tear ran down Molli's plumb cheek.

"She understood you are a bad person. She loved you. All you did was use her, take from her. You used her love for you against her."

"Someday you'll understand," Abby grunted.

"You don't understand!" Molli said, her voice rising. "I would rather live in a rat hole than live with you. And you have the nerve to try and bribe me with skiing and snowboarding."

Her face was crimson as she motioned to my parents.

"These people, Uncle Geoff, Aunt Karen and Max, they love me! And you want to take that away from me after I've lost my whole family? God, you're horrible!"

Abby's face was tense with anger.

"I told you I love you!"

She threw her hands up.

"I loved your mother like a sister. No, I mean she was like a sister to me. I mean…"

Fury flared in Molli's blue eyes.

"You and those like you are the destroyers of families," she screamed. "If I have to go with you…this is what I promise to do…

run away…the very first day…you'll never find me…i'll live in a tree…we'll never be three…understand…you could search the land. I'll come back when I'm eighteen and take it from there. You'll never get another penny out of my family. Never! Do you understand?"

She leaped from the table and stormed out the screen door, slamming it shut. My mother jumped to her feet and went after her.

"She's obviously upset, but all that matters is what the court says," Abby grinned evilly. "She'll get over it. You said she was real bad when she got here, and who's to expect anything different in Colorado?"

"She'll adapt," Bruce added smugly.

There was a wrath in my fathers' eyes I had never seen before. He brought his fist down heavily on the table.

"You mean to tell me that after what she's just told you, you're still going to continue this ridiculous charade? My God, woman, the girl could not have made it more clear if she had written it in the sky. She hates you! She'll run away! You can't be serious. You can't be that cold hearted."

"Teenagers hate everyone," Bruce said smugly. "We're serious, alright. The court will decide what's best for Molli."

He stood up.

"Come on, Abby, let's go. Your niece is too upset to see things straight. Give her time."

They left, and my father and I sat in stunned silence. I could not believe what I had just witnessed. We all have many sides. Shades of dark and light. A loving and giving person can turn hateful and selfish if the circumstances are right. But this was the first time I witnessed firsthand how greed and the relentless pursuit of money bring out an evil, devious and callous side of people.

"What happens now, Dad?"

He exhaled loudly.

"The court will decide."

He went upstairs to lie down, and I went out on the deck to decompress. After a while I saw Molli and my mother climbing the grassy slope toward our house. They looked drained and gloomy.

"Abby and Bruce left," I said. "Dad's upstairs resting."

"I'm going to check on him," my mother said as Molli dropped into a seat beside me.

"Are you okay?" I asked after my mother had gone inside.

The breeze was playing with her hair.

"I've had better days."

"What are you going to do if the court says you have to live with your aunt and Bruce?"

"I don't know," she sighed. "That 'I'll run away, you'll never find me' stuff was for dramatic effect."

She glanced at me, a wounded look in her eyes.

"I was hoping she'd back off, see that there was no point trying to get me. I can't live on the street, and if I come back here, they'll just come and take me back to the states."

She exhaled sharply.

"I don't know. I guess there could be worse things than moving back to Colorado."

I was beyond surprised. *Why on earth would she even consider the possibility?*

"Is that what you want?"

She looked as if I had insulted her.

"I didn't say that."

"Well, what would you do if you could choose where to live?"

She slumped in the chair and her eyes narrowed.

"That's a hypothetical question."

I was sick and tired of her evasive answers.

"What's the freaking hypothetical answer?!"

She sliced the air with her hand.

"Can we stop talking about it? I have no say! The court will decide."

"Isn't life wonderful?" I muttered sarcastically.

"It's like a recipe."

"What is?"

"Life."

"If you say so."

"Really, Max, it is. I've been thinking about this. I love homeopathic recipes, and I've come up with one for life."

I tried to read her expression. Was she kidding, serious, or a bit of both? As usual it was impossible to tell.

"There's a recipe for life?" I asked weakly.

"Yes," she nodded. "It calls for one part person. Two parts pain. One part disappointment. Three parts unexpected shit. Two and a half parts luck. Then you take it all and carefully mix it together."

She paused and gazed at me.

"You cook it all up, and then you throw it against the wall and see how it lands!"

She stared at me, waiting for a reaction.

I scoffed.

"Sounds delicious."

"I'm not finished. You do the exact same recipe and add one part "God," and that's the secret ingredient. It really is. There's only one extra ingredient, but it's a totally different recipe."

Yet another one of her crazy notions. I couldn't help but chuckle.

"Make sure you tell that to the judge who'd deciding your future."

And so the stage was set for a nasty custody hearing. When all this started my father's attorney had said that Abby's custody case was weak and that having the court rule in my parents' favor would be a "slam-dunk." In just a few weeks it went from being a "slam-dunk" to "maybe I spoke too soon," to "I don't know how she got that big shot as her attorney," to "maybe she promised him money from the estate but that's illegal," to "there's actually some precedent for her case," to "we're going to have to push back hard," to "I'm sorry, but this is no 'slam-dunk.'"

-54-

When is it okay to kill someone? Today…it's okay.

A half hour before I was supposed to meet Mister D, I carefully slid Ricky's shotgun into a garbage bag…its dark surface shiny in the sunlight. I rode to the fire road and hid the gun under a bunch of dried leaves and sat waiting by a maple tree under a perfect blue sky. I was surprised at how calm I was. When I heard Mister D's car rumbling up the road, I slowly got to my feet and brushed dirt and leaves from the back of my cutoffs. The hinges on his car door squeaked and moaned as he flung it open.

"Hey there, dickwad," he scowled as he climbed from the car.

"Hi."

"I almost tore my suspension off on that road."

I shrugged.

"You got my money?"

"Yeah."

We looked at each other for a second without saying anything.

"Well, where is it?"

"I hid it, you know, in case…"

"You hid it? What for? Where?"

"Just in case…"

I motioned to the side of the road.

"It's over there. I'll get it."

Suddenly my calm nerves gave way…sheer anxiety…something…loose inside of me…willing myself over to the pile of leaves…kneeling…I slipped the shotgun out of the garbage bag…cocked it…turned…leveled it at Mister D.

"This is over!" I screamed. "I'm not giving you another thing!"

He smirked.

"What really? You're pulling a gun on me?"

I was hyperventilating...palms slick with sweat.

"You leave me no choice! You said you'd burn our house down. I can't..."

He cut me off.

"Relax, kid," he said, his smile hard. "I was just yanking your chain. Let's talk this out. I don't want anything else from you."

I tightened my grip on the shotgun to stop my hands from shaking.

"Liar!"

He held his hands up in mock surrender.

"Relax, kid. Put the gun down."

"I'm not letting you hurt my family!"

His bloodshot eyes narrowed.

"No one's hurting your family. I was just messing with you."

"You're the king of liars!"

He took a step forward, and I stepped back.

"Stop this. Let's go have a beer."

I shook my head and cursed at him through clenched teeth.

"Screw you! I'm ending this right now!"

He took a few more steps toward me.

"Kid, come on. You don't have to give me another thing, I promise."

I raised the shotgun to my cheek and aimed it at his face.

"'You promise?' You're a liar, and I'm going to blow your head off!"

"Kid, settle down. You're making a big deal out of this."

"It is a big deal! I can't...you can't..."

He took another step forward...i tried to move...my back pressed up against the trunk of a tree.

"Don't come any closer! Or I swear..."

He was less than two feet from the end of the gun barrel now.

"Max, buddy," he smiled wickedly. "I know I'm an asshole and I stressed you out. Let's go have a beer, okay? No one has to know anything."

I continued gripping the barrel of the gun.

"You'll never stop blackmailing me!"

"Max," he said, inching forward. "There no reason to..."

God, how I wanted to pull the trigger...I couldn't. All the muscles in my body went limp. What a wimp! I lost my death grip on the barrel of the gun. It slipped from my hands and fell to the ground. Mister D grabbed the gun and pointed it at me.

"Go ahead!" I cried. "Do it! I'd rather be dead, anyway. Just do it!"

A depraved grin crossed his face as I sank to my knees.

"You don't have the balls it takes to look a guy in the eye and pull the trigger," he sneered as he towered over me. "You could never run with the big dogs like me. You're a pathetic pussy. Screw you! I'm keeping this shotgun, and I want two hundred bucks. I don't care where or how you get it. Just get it, you pussy."

He laughed manically and kicked me hard in the side.

"I should beat your ass for pointing a gun at me! Get me that money, or I'll rape your cousin and burn your house down. I'm not kidding, you pussy. Understand?"

"Yes! Yes!" I sobbed.

"Good. And if you try anymore of this tough guy shit..."

He shook his head.

"I'll show you what *real* pain is."

He jumped into his car and drove off.

I slowly tried to get to my feet but my legs were useless. Pulling my knees to my chest...i stayed on the ground sobbing uncontrollably.

-55-

There is a weight so great that is as invisible as it is immeasurable. You stagger under its immense burden. It's like trying to lug around a house...a burning house. I didn't care about living. I wished Mister D had killed me. He was right. I was a pathetic pussy, a coward. In the span of eight summer weeks, I had gone through a hideous transformation, a repugnant metamorphosis. From hopeful light...to baleful dark...no doubt...no way out. If given the chance, I would have gladly run into death's outstretched arms. I lay in bed longing for a diagnosis of inoperable and aggressive brain cancer... to be stricken by a mysterious illness...crushed under the wheels of a dump truck...clobbered by a meteor from space! All of the above would have been even better. Everything would be behind me! No more guilt! No more fear! No more blackmailing by Mister D! Just nothingness. I'd never have to face another day or the consequences of my insipid actions.

Then there was the party.

It was going to be the event of the summer. A late-August, pre-back-to-school, no-holds-barred blowout. Adults never got wind of parties like that, and they wouldn't know about this one until later, when the cops got involved.

The party was posted on Facebook, an open invitation. Never a good idea. Everyone from Sambro to Armdale was going to be there. I had a bottle of tequila, and as usual, I had carefully hidden it in the A-frame. My mother was feeling a little better, so my parents had gone to a party in Halifax. I figured they wouldn't get home until after 11 o'clock.

The only thing that fueled me...other than alcohol...my bottomless guilt and profound self-loathing. I started sneaking shots of tequila that afternoon and was loaded by 5 o'clock. My parents had left for town. Molli was in her room getting ready, and I was watching TV when Ricky, Janet, Chen and Phil arrived. We were in the kitchen when Molli came down the stairs...wearing makeup and glitter...dressed in a red hoodie...jeans and hiking boots... she looked older and worldly.

"You look great!" Janet smiled.

"Thanks," Molli replied shyly.

"What's Hua up to tonight?" I asked Chen.

"Studying, I guess."

He shot me a sideways glance.

"Dude, why are you always asking about her?"

"I didn't know I was," I lied.

"Yeah, you do," he grinned. "Are you stalking her?"

Everyone stared at me, waiting for a reply. I could feel heat rising in my face.

"No."

"She has a boyfriend, you know," Chen said.

I felt like I had been punched in the gut and kicked in the head at the same time.

"She does?" I asked weakly, trying to hide my unfathomable disappointment.

"Yeah, that Brad guy with the Beamer."

"I don't think he's a 'boyfriend,'" Molli said, holding up her fingers like quote marks.

She glanced at me.

"He's her friend. They're in a study group."

"Whatever he is, he calls every night," Chen said. "I guess he's a 'wannabe boyfriend.'"

"Is she coming to the party?"

He shrugged.

"I doubt it."

I pulled the tequila from my backpack and took a big swig. It burned going down, but it immediately calmed my anxiety. Was I self-medicating? Yes, of course. I didn't care. All I knew was that I felt better when I was blasted drunk and numb.

"Take it easy, Max," Molli said.

She stepped forward and tried to grab the bottle, but I pulled away.

"Back off!" I snapped.

She stepped away and scowled.

"Jerk."

Slipping the bottle into the backpack, I zipped it shut and stood.

"Let's go!"

We left our house and headed toward the path that would take us through the woods…past Champayne Dam to the bluffs where the party was. Ricky had beer in a backpack and Janet was sipping from a pint of lemon gin, which she held out for everyone to see.

"I love anything with lemon," she cooed.

"Hey," Ricky said playfully. "If you get to the bottom of that bottle, you better be careful."

Janet turned to Molli.

"Molli, you'll help me drink it, right?"

I glanced over at Molli.

"Sure," she nodded.

I stopped walking and glared at them.

"No way! She can't have anything."

Molli looked at me defiantly.

"You're not my parents. They're dead. And you're not your parents. You can drink, so can I."

I scoffed.

"You're too young."

"Relax, Max," Janet said. "A sip or two isn't going to get her loaded."

"I'm not going to relax! She's fifteen, too young. If my parents find out she had a single drink, there'll be hell to pay!"

"They're not going to find out," Janet grinned. "What are you going to do, tell them?"

Molli laughed viciously.

"Yeah, Max, that's a good idea. Why don't you 'tell them?' Hey everyone, do you think Max should tell them?"

"Hell yeah, Max, tell them," Ricky chuckled. "Tell them you got your cousin good and drunk!"

"Yeah, Max, why don't you tell them everything?" Molli smirked. "Just go ahead and tell them!"

My blood pressure spiked as I frowned at Molli through the twilight. She was so good at that type of thing. She was like a cat with a mouse, and she knew it. She was torturing me. She'd use any situation to her teenage advantage.

We walked a little further and reached the spot where the dirt and gravel road turns into a narrow and rocky footpath winding through the woods. I had been walking that path forever, but it was narrow, uneven and littered with half-buried boulders, pine needles and leaves. There was no moon, and the sky was a deep black. Treading carefully, we made our way over the snake-like tree roots and rocks crisscrossing the narrow path. If you tripped and fell…half-buried Nova Scotia granite would gladly…take a bite out of your arm…leg or face.

The previous day Ricky and Chen had spent two hours gathering driftwood, which was plentiful thanks to a storm two days earlier. The party was near where Kevin had died, and as we made our way through the darkened woods…a sense of deep dread enveloped me. I stopped in the middle of the path and took another big swig from my bottle.

"Careful with that shit," Ricky said. "You're going to finish it before the party starts."

"Fine," I grinned, "then I can start in on your beer."

"No chance of that!"

Phil and Molli were hanging back a little...walking...talking. I don't know what they were saying, but every once in a while I'd hear Molli laugh, which I've got to say was a welcome sound. Within twenty minutes we reached the open area above the bluffs where the party was going to be. Ricky dropped his backpack on the ground, pulled out a beer, cracked it open and held it up in a toast.

"Let the festivities begin!"

We were only fifty feet from...the crack...the black...the exact spot where Kevin had gone over the edge...thoughts...swirling...twirling...churning...turning...like the boiling ocean at the base of the bluffs. I took a long, slow drink of tequila, wiped my chin with the back of my hand and then slipped the bottle into my backpack.

"I'm going to scavenge for firewood."

Chen pointed to the large pile of branches and driftwood he and Ricky had collected the previous day.

"We have plenty."

I waved him off.

"We'll burn through that in a few hours."

The warm and familiar sensation of the booze working its way into my blood was comforting as I lumbered off toward, the crack, the last place I had last seen Kevin...alive. I came within ten feet of the edge, but my fear of heights kept me from getting any closer. Below me, the tide brought in chunky waves that crashed and gnashed...into the crack...a deep baritone voice summoning me to the edge. Looking out over the twilight tinted ocean, I was filled with guilt...remorse...I saw my course. People say suicide is a permanent solution to a temporary problem. They're right, but I couldn't stand one more night in fear's suffocating embrace. I wanted a permanent solution, and it was right there in front of me.

*Why not just step off the edge? All my pain would disappear, just like my life. Why not? Molli was right. What was the point of going on? Life had become too painful. Too complicated. It would be so easy...*I hit the bottle again and took a few steps forward.

"What's up, Max?"

I turned to my left. Molli was standing there, her blue eyes wide.

"Are you okay?"

"I'm fine."

"I don't see any firewood out here."

"Yeah, I guess not."

She motioned back to where the others were gathered.

"They got the fire going. It's nice."

"Yeah? Let's head back."

My God, what did I almost do?

Someone had started two additional bonfires nearby which were in full blaze...sparks leaping...flames creeping...into the evening air. I sat on a log by one of the fires swigging from my bottle, the heat from the flames warming my face and hands, the smell of the smoke comforting like an old blanket. Within half an hour another twenty people arrived, including two guys who brought guitars.

"'Go ahead," someone yelled to them, "play, Out on the Mira!'"

A girl from school passed me a joint, and I inhaled deeply. I was sitting there drunk and stoned when Phil claimed a seat next to me.

"How's it going, Max?"

I glanced at him through bloodshot eyes.

"Okay."

"Did you mention anything to Molli about the Bar Mitzvah party?"

I had no idea what he was talking about.

"Huh?"

"My brother's Bar Mitzvah, remember?" he asked keenly. "I'm inviting you and Molli, remember?"

"Oh yeah, right. I didn't mention it. Why don't you ask her?"

"Okay."

He got up to leave, but I called him back.

"Do me a favor," I slurred. "Help me keep an eye on her tonight. There's going to be a ton of people here, and I don't want her getting in trouble or drinking, okay?"

He nodded and smiled.

It was exactly what he wanted to hear.

-56-

Night rolled in like shadowy waves across the ocean's far edge. It was the fire's time.

Stragglers showed up as ghosts...mere silhouettes...unless they were beside the fire it was difficult telling who they were. Within an hour there had to be a hundred people, partying and laughing. I stayed where I was, staring into the fire...getting higher...staggering off into the darkness once in a while to take a piss. I tried to keep an eye on Molli, but pretty much left that task to Phil. The guys with the guitars were sitting across the fire from me playing and singing. Every once in a while someone would throw more wood on the fire, sending sparks dancing up into the inky night sky. I loved those parties. There was something tribal and ritualistic about them. Or maybe they were just fun...like a circus...players in shadow... trained animals.

I leaned back and looked up.

No moon or stars. Guilt blocks the stars. It robs and assaults you, leaves you exposed and weak. I wish I didn't have any feelings. Ridiculous! I see it now. Reality! Life, is a pathetic circus!

Teetering to my left I gazed out over the ocean's black surface.

There are seven stages of night. At dusk they creep in from the east. Where's Hua? What's she doing? Who's she with?

I snatched my bottle and chugged down a drink.

Screw you, Kevin! I don't care if you're an anchor around my neck forever!

Within an hour the weather turned as nasty as my mood. The wind shifted to the north, and a damp fog pounced on us, painting the darkened landscape in an otherworldly quality.

"Hey, Max, buddy, you okay?"

It was Ricky. He sat down beside me and took a swig of beer, the light from the fire dancing over his face.

"I'm okay."

"Molli's not. She's had a few drinks, man. I saw her a while ago."

I sat up.

"What?"

"I told her to stop, man!" he slurred, his breath reeking of beer. "She was real tight after four small drinks."

"Four drinks? What!"

That sobered me up like a bucket of ice water over my head.

"Where is she?"

"I'm not sure."

He looked around.

"She was here a while ago."

"A while ago?!"

I stood but fell over the log and onto the ground. Staggering to my feet, I brushed dirt from my shirt.

"I saw Mister D and one of his dumbass friends talking to her by the other fire," Ricky continued. "She was right in his face! She was pissed off about something, man. I went over, man, and put my arm around her and pulled her away. That was twenty minutes ago."

He looked into the darkness.

"I lost track of her."

My pulse quickened.

"Mister D's here, at the party?"

He waved his hand through the air.

"Yeah he was here. That idiot. If you could spell asshole with a third 's,' he'd be the guy."

Once again I desperately tried to see through the darkness.

"Where's Molli?"

He looked around.

"Probably talking to people."

"Where's Phil?" I blurted. "I bet she's with him."

"I don't know. There's a lot of people here, man. I saw him a while ago."

"I've got to find him. You start looking for Molli, okay?"

"Okay."

"Yell if you find her."

"Okay."

"Molli! Molli!" I yelled into the darkness. Nothing.

I finally found Phil standing with a group of people.

"Where's Molli?" I asked breathlessly.

He looked bewildered.

"I thought she was with you."

"She's not with me! I thought *you* were keeping an eye on her."

He was completely sober.

"She said she was cold and was going to sit by you next to the fire."

"By me? She didn't sit by me."

I looked around frantically, but it was impossible to see through the darkness.

"Where is she?"

We started racing from group to group, asking if anyone had seen her.

"Red hoodie, and jeans?" a guy finally asked.

"Yes!" I blurted.

"She left a little while ago. She was pretty drunk and said something about being cold."

"When was that?

He shrugged.

"I don't know. Twenty minutes ago?"

Shit!

I grabbed Phil's arm.

"I'm headed back to look for her."

"I'll come with you."

"No! Stay here with Ricky in case she comes back. Call me if you see her."

•   •   •

I have this recurring dream...same old theme...in a panic...hurrying through the woods at night...impossible to see left or right...drunk...darkness...has left me totally disoriented...hiked that path a thousand times...without crimes...but as I try to rush...find my way...it seems strange and unfamiliar...tree roots like black boots...intentionally tripping me up.

But it's not a dream, is it? I don't dream anymore. It's real.

Where the hell is Molli?

I tripped over a rock and went flying into the bushes. Staggering to my feet I took a few more unsteady steps before tripping again. By the time I got to the narrow dirt road leading into Chandler's Cove, my knees, elbows, shins and face were covered with painful cuts and scratches.

"Molli!" I yelled into the night. Nothing.

Exhausted and battered, I quickly made my way up to the road.

"Molli!" I yelled again, then stopped to listen.

Drunken voices in the distance, coming from a spot in the road where people parked. I followed the voices. That's when I saw them. Molli was slumped on the ground beside a car. Her hoodie was pulled up to her neck, exposing her bra and naked torso. Mister D was standing over her, unzipping his pants while another guy looked on.

"Stop!" I yelled, racing toward them. "Get away from her!"

"Get him!" Mister D shouted at the other guy.

He smashed me hard in the face, and I fell dazed to the ground. I tried to get up, but he kicked me in the side, and I collapsed. Mister D grabbed Molli's head and pulled her toward his crotch. She was barely conscious, her eyes half open. Suddenly she puked a torrent of vomit...like something out of *The Exorcist*. Then she started laughing maniacally. Mister D slapped her brutally across the face, and she flew backwards.

"You little bitch!" he sneered.

Once again I desperately tried to get to my feet. But Mister D's henchman kicked me, this time knocking the air out of me as I slumped to the ground.

"Molli!" I managed to shout between gasps for air.

Mister D turned toward me.

"This little bitch carpenter's dream told me to leave you alone," he growled.

"Don't hurt her!"

"Give it to her D," the other guy smirked.

Once again I desperately tried to get to my feet and once again I was kicked viciously in the ribs. I landed next to a shed. That's when I saw it...half an oar in the tall grass...as if it had been left there for me. I lunged for it and came up swinging, slamming it violently into the side of the head of the guy who had been beating me. He flew backwards as if I had blasted him with a shotgun.

Then, wailing like a madman and swinging the oar wildly, I ran at Mister D. He took a blind swing, which knocked me to the ground. But my adrenaline was pumping now and I bounced right back up and landed a blow that knocked Mister D down. Then I started beating him unmercifully with the oar.

"You like raping fifteen-year-old girls?" I yelled, as I brought the oar down hard on his arm. "You blackmailing asshole! I'm going to kill you!"

He tried to get up, but I kicked him squarely in the face and he fell backwards. The other guy tried to get up too. Before he could, I strode over, kicked him in the head and he fell to the ground, moaning. Then I started beating them both with the oar, the blows landing heavy and hard.

"You jerks. I'm going to kill you!"

An evil and primitive joy welled up in me as if I was pounding my guilt driven fear to death...a completely different person... transformed...in a frenzy...reveling in the brutal viciousness of it...as i raised the oar into the night air...poised to bring it down as hard as I could on Mister D's head...someone grabbed me from behind and pulled me away...Ricky.

"What did you do that for!?" I seethed, as I struggled for breath.

"You're going to kill them!"

"Damn right? They were going to rape Molli!"

"Max," he said trying to calm me. "Stop. They've had enough."

What had been sheer primal rage only moments earlier...was now subdued fury.

Mister D and the other guy were semi-conscious on the ground, bleeding and moaning. Ricky strode over and kicked Mister D hard in the ribs. I dropped the oar in the grass, crouched beside Molli, pulled down her hoodie and carefully turned her face toward mine. Vomit was on her chin, blood was running from her nose and her eyes were half-open and distant.

"Molli, are you okay? Did they? Did he…"

"I don't feel good."

I gently grabbed her arm.

"Come on, let's go inside."

She slowly got to her feet and leaned into me. We had taken a few steps when she stopped, pulled away, staggered over to Mister D and stomped him.

"Jerk," she muttered.

"Get Molli inside. Then come back and give me a hand," Ricky said.

"Why? What are we going to do?"

He grinned.

"We're going to throw them into the crack."

For a second it sounded like a very good idea. But then I came to my senses.

"No way! You were right. There's no point killing them…it's murder!"

"No, it's not! They were going to rape Molli. It's justice."

"No way, that's…"

He flashed his shit-eating grin as he playfully pushed my shoulder.

"I'm just yanking your chain, man. You're so gullible."

A heavy fog had rolled in and people from the party started straggling back to their cars. Someone who knew Mister D and his asshole flunky loaded them into a car and left in a hurry.

I carefully helped Molli inside, cleaned her up in the bathroom as best I could, carefully put a washcloth soaked in cold water on the bridge of her nose, poured her a glass of water, put her to bed and placed a wastepaper basket by her side in case she got sick again.

"How you doing?" I asked softly.

"Not good."

"Trust me. You're going to feel it tomorrow. Go to sleep. I'll see you in the morning."

I got up to leave, but she grabbed my arm.

"Max, why does life happen?" she slurred weakly.

"What do you mean?"

She took the washcloth off her nose, tried to sit up, but collapsed back onto the bed and rolled onto her side facing me. Fat tears throbbing with an unimaginable pain rolled down her plump and pale cheeks as an aching sadness filled her smoky blue eyes.

"Why does life happen?" she wept. "Why do people die? What about Mister D and his friend? They're evil. What about Abby? She's heartless and greedy. What about the guy with the lost dog? He didn't care. Why are people so vile and self centered? All the hate! It doesn't make sense."

"Molli, don't think about it right now. Go to sleep."

I tried to stand but she grabbed my arm again...tears streaming onto her pillow.

"I don't get it," she whimpered. "What is life?"

"Don't think about it right now," I repeated softly. "Go to sleep, okay?"

"But why?" she moaned. "Why..."

I knew I had to answer her somehow. She was right. The world is full of evil...injustice...hate...greed and every other type of destructive sin...gin...as if there wasn't anything decent in the world...and...any of us could all be swept away without warning.

"People don't die," she chocked. "They just go to live in the sky, right? Like my family. Like Kevin. They're not dead. They're living in the sky, right? They're with God right? They're in a better place right?"

"Right," I offered weakly.

"But why does life happen?" she insisted.

There she was in front of me in all her raw grief...loss...confusion...laid low...much too low for any fifteen-year-old girl...defenseless...heartbroken...lost. I sat on the edge of the bed and gazed down at her in the half-light.

"I don't know why life happens, Molli," I replied gently. "All I do know is my parents love you like their own daughter. They want to take care of you, make you part of our family. Is that enough? Who knows? Maybe it should be."

"They love me?" she asked weakly. "You love me?"

I paused.

"Yeah we do," I smiled. "A little."

She laid her head on the pillow.

"That's good, I guess."

I handed her the glass of water.

"Drink this."

She was passed out, her mouth half open and crooked.

Back outside a chill in the night air hinted at an early fall. Ricky was smoking a joint, talking with a group of people from the party under the weak glow of a streetlight. He was swinging his arms wildly through the air, obviously reenacting what had happened. I walked up to him and saw Phil heading toward me.

"Max, I'm so sorry," he said, his eyes pleading. "I just heard what happened. I don't know how I lost track of her. It's my fault. I should have..."

I cut him off.

"It's not your fault, Phil. She's my cousin. I should have been looking out for her."

"Is she okay?"

"She's sleeping."

Ricky came over and offered me the joint. I shook my head.

"Those assholes. I should have let you finish them off."

"Yeah," I replied, with a half laugh. "They deserved it."

I looked him in the eye.

"I'm real glad you came back when you did, though. Real glad."

He took a hit off the joint and then exhaled a huge bloom of smoke.

"I was at the party thinking 'I hope they're okay and that Molli didn't fall or something.' Suddenly I knew I had to get my ass over there as fast as I could. I didn't know why. It's weird."

He grinned then pointed at my face.

"You're all messed up, man"

"Huh?"

"Your face, Max," he chuckled. "It's all scratched, cut and shit."

I raised my hand to my cheek. He was right. I was so amped up from the fight and drinking I never felt it.

I playfully pushed his shoulder.

"I'm not as messed up as Mister D and his asshole buddy are."

-57-

The next morning came early...painfully. My head throbbed from drinking, from falling over the path and from the blows to my face and body. There was no way to keep what had happened to Molli from my parents. It was too serious. I wearily explained everything to my father, leaving out the part about our drinking, although I'm sure he suspected something. He called the police, and two cops came to our house. One of them was a woman in her thirties. She took Molli aside and talked to her for twenty minutes while my father and I talked to her partner. As they were leaving, the female cop handed Molli something.

"That's my card," she smiled. "It's got the detachment phone number. You can call anytime and leave a message for me. Call 911 if you see either of those two creeps again, or if there's an emergency. Okay?"

Molli took the card and slipped it into her pocket.

"Thanks. I will."

Mister D and his buddy heard the cops were looking for them and took off for Alberta the next day. Needless to say, I was greatly relieved. It must be the same way people feel when they have a cancerous tumor removed. Still, there was a malignancy there. Kevin continued to haunt me, and there was no way to rid myself of that.

My mother and Molli went to Walmart, and I started toward the stairs. I wanted nothing more than to sleep off my wicked hangover.

"Max," my father said, standing in the middle of the kitchen, "I want to talk to you."

He dropped onto a seat at the table and I did the same. I could tell by his grim expression that he was pissed off.

"Do you have any idea what will happen if Molli's aunt hears about last night?"

I sat up.

"I know, Dad. I'm sorry."

He leaned forward and examined my face, his expression a mix of concern and anger.

"You're cut up but it doesn't look too serious."

He exhaled loudly.

"Thank God you weren't killed."

"I'll be okay."

A stern look formed on his face.

"Was Molli drinking?"

"No."

His eyes narrowed.

"And you?"

"No."

He jumped up, went to the recycling bin and pulled out three empty beer bottles.

"Who do these belong to?"

I shrugged.

"I don't know."

"They were in your mother's garden this morning!"

Shit! I turned my palms up.

"Someone from the party must have left them."

"You just said there wasn't any drinking."

"I don't know? There were a lot of people there. It's…

"Lies! More of your lies!"

He glared at me angrily.

"This is on you, Max! Do you understand? I blame you for this! I haven't asked much of you. You let me down in a big way when I was counting on you."

I was deeply wounded by his tirade.

"Dad, I'm sorry," I choked.

"You're sorry? Do you have any idea how difficult the last eight weeks have been?"

You have no idea...

"I know. It won't happen..."

He interrupted me.

"Who are you, Max?"

"What?"

His forehead was creased in anger, his face was beet red and the tendons in his neck were popping out.

"You heard me," he yelled. "Who are you? Some ass-clown who's always going to be in trouble? A loser who drinks and blames the world for his problems? Is that who you are? That's not the son I raised. Who are you?"

"I'm...me," I answered weakly. "Dad, I'm sorry. I promise..."

"You promise?" he scoffed. "We've seen how good your promises are! I have never been as disappointed in you as I am right now. I have no idea who you are."

It was the second time since Molli arrived, that I thought he might actually hit me. It was the stress of everything. He was exhausted, at the end of his rope. We all were. I was speechless, beaten and sick with another hangover. I buried my face in my hands.

"I'm sorry."

"My lawyer's coming out this afternoon," he said crossly. "I want you and Molli both here when he gets here. He's going to have an update."

"What is it?"

"I don't know!" he snapped. "He'll tell us when he gets here."

"Okay," I replied feebly.

I slowly got to my feet and staggered toward the stairs, my head pounding. My body, my soul, were dehydrated like a man who had spent days crawling through the desert. It was the lowest moment in my life...but it suddenly got a lot worse.

"Where do you think you're going?" my father asked, his eyebrows arched.

"Back to bed."

"Back to bed? No, Max. I need you to rotate the tires on my car."

He might as well have kicked me in the gut! Rotating his car tires would be hard, dirty work and take hours! I'd have to jack the car up and down four times. It was beyond punishment. It was torture. He knew how sick I was.

"Dad, I'm in pain from last night. Get them to do it at Murphy's."

"You're in pain, alright, but it's not all from those two criminals," he scowled. "Besides, Murphy's is too expensive. I want you do it right now!"

Thanks, Molli, for ruining my life!

There was no arguing.

The lug nuts on the tires...like the fires of hell...and the smell...road kill...not a thrill...shreds of skunk...porcupine...raccoon...who knows what else was embedded in every tread...wished I was dead...every disgusting tire weighed forty pounds...wrapped my sweaty arms around them in a sickening embrace...a race... to wrestle them off and back on the car...sun like a scar...hot and unforgiving...I didn't feel like living...torture...a scorcher...perspiring like a madman...sweat stinging my eyes...my soul cries....a deep thirst...not the first.

There's a separate level of hell for a job like that, especially when you're sick with a wicked hangover. Long, frequent guzzles from the garden hose were the only things that saved me. I staggered down to the cove twice to get sick, slipping all over the kelp-covered rocks. It was low tide, so the seaweed and kelp were exposed to the air, their salty fragrance adding to my misery. Dropping to my knees, I puked until I dry heaved. At one point, I glanced up and saw a seal ten feet from shore, staring at me in a weird way. Its brown eyes were liquid, huge and judgmental. Like all seals, it was smiling, its long whiskers hanging over the sides of its mouth.

It must be a curse to be smiling all the time!

"What are you looking at, dickwad?"

It kept staring at me, so I grabbed a stone and threw it in the water.

"Get outta here."

It slipped silently below the surface. I looked out across the cove. I wanted a drink of alcohol. Badly. It would help me feel better. Still, there was no way I'd be able to sneak anything from my parents' liquor cabinet.

I was slaving away, wrestling on the last disgusting tire, when I heard a car in the driveway. It was Hua in shorts, sandals and a green halter top. He hair…in a ponytail…swung back and forth like a pendulum as she approached. Pink-framed sunglasses hid her eyes.

"Max, you look like crap."

"Thanks."

"Can we talk?"

I looked around.

"Sure."

She slipped off her sunglasses and knelt beside me. I could tell from her bleak expression that something was on her mind.

"I heard about the party and Molli and you getting beat-up and that shithead, Mister D!"

"I don't care about getting beat-up. I'm glad I got there before they raped Molli."

"So am I," she exhaled.

There was a pause.

"My pregnancy scare was a real wakeup call."

I forced a smile.

"Thank God it was the wrong number."

"It was a wakeup call," she repeated.

My forehead, the back of my neck and my armpits were slick with sweat and grime.

"Right," I replied wearily. "We'll have to be more careful."

"Max," she said quietly. "I don't know how to say this, so I'm just going to say it."

She paused, looked up at the sky and then stared down at me.

"We can't see each other anymore."

I was stunned. I raised my hand to shield my eyes from the sun.

"What? Why? Just because you thought you were..."

She cut me off.

"It's not just that."

Once again she exhaled heavily.

"These summer courses are really harsh, and I go back to school fulltime in a few weeks."

I sat up.

"You're just stressed!"

"Max, if my father found out that we're...he'd kill me. And if your parents found out, they'd be so disappointed."

I shook my head.

"No one will find out."

"That's not true. Molli knows."

"She's not going to say anything!"

She paused as if collecting herself.

"Max, I'm sorry, but I've made up my mind."

She frowned.

"This is the way it's got to be."

"Says who?" I blurted.

She stood and gazed down at me.

"I do. I'm sorry, but there's no other way."

She turned and strode to her car...never once looking back. I was too sick and exhausted to go after her. Sitting on the ground in bewildered silence, I watched as she drove away for the last time. I was beyond devastated. I had puked a lot that summer, but slouched there, weak and heartbroken, I felt as if my soul were emptying out. It was a powerful emotional beat-down. Our yin and yang wore out...shifted...did whatever yin and yang do. The leaves on the trees turned from green to red and fell to the ground the same way Hua's interest in me did. I saw her on occasion at Chen's house, but she was always in a hurry on her way to somewhere better.

-58-

I finished rotating the tires from hell, crawled into the A-frame and collapsed on the floor. Following a fitful ninety minutes of something like sleep, I heard the sound of a car on our gravel driveway. Peering through the window, I saw my father's attorney. He grabbed his briefcase and strode toward the backdoor. Within seconds I heard the familiar sound of Ziggy attacking him. I ran to the backyard and the attorney was doing the same thing everyone did when Ziggy attacked: Duck, wave their hands frantically above their head and scream. I grabbed what we called the "Ziggy broom" and shooed the bird away.

"What was that, a falcon?" the attorney asked as he patted down wrinkles on his suit coat.

"There aren't any falcons around here. It's a Cyanocitta cristata bromia."

He looked horrified.

"A what?"

"Never mind."

Inside the kitchen…I was parched and woozy…my mouth like a paper bag. Pouring myself two large glass of fresh lemonade, I greedily downed them. It didn't help much. My father, mother and Molli came into the room as I poured myself a third lemonade. We all sat gloomily around the table as the attorney pulled a pile of papers from his briefcase.

"I've got news," he smiled. "Big news!"

"What is it, Glen?" my father asked.

"I've been looking at provincial family court and child custody case law, and I found something."

He pulled a single page from the pile and slid it across the table for my father.

"That's the Fisherman's Orphan Statue of 1846," he said.

I drained the glass of lemonade as my father studied the document.

The lawyer cleared his throat.

"It states that in the rare circumstance when a fishermen and his wife die together, and have a single surviving child under the age of 18 but beyond the age of 14, the child being of sound mind and body, in the presence of witnesses, can choose where to domicile."

We all looked at him blankly.

He smiled widely.

"'Domicile' means where to live."

"I know what domicile means," my father replied.

What did the law mean? We weren't fishermen.

He obviously read our collective expressions of confusion.

"It was written for fishermen, but we can use it too," he said triumphantly. "It was never taken off the books. I've checked with a family court judge I know. He agrees with me. Molli decides where she'll live."

My mother gasped and raised her hands to her face. My father seemed to be taking it all in, as if he was unsure of what he had just heard. Molli's expression didn't change. She looked bored or even indifferent. I was staggered.

"Are you sure?" my father finally asked.

"I can start on the paperwork tomorrow," the attorney said. "I'll need a sworn affidavit from Molli stating that she wants to live with you, but that's basically it. The judge's ruling will be perfunctory."

"Awesome!" my father said.

He placed his hand on top of Molli's hand.

"What do you think? Great news, eh?"

You wouldn't think it was "great news" from her distant expression.

"You know what?" she replied softly. "It's a lot to take in and well...I'd like some time to think about it."

An awful silence...as if the light in the room suddenly dimmed. I was as shocked as my parents. The color drained from my father's face. I was completely ambushed by her response. We'd shown Molli true love and accepted her into our home, our family. What a slap in the face! She needed time to think about what? Living with her addict aunt and her loser fiancé? They'd spend Molli's inheritance and leave her broke. What was there to think about, for God's sake?

"Oh," the attorney finally replied. "Well that's, yeah, that's, you know, okay. I understand it's a big decision best not made in haste."

He looked at my father.

"I just thought that, you know, we were all headed in the same direction and that..."

Molli stood, her face void of emotion.

"I'm going for a walk."

She strode out the door as my father slumped in his chair like he had been shot through the heart. My mother took his hand.

"It's okay, Geoff," she said softly. "She's been through so much. It's been so hard for her."

I jumped up.

"Where are you going, Max?" my mother demanded.

"For a walk."

"Leave Molli alone," she said sternly. "This is not a time for confrontations!"

I barely heard her because my anger was soaring.

-59-

What matters in this world, this life? Loyalty? Family? God? Money? Truth? Sex? Power? Love?

All of the above? None of the above?

What matters is doing "the right thing." Right? Because if we all did the right thing...but it's impossible to do the right thing all the time, and *so* easy to do the wrong thing! Sometimes things are as clear as the night sky, and even then we do not do the right thing! Right. Wrong. Up. Down. None of it made sense anymore.

I caught up with Molli on the Chebucto Head Road.

"Molli" I yelled when I was about twenty meters away. "Wait for me."

She turned and stood by the side of the road as I rushed up to her.

"Thanks!" I said breathlessly as I reached her side. "You really have to think about it? That's unbelievable! We've done everything for you. You ungrateful little..."

She cut me off.

"No, Max, I don't have to think about it. I made my decision weeks ago. I decided that if I had a choice of any kind in all of this, I want to stay here with you guys."

For the second time in minutes I was completely stunned.

"Then why on earth would you..."

"First, let me ask you a question. When I was drowning at Champayne Dam why did you risk your life to save me? The only thing I remember is drowning and your frantic yelling above the storm, the wind and the rain. I heard you yelling, 'Take my hand!'"

"Why did I save you?"

She planted her hands on her hips and glared at me.

"Yeah, why?"

"Why?" I replied angrily. "Why not? It wasn't like it was an important life or anything! Besides what's that got to do with it?"

Her face was stern, not even a hint of a smile. She was obviously expecting more of an answer.

"I don't know why."

I turned my palms up.

"It was pure reaction. Was I supposed to watch you drown?"

She looked at the ground and then back at me.

"Abby would never risk her life for me. Never! She would have let me drown. You and your parents care for me. Maybe you even love me."

I was astonished. Hadn't we made that abundantly clear?

"You know that's true. You don't have to ask me, you know. We've done everything for you."

She seemed to be studying me.

"Like I said, I want to stay here, but there's one condition, and I mean it. If you don't agree, then I moving with Abby."

"What do you mean, 'if you don't agree?'"

She folded her arms across her chest and stared at me.

"I mean if you don't agree to my one condition, I'm leaving. I'm going back to the states."

My head was spinning.

"What's your 'one condition?'"

She paused and then looked me squarely in the eye.

"Max, tell your parents and Kevin's parents what really happened that night, when he fell, when you pushed him. Tell them, and I'll stay."

I was appalled. I wanted to grab and shake sense into her.

"I told you I could never face them!" I blurted. "I'm too ashamed. I'll go to jail."

"You're afraid, right?"

"You're damned right I'm afraid!" I seethed. "I never should have told you."

She stepped forward until she was only inches away.

"Face down your fear, Max. Face it down. Go to the edge. Do what's right."

She was right. I was at the edge...of something. Losing my temper. Losing my mind.

"Kevin's dead! Gone. Telling them won't bring him back!"

"Yeah, but it might bring you back! I can see what your secret is doing. It's destroying you, eating you alive. I'm not going to stay and be witness to that."

I buried my face in my hands.

"I can't believe this...after all we've done for you."

"If you choose not to tell them, I'll go away with Abby," she continued matter-of-factly. "I can handle her and her bullshit fiancé for a few years. I promise to God I'll never tell anyone what happened with Kevin. I swear. But if you tell your parents what happened...I'll stay. That's my condition, Max. It's up to you. Your choice."

I looked at her, trying to gauge if she was serious.

"That's blackmail!"

She threw her hands up.

"Call it whatever you want! I don't care, and I'm not kidding. I have no desire to stay here and watch you turn into an alcoholic and kill yourself."

I was so infuriated I wanted smash her in the face!

"Go to hell!" I screamed. "Do whatever you want!"

I stormed home and spent the rest of the afternoon in the A-frame, staring at the ceiling, fuming and thinking...

The best thing is for Molli to go with her aunt. It would make everything so much easier. The baby's coming, and our house is too small for all of us. Molli would be happier in Denver, snowboarding with her friends, even if it was with her shithead aunt.

It wasn't her pathetic attempt to blackmail me with the true story of what happened to Kevin. She'd be happier in Denver, even though she said she wanted to live with us. She wouldn't tell anyone about Kevin. She was a pain in the ass, but I knew I could trust her.

What would my father do? What would he want? I knew hands-down. He wanted Molli to stay with us, for us to be her family. He believed that people need a family and that if they're lucky and blessed, that family will help them in life. My father meant it when he said he wanted Molli to stay with us. He knew it would present hardships, but he was willing to endure it because "family" was essential to him. He had loved his brother and parents. The same with my mother. She knew that if Molli stayed, it would be difficult for everyone, but she was perfectly willing to treat Molli like her own daughter. My parents were willing to sacrifice.

And me? I was torn, to say the least. Molli was "blood." She had suffered a great loss. We were the only real and loving family she had left in the world. She knew that. But my life would be a lot easier without her around. Anyone could see that. It would go back to normal. She'd adapt. She was smart, tough and capable.

But but but…

-60-

Molli was in her room with the door shut when I went inside. My father was in the kitchen tying a fishing fly under a bright lamp. My heart…hammering…as i…knocked on the doorframe… he looked up…his eyes huge through the magnifying glass.

"Dad, can we talk?"

"What is it?" he asked impatiently.

"I need to talk to you."

"Right now?"

"Yeah."

He must have read my stressed-out expression, because his look softened.

"Okay, Max. Sit down."

He leaned forward.

"What is it?"

I told him everything. Every word. Every painful detail of what had happened with Kevin. The robbery. The fight…Kevin's fall that night. My heavy drinking to dull my immense guilt. Everything poured out of me. The dam holding back my guilt driven fear burst. I tearfully confessed to stealing his painkillers. I told him about Mister D blackmailing me. He sat and listened intently, hanging on every word. When I finally finished I actually felt a little better, as if a slender beam of light had found its way into a shadowy place.

"Max, you should have told me immediately after it happened," he said softly. "Kevin might have still been alive."

I shook my head in shame.

"He fell into the crack. He wasn't alive, Dad. No one could survive that."

He rubbed his eyes.

"Why now, Max? I'm glad you're telling me, but why now?"

I didn't tell him what Molli had threatened. What was the point? She was right. I couldn't live with that secret around my neck. Sooner or later it would have dragged me to the bottom.

"It's just time," I replied, my voice cracking. "I'm so scared. But Dad, it's killing me. I feel *so* guilty."

Weeping uncontrollably…a steady stream of tears…fears…saliva…snot flowed from me like truth. Never had I been that weak and exposed. My father got up and wrapped his arm around my shoulders, tears running down his own cheeks.

"I'm glad you told me. We'll get through this, son. I promise."

"Are you going to tell the police?" I sobbed. "Am I going to jail?"

I really didn't have to ask. I knew my father. Right or wrong, he'd do the right thing.

"One step at a time Max," he replied wearily. "This is very complicated. I'm going to have to think about this, where we go from here."

"But am I going to go to jail?" I repeated tearfully. " I killed him. He's dead because of me."

He exhaled heavily.

"You didn't…it wasn't."

He slowly shook his head.

"I'm going to talk to some people…to see…to check what…"

He stood without finishing.

"Right now I'm going to talk to your mother about it."

"Why do you have to tell Mum?" I gasped. "Can't we just…"

"Max please. This is *very* serious and we can't keep it from your mother."

He went upstairs and told her. She was in bed and started crying.

"Max, what a terrible secret. You can tell us anything. You should know that."

She sat up in bed and hugged me like she was never going to let go.

"Mum, I'll face whatever I have to for this. It's better than keeping it hidden."

• • •

I had never seen my father so troubled and somber as he was that black day. All of it was visible in the tautness of his face and tightness of his shoulders. Obviously he was wrestling with what to do with the toxic information I had given him. He was sharing my terrible secret, and like me...he felt the appalling weight of it.

In a daze, I went outside and crossed the yard to the A frame. Stepping through the door, I found Molli typing on her laptop. She looked up, her sad round face, black-and-blue.

"Mum and Dad know everything," I said flatly. "I just told them."

Her eyes widened.

"Really?"

"Yes."

She jumped up and hugged me tightly, but I was numb, my arms hanging limply at my side.

"Thanks, Max," she smiled, her smoky blue eyes beaming. "You saved me. I would have gone crazy with Abby."

I stepped back.

"I'm probably going to jail for the rest of my life and..."

I collapsed onto the bench and looked over at her.

"You really were going to leave if I didn't tell them, right?"

She glanced at the floor and then looked at me, her gaze unwavering.

"Yes...no. I don't know. I'm glad it didn't come to that."

"I actually feel better. A little, anyway."

"I knew you would."

A sacred second...all we had was the fragile outline of our youth...family...and the unknown path ahead of us. For better and worse...the future was ours.

Molli sighed.

"I loved my family, living in Denver, being in the mountains, snowboarding with my friends, hanging out. All that's been taken away from me. There's no way to reclaim it. It's gone."

She paused as a look of painful resignation rested in her tired eyes.

"Mom and Dad would have wanted me to stay with you guys, not Abby."

That moment...locked in time...an endless chime...lifelong memories forged in the warmth of a single instant...i gazed at Molli...a stew of thoughts...connecting the dots...questions...simmering in my mind...

Does life have meaning? Is it just some random drop of a cosmic roulette ball in the endless wheel of time? Is there a master plan? If so, what is it? Does tragedy have meaning? Maybe it doesn't, but we mold it with our minds until it has one. Maybe it does, but we can't fathom what that meaning is. Maybe we have to hope and pray that tragedy is not visited upon us or those we love. But sooner or later it is. No one is immune. Maybe we have to love and support people when they are forced to face the most painful things in life. When hatred, pain and loss arrive, we have to confront them with love and compassion.

But why why why is there so much pain, suffering and injustice in the world? Why? If there is a God, and he loves us so much, why does He allow bad and evil things to happen to good people?

Maybe life is about having the guts to say 'This hurts too much! I can't take anymore!" Maybe it's about leaning on people who love you enough to help you through whatever horrors life throws at you. Maybe it's about taking responsibility for your actions no matter the consequences. Maybe it's about finding and having a relationship, a friendship with, God.

Maybe it's all of the above?

I buried my face in my hands.

"After all this, I need a drink."

Molli pushed me playfully.

"No, you don't."

She pointed at me and smiled.

"I'm keeping an eye on you."

Her face…a bruised and battered mess…not from playing chess…cheek swollen purple…a fat lip…her tooth was chipped… the white of her right eye…blood red…but thank God…she wasn't dead! She was only fifteen, but life had knocked the crap out of her.

I scoffed.

"Good luck with a hideous eye like that!"

I moved closer to her on the bench.

"When are you going to tell my parents you've made a decision, that you're staying?"

She stood.

"Right now."

Together we did.

• • •

The next morning my father called me into his tiny study, his face unshaven, drained and fatigued.

"How you doing Max?"

"Tired."

"We all are."

He rubbed his temples.

"I talked to, Glen, our attorney. I told him what happened with Kevin, the fight."

He didn't have to say anything else. I could tell by his bleak expression what was coming next…my death sentence.

"Max, you're in very deep trouble. Your mother and I will do everything we can for you. This is going to the hardest thing in your life."

"Dad," I choked, "am I going to jail?"

He fixed his gaze on me.

"Max, Kevin is dead. This whole thing is beyond our control."

He paused.

"God how I wish I could turn back time or switch places with you! But I can't son."

His eyes were heavy with something…pain…heartbreak…hurt…a bleak and relentless reality.

"Max, your mother and I love you very much. More than you know. We will be with you every step of the way through this. I promise. You're not facing this alone. I want you to know that. We're going to go through this together."

"You're turning me in?"

He seemed to be collecting himself.

"It will be the hardest thing I've ever done son."

He inhaled deeply.

"We're going to tell the authorities what happened. The whole story."

He paused and our eyes met.

"The truth."

My stomach heaved.

"The truth? That I killed my friend?"

He leaned forward, his face inches from mine.

"The truth is that you robbed the gas station together, you fought and Kevin fell to his death. The truth that you never intended to hurt him. The truth that he struck you first."

"But Dad I'm scared. What's going to happen?"

His face was pensive.

"Honestly Max, at this point, I don't know."

That afternoon he called Kevin's parents and asked if we could stop by. Facing them was the most difficult thing I had ever done. I wasn't hung over, but I thought I was going to puke. I cried and choked my way through the story. I tried to answer their questions as best as I could. Who knows what they thought. I was too ashamed to even look at them.

The truth may set you free…it can also bring you to your knees… break hearts…leave you bewildered…bitterly disappointed. But you know what? My father fought for me with everything he had. He came to my side when I needed him the most, stepping up for me at a critical crossroads in my life.

"My son didn't mean to hurt your boy. It was an accident," my father said to Kevin's parents, his voice cracking. "Nothing I can say or do will bring Kevin back. All I can do is offer you a deep and profound apology. We'll do whatever it takes. We're not hiding from this anymore."

He turned to me.

"Wait in the car. I want to talk to Kevin's parents in private."

After fifteen minutes he came out and we headed home in what was the longest drive in my life.

- 61 -

People who are always conniving...scheming...plotting...sometimes get what they want. But it comes at an atrocious price. They also end up as spiritually sick sociopaths, burned out, friendless and beyond bitter. All the money in the world can't buy what everyone really and truly wants...needs.

The day we went to sign the papers making Molli legally part of our family, we stopped to see Abby and Bruce. We were shocked when Abby called, telling my father she had something for Molli.

I was skeptical. We all were. Abby tried to hijack Molli's life because Abby's life was stalling. She desperately needed money and drugs to keep it going.

When we got to the hotel where Abby and Bruce were staying, their beat-to-shit bags were by the door and a taxi was waiting. Abby's eyes were bloodshot, and it looked like she had aged ten years since I first saw her.

"Bruce," she said motioning to the parking lot. "Wait in the taxi."

He grunted a response and left...barely acknowledging us.

Abby turned to Molli.

"I've got something for you."

She pulled a tattered velvet ring box from her suitcase and opened it, revealing an ornate silver ring with a translucent blue stone. It was magnificent...the endless blue Nova Scotia sky and Atlantic Ocean.

"This belonged to your mother," Abby said, her face crimson as a sunset. "She gave it to me when I was fifteen. Your age. She said..."

She paused.

"I always treasured it. No matter where I lived, I took it with me and made sure no one stole it."

She thrust it toward Molli.

"I want you to have it. It belongs to you now."

Molli looked stunned. We were all standing there unsure what to do. I shoved my hands deeply into my pockets.

"No, Abby, it's yours," Molli replied softly. "Mom gave it to you. I can't…"

"I want you to have it," Abby insisted.

Once again she tried to hand it to Molli.

"Please, take it."

"You keep it."

"Please, take it," Abby repeated, her eyes pleading.

"Go ahead and take it, Molli," my mother said gently.

Molli reached out and took the ring. She gazed down at it for a second, wiped a tear from her cheek, then slipped the ring into the pocket of her blue jean jacket.

"Thank you," she said softly.

"Do you know what I realized yesterday?" Abby said, her expression miserable and drained.

No one said anything.

"I realized I no longer have a family," she continued. "Beth, my big sister…she's…gone."

There was another awkward silence…then Abby started crying…tears sprinting…in tiny rivulets down her cheeks…as she… collapsed into a chair…burying her face in her hands.

"There'll be no more Christmas invitations," she cried, her mascara a mess running down her cheeks.

She looked like a raccoon…a weeping raccoon.

"No more birthday phone calls from my sister. No more reassuring words over the phone."

She hung her head in despair.

"No more love."

She glanced up at Molli.

"I'm glad you're staying here," she blubbered. "You need to be with people who really love you and can take care of you. That's what your mother and father would have wanted."

She started bawling again, her tears falling onto the floor, her nose running. Her heart was really breaking in the sudden realization of what had happened to her only sister.

My mother knelt and gently placed her hand on Abby's shoulder.

"What about Bruce?" she asked softly. "You're getting married. You can start a family. You can…"

"Bruce?" Abby choked. "He'll be gone a week after we get back! He doesn't love me. He's…"

Her crying got louder and she started convulsing as her tears committed to their dreadful downpour.

"I'll be a ghost," she bawled. "No one will know me. No one will care."

"Go get Bruce," my mother whispered urgently to my father.

Bruce came in, knelt beside Abby and put his arm around her.

"What's the matter, babe?"

Abby shoved him.

"Leave me alone! This whole trip was your idea!"

Bruce turned to us and motioned toward the door.

"You should go. I'll make sure she gets home okay."

We turned to leave, but Molli rushed over, knelt beside her aunt and gently took her hand.

"I want you to know something," Molli said, her eyes swelling with moisture. "You're not alone. I'll always be your niece."

Molli leaned in and hugged her.

"I…I…I love you."

What an unbelievable act of compassion! It was as if Molli had bandaged a gaping wound in her aunt's damaged soul.

"Thank you, Molli," Abby sobbed. "I love ahhh. I love…"

She started to mumble something…but her words…were swept away in a river of tears. She couldn't have stopped bawling if she wanted to. Watching a person fall to pieces like that is beyond painful. It's like watching someone slowly die. In a way maybe they are dying. If tears really are cathartic…she must have felt a lot better when she stopped…if she stopped.

"Go," Bruce said, ushering us toward the door. "She'll be okay."

The drive home was quiet for the most part, each of us deep in our own bottomless thoughts.

"People will surprise you, for better or worse," my mother said at one point. "Abby finally had a heart."

My father's face turned scarlet and he started cursing under his breath, but he reeled it in.

We stopped at a red light, and he turned toward the backseat.

"I want you two to know something. I'm checking myself into hospital for a short period of time."

He cleared his throat.

"Your mother and I have been talking. I've been abusing my pain medication, a little. I'm taking too much."

Too much? Ha! He was eating it like candy.

He placed his hand on top of my mothers.

"I've had a small problem for a while. I didn't want to enter into treatment until I was sure it wouldn't impact the custody battle over Molli."

He paused.

"Anyway, I'm getting inpatient care."

-62-

Tell the truth about an idiotic fake robbery and confess to killing your friend...you're sentenced to three years in jail. That's what justice hit me with. They didn't call it murder. They called it "involuntary manslaughter." I had killed Kevin by accident.

In jail everything was taken from me: Freedom. Christmas, holidays, graduation, summer vacation and Grace's birth. I still got more than Kevin. My time in jail made our living conditions easier. We didn't get a new house. My father had been bluffing Abby. He built an addition on our house instead. He'd come to visit me in jail all the time and show me pictures of it being built. In jail you have a lot of time to think...then you try not to think because it's driving you crazy. How is it that someone can know you better than you know yourself? Molli knew I couldn't live with a horrendous secret. My life was in a downward spiral. I spent time in prison... but stifling the truth...would have taken twenty years off my life.

To everyone who knew Kevin he'll always be seventeen...a defining age. It was that summer that helped define me as a person. My blind and feeble justifications led to petty crimes...that conjured hideous lies...summoning death...spawning appalling secrets...generating insidious tribulations...turning into endless quandaries...giving birth to fear and tears...sprouting heartbreak...begetting truth...speaking love...finally delivering...all of the above.

Life was definitely more complicated...that summer...was like a birth...painful and miraculous at the same time...i saw the world differently...tragedy...death...fear...love forced out the innocent edges of my life...making it bigger.

• • •

That fateful fall, while the courts were still deciding what would happen to me, Molli, my father and I were at a completely boring fundraiser for the Halifax Symphony when a guy I didn't know started chatting with Molli and I. I started to introduce Molli as my "cousin," like I had so many times before. But I stopped.

"I'm Max, and this is Molli, my sister."

Molli and I locked eyes. I'll never forget her expression. Simple contentment and acceptance.

The guy moved on, and Molli gently grabbed my elbow.

"Your 'sister?' Really?"

I shrugged.

"Why not? It's easier, that way we don't have to get into the whole story."

I smiled and playfully pushed her shoulder.

"But you know, it's not like my family accepts you as our own."

She grinned and slapped me on the arm.

"Shut up!"

I got two new sisters that year. Molli and Grace.

Grace was born...blind...as an appalling guilt settled on my mother. She blamed herself and moaned she hadn't rested enough while pregnant. Her obstetrician assured her it was not her fault. It was just one of those sad...unexplainable things.

Molli will have those three stars tattooed on her hand forever. She'll treasure them. Gently stroking them in remembrance. What if everyone had their tragedies...losses...disappointments tattooed on them?

Molli's pain receded in time like a retreating tide. The immense heartache and grief faded from her smoky blue eyes...but...there were always hints of hurt and fury there, lingering in the corners like shadows of fire.

-63-

Sooner or later *everything* flies…floats…swims…or is swept into Chandler's Cove.

Trying to stop it is like trying to stop the tide. It's not going to happen.

Death came…so did life…greed…lust…love…so did Molli.

Molli loves the mountains. I love the ocean. They're not that different. We're not that different. We bring the same things to the mountaintops we bring to the depths of the ocean. Molli navigated a deep ocean of grief. She made it. Bruised. Battered, wounded and hurt…but she made it.

The ocean tried to kill me a few times. I don't judge or hold a grudge. It's given way more than it's taken. There's no worry there. Only truth. Like Father Morris said…it's all part of God's general revelation!

But there's another general revelation! A much larger and infinitely more powerful and precious one. I never believed that until Molli came. That summer I was witness to its immense and timeless power. Black ocean waves…angry seas of the soul…greed…grief…hatred…death…all bowed down before it.

Molli asked, why does life happen?

I ask, why does life happen?

What do you do when the world turns cold and bleak…when the pain is so deep all you can do is weep?

Go on when all your dreamy illusions are shattered by the ruthless realities of life…time…death?

What's it like to...discover...uncover...unfathom...understand...the multi-layered...real truth of another person? It's like discovering a new country...an alternative world...a fifteen-year-old girl. Maybe it's like seeing them as God sees them.

Is life good? Bad? Indifferent?

Is it all of the above?

It's like the ocean, filled with endless wonders, mysteries, life and death. Just like the ocean, life offers fleeting moments of transcendence. But if you drained the briny water out of all the oceans and tried to fill the timeless void with all the pain, injustice, suffering and loss in the world...there wouldn't be enough room for it. It wouldn't be close.

What's the cure for that...for life?

Ask Molli. She's the queen of one-word answers.

She'd have an answer for that.

87498039R00211

Made in the USA
Lexington, KY
25 April 2018